The Spirituality of the Psalms

Carroll Stuhlmueller, C.P.

Foreword by
Donald Senior, C.P.

Edited by
Carol J. Dempsey, O.P.
and
Timothy Lenchak, S.V.D.

THE LITURGICAL PRESS
Collegeville, Minnesota

www.litpress.org

Cover design by Greg Becker. Photo: Cleo Freelance Photography.

1	2	3	4	5	6	7

Library of Congress Cataloging-in-Publication Data

Stuhlmueller, Carroll.
    The spirituality of the Psalms / Carroll Stuhlmueller.
      p. cm.
    Includes bibliographical references and index.
    ISBN 0-8146-2599-1 (alk. paper)
      1. Bible. O.T. Psalms—Devotional use. I. Title.

  BS1430.55 S78 2002
    223'.206—dc21   2001033744

Contents

Foreword

Carroll Stuhlmueller, C.P., was one of the giants of American Catholic biblical scholarship. His teaching and writing career spanned an extraordinary period in American Catholic life, beginning with the resurgent biblical renewal in the early fifties and continuing into the glories and turbulence of the post–Vatican II Church. Carroll was a vital part of this history, teaching in the many summer biblical programs that sprang up across the country, active in the new translation projects, a consultant on the revision of religious education materials, a champion of women's roles in the Church, and a prolific writer of both scholarly and popular publications.

But the Carroll Stuhlmueller so many of us knew and loved would not be accurately portrayed only in terms of his remarkable productivity and professional success. I think it is safe to say that Carroll was a saint. Born of a sturdy German family in Hamilton, Ohio, Carroll never lost his way. He was ordained a Passionist priest in 1943 and immediately began his biblical studies at the Catholic University and the Biblical Institute in Rome. He later would earn a doctorate before the Pontifical Biblical Commission. His dedication to his ministry of teaching, lecturing, and writing was legendary. He taught at Catholic Theological Union from the time of its founding in 1968 until his death in 1994. For most of those years I was privileged to have the faculty office next to his. I would hear his typewriter pounding away non-stop until late at night. In later years, that intimidating sound would be replaced by the soft click of his computer keyboard, which he courageously took up long before it was common. During the day there would be a stream of visitors to Carroll's office: students seeking help, graduates returning to greet him, publishers trying out new projects, and always, lost souls desperate for guidance whom Carroll never turned away.

Carroll had a unique blend of gentle humility and fierce, uncompromising strength. Some of us used to joke that we were glad that Carroll was "on our side"! I think that the spirit of the prophets he loved to study had become incarnate in him. When he was convinced of the rightness of a cause—as for example the Church's need to be more inclusive of women—

he would speak and act without compromise or hesitation. Carroll had a potent set of virtues for a prophet: courage, a profound, almost childlike piety, love and loyalty for the Church, and complete integrity.

His students will readily testify that Carroll was an inspired teacher, particularly in the two areas of Old Testament studies he loved the best: the prophetic literature—especially Isaiah and Jeremiah—and the psalms. He had a poetic, passionate nature and it came through in his lectures where the boundary between scholarly exposition and profound, heartfelt spirituality was always blurred. To sit in Carroll's classes was like being on a unique retreat. Toward the end of his life, teaching the psalms was his greatest satisfaction. The passion and poetry of the psalms gave voice to Carroll's own tenacious love of God and a rigorous fidelity to prayer.

When Carroll died suddenly of a stroke in February 1994, it fell to me and my Passionist colleague Fr. Ken O'Malley to do the poignant task of clearing his personal effects from his office. Carroll had often talked of wanting to do an introduction to the psalms that would also highlight their spirituality. I knew he was working on a manuscript among the many writing projects to which he was committed, but I had not yet had a chance to see any of it. When I was going through his papers and checking the files on his computer, I could not find any evidence of it and I began to wonder if he had ever had the chance to put his thoughts in writing. Then one day I noticed a stack of papers on a bookcase in his office. It was the manuscript on the psalms—hand written, not yet completed, but substantially intact. Thus began the process that led to this book. Thanks to The Liturgical Press and the patient editorial work of Timothy Lenchak, s.v.d., and Carol J. Dempsey, o.p., Carroll Stuhlmueller's labor of love is complete. Carroll had a special place in his heart for The Liturgical Press, serving as one of the original editors of *The Bible Today* and publishing many of his works with The Press. How fitting it is that Carroll's last book would be published there. Readers will discover here his signature approach: solid scholarship, genuine piety, and a commitment to making the Scriptures come alive for a wide audience.

For those of us who knew and loved Carroll Stuhlmueller, it has been hard—even now—to think of him as gone. His humane spirit and his genuine holiness touched people deeply. He worked hard, teaching and writing right up to the end of his life. And now through this book and through Carroll's passionate reflections on the psalms he loved so well, his great work still continues.

Donald Senior, c.p.
Catholic Theological Union

Editor's Preface

The death of Carroll Stuhlmueller, C.P., in February 1994 was a sad experience for his students, friends, and biblical colleagues. A scholar of great insight and profound thought, Carroll was a prolific writer who, up until his last days, was busy working on articles and manuscripts, including *The Spirituality of the Psalms*. He had completed a first draft of all the chapters but two—Chapters 12 and 13—which Timothy Lenchak, S.V.D., supplied from Carroll's commentary *Psalms 1 and 2*.[1]

This text on the spirituality of the psalms represents the thought and work of Carroll Stuhlmueller, C.P. Because the incomplete manuscript was fifteen years old when I received it, the work needed some editing, revising, and updating, all of which I have done with care so as not to lose Carroll's "voice" and "hand" in the text.

It has been a privilege for me to work on Carroll's manuscript, and I am grateful to Linda Maloney of The Liturgical Press, who invited me to bring Carroll's work to completion. I am also grateful to Timothy Lenchak, S.V.D., who read and edited the first draft of this work, prior to my receiving it. I would also like to acknowledge Lissa Romell who worked untiringly to type out Carroll's hand-written manuscript in preparation for editing and publication. I would be remiss if I did not express sincere gratitude to Donald Senior, C.P., who was one of Carroll's revered colleagues at the Catholic Theological Union in Chicago where Carroll taught for many years. Don has advocated consistently that Carroll's unfinished projects be brought to completion.

Finally, this work is dedicated to the memory of Carroll Stuhlmueller, C.P., who, in the company of saints, proclaims:

---

[1] Carroll Stuhlmueller, *Psalms 1 and 2*, Old Testament Message 21 and 22 (Wilmington, Del.: Michael Glazier, 1983).

How lovely is your dwelling place,
    O LORD of hosts! . . .
my heart and my flesh sing for joy
    to the living God (Ps 84:1, 2b).

Carol J. Dempsey, O.P.

Chapter One

The Psalms within the Bible and Christian Community

"Everything written about me in the law of Moses, the prophets, and the psalms must be fulfilled" (Luke 24:44).

In many ways the psalms are at the heart of the Bible, or at least at the start of important places in the Bible. Not surprisingly, then, one finds the Gospels portraying Jesus frequently turning to the psalms to experience peace in the desperate moment of dying (Luke 23:46; Ps 31:5), as earlier in difficult times of controversy (Matt 22:42-44; Ps 110:1) or temptation (Matt 4:3-11; Ps 91:9-13); or for inculcating trust in God's loving care (Luke 12:22; Ps 55:23). In the Gospels, Jesus continues to give important emphasis to the psalms after the resurrection. In an appearance to the eleven apostles, Jesus calmed their fears and started them on the long trek to understand his life and especially his death:

> Then he said to them, "These are my words that I spoke to you while I was still with you—that everything written about me in the law of Moses, the prophets, and the psalms must be fulfilled." Then he opened their minds to understand the scriptures, and he said to them, "Thus it is written, that the Messiah is to suffer and to rise from the dead on the third day" (Luke 24:44-46).

The reference to "the law of Moses, the prophets, and the psalms" follows a Jewish style of naming their Bible by its major sections. "Psalms" stands for the entire third part, everything not contained in the five books of Moses (the "Law") and in the former and latter prophetic books.

The psalms have continued to maintain a prominent position in the lives of believers today. They offer a harmony to life and a rhythm that keeps us peacefully in tune with the intense fervor of life.

1

Walking through the Book of the Psalms

In order to grasp a sense of the content, the melody, and prayers of the psalms, a preliminary walk through the Bible is necessary. Several external features are considered not only to satisfy one's curiosity but also to begin appreciating the family background, origin, and life of the psalms. Is this not what friends invite other friends to do when they first have the privilege of visiting them at home? Friends show their guests through their home and, as they slowly move from one room to another, they explain the pictures and paintings on the wall, the family memorabilia, the photos of their children or parents or of themselves. They direct their guests' attention along the way, for instance, to gifts from distant places or other items purchased on vacation or holiday; to the children's first assignments from school, most elementary yet very precious to the parents; to a piano or musical instrument, the occasion to invite someone in the family, generally one of the children, to play a piece; to alterations in the structure of the home, like a new porch, or to the redecorated kitchen or den. Such a tour of the home becomes a mark of honor and trust, for there is a sharing of family life and history, in its secret joys and sorrows, in its small but important accomplishments, in its hopes and dreams.

As indicated already, the psalms reflect the life and beliefs of the ancient Israelite community, and they played a prominent role in the early Christian community, particularly in the community's prayer, preaching, and worship. Paul's words, in his epistle to the Romans, challenge readers and listeners today to respect and ponder even what at first seems odd or useless. After quoting from one of the most difficult lines of the psalms, a selection from a "curse psalm" (Ps 69:9), Paul proceeds to say:

> For whatever was written in former days was written for our instruction, so that by steadfastness and by the encouragement of the scriptures we might have hope. May the God of steadfastness and encouragement grant you to live in harmony with one another, in accordance with Christ Jesus, so that together you may with one voice glorify the God and Father of our Lord Jesus Christ (Rom 15:4-6).

Paul stresses an appreciation for the Scriptures and a reverent attention to the tradition, "For I handed on to you as of first importance what I in turn had received" (cf. 1 Cor 11:23; Phil 4:9). And yet, because the tradition is a living one, it needs to be read and reread and heard anew in the context of contemporary life.

The Bible, and specifically the book of Psalms, has been handed down to us, divided into separate sections, with enumeration of psalms and verses. A look now at this environment and the structure of the psalms will release secrets "so that by steadfastness and by the encouragement of the scriptures we might have hope" (Rom 15:4).

The Psalms: A Book with Many Books

The psalms contain any number of details for a game of trivia. Such incidental, and at times accidental, details provide the stuff not only for humor but also, like humor, for important aspects of anyone's personality. For instance, types of clothing or hairstyle, hours for rising from sleep and retiring to sleep, stories that suppress some details and enhance others, these and many other trivial tidbits can turn out to be very illuminating about a person. Still other aspects of a person's life may be inherited, like being prone to sickness, or happen accidentally, like a broken leg or, worse still, the severing of an arm or leg—yet these events have the potential of profoundly changing someone's attitude and eventually one's personality.

Accordingly, one needs to observe the external aspects of the psalms, even if these details seem boring and irrelevant to us today. Paying attention to the psalms in this way prepares a person to meet, with solicitude and openness, an ancient people and culture. It is possible for a contemporary reader or listener to enter the heart and life of early Israel and come to see what the Israelites considered to be important, and come to an understanding of how the psalms reflect certain salient features of the community's personality. One can make friends and influence strangers by meeting them on their own grounds and not evaluating their usefulness or importance. How one reads the Bible, and the psalms within it, prepares that person for life and work within the Christian community and the world.

The book of Psalms alerts readers of the text to unique features about the Bible. It consists of five books, and its organization informs readers of major stages of its growth. As new groups of psalms were collected and added to an earlier collection, what at first may have been an appendix to a preexisting book became itself a new book of Psalms. For many reasons—practical reasons in order to remember (in an oral culture where most things were passed down by word of mouth and memory) and to preserve (lest some psalms get lost in the shuffle), and topical reasons in order to cluster together similar groups of psalms—a new book was attached to an earlier book. Gradually, the one book of Psalms grew into five books.

Each book was drawn to a close by a doxology. The entire Psalter closes solemnly with Psalms 146–150, where one finds the phrase "praise the Lord" repeated often. One curiosity in these dramatic conclusions to each book occurs at the end of book two (Psalms 42–72). Here one reads: "The prayers of David the son of Jesse are ended." Either this means simply that one of the series of David psalms so ended or else that a religious authority decided, after allowing a second book of psalms into the sacred collection, that there would be no more additions. Like any disciplinary decree this one too could be, and actually was, reversed.

The clear division of the book of Psalms stands in contrast to another case in which new books were added without any such clear indications. Scholarship has struggled long and persistently to decide major changes and new "books" in the prophecy of Isaiah. There is a popular consensus that the one book of Isaiah consists of three books, called First (chapters 1–39), Second (chapters 40–55), and Third Isaiah (chapters 56–66). All, of course, are equally inspired. Consequently, it is helpful to think of an Isaian tradition rather than a single Isaian author. The book, on several occasions, refers to disciples who were preserving the teaching of a gifted prophet (see Isa 8:16; 30:8; 50:4). Preservation included authentic accounts, perhaps verbatim, but it also demanded adaptation to new circumstances.

Returning to the five books of Psalms, one discovers telltale signs of such adaptation. It is not that one account is wrong and the other correct, but rather that people lived in different circumstances and pastorally had different needs. One example in which parts of two psalms were joined to form a psalm that is new and different from the parent stock is Psalm 108, which includes verses also found in Psalm 57 (see, e.g., Pss 108:1-4 and 57:7-10).

Psalm 108 closes with very different lines from Psalm 60. This latter psalm explodes with the thunder of war and the deadening silence of defeat. So different from the generous outreach to the foreign nations, just quoted from Psalm 57, the psalmist reels with anger or disdain:

> "Moab is my washbasin;
>> on Edom I hurl my shoe;
>> over Philistia I shout in triumph."
> With God we shall do valiantly;
>> it is he who will tread down our foes (Ps 60:8, 12).

It seems that the editor of Psalm 108 considered Psalm 57 too gentle or passive under oppression and Psalm 60 too militaristic and angry. By combining parts of both psalms, the editor produced a new psalm in which Psalm 57 subdues the sounds of war, and Psalm 60 adds strength and teeth to the meek patience of the former. Psalm 108 comes from a later period when Israel no longer possessed an army of any significance, yet, nonetheless, from a time when people were not to submit silently to oppression. The collector of psalms in the fifth book (Psalms 107–150) evidently saw a need of balancing Psalms 57 and 60 in the second book (Psalms 42–72) with the new Psalm 108.

This example advises us to take our own pastoral commission seriously, that is, with similar ingenuity. As a matter of fact, the members of the Christian community who have helped to shape various church lectionaries have frequently taken such initiative by combining various biblical selections to help communicate the mysterious graces of a feast day or of a liturgical cycle like Advent or Lent.

Psalms, Numbered Differently—Why?

If one compares different editions of the Bible—for instance, Psalm 51 in an old Catholic, "Rheims-Douay" version, in the NAB, and in the New Revised Standard Version (hereafter, the NRSV)—one comes up against a confusing set of differences. To compound the complexity still more, we note in passing that the English edition of the New Jerusalem Bible (hereafter, NJB) does not conform with original French editions in numbering the verses within many psalms. What is Ps 50:1 in the Rheims-Douay Bible turns out to be Ps 51:3 in the NAB and Ps 51:1 in the NRSV. Here one is dealing with various traditions for numbering the psalms and for numbering the verses within individual psalms.

Already in Old Testament times two traditions emerged for enumerating the psalms. One of these shows up in the Hebrew Bible, another in an ancient Greek version called the Septuagint. Chart 1.1 points out how some verses within the two versions are numbered differently:

Chart 1.1

Hebrew	Greek
Pss 1–8	1–9
9–10	9
11–113	10–112
114–115	113
116	114–115
117–146	116–145
147	146–147
148–150	148–150
—	151

The Hebrew numbering is followed by Jews and Protestants, as well as by Catholics since Vatican II and, therefore, by the NAB and NJB.

The question naturally arises: Which enumeration is better? Each has its strengths and its weaknesses. All agree that originally Psalms 9–10 (Hebrew) were a single psalm as in the Greek, and that Psalm 113 (Greek) combines the originally separate Psalms 114–115 (Hebrew). Furthermore, both systems separate Psalms 42–43 (or Psalms 41–42 in Greek). Yet, the original unit had to combine both psalms. The same refrain and many key phrases run through both psalms. It is not a question, then, of which system is superior. Rather, each represents a valid, acceptable liturgical tradition. For some, Psalm 9 (Greek) may have seemed too long and so became Psalms 9–10 (Hebrew), a manual of prayers and sacred readings just as today in the *Christian Prayer Book*. The longest of all psalms (Psalm 119, Hebrew) is spread throughout this prayer book in twenty-two segments.

Evidence from ancient Jewish writings indicates that Psalm 113 (Greek) was divided into Psalms 114–115 (Hebrew) so that in singing what is known as the Hallel or Praise Psalms (Psalms 113–118, Hebrew) on the three major feasts of Passover, Weeks, and Tabernacles, Psalms 113–114 (Hebrew) were sung in the first part and Psalms 115–118 (Hebrew) toward the end.

Psalms with Their Titles and Setting

As mentioned above, the situation becomes even murkier, for there is also a double arrangement for counting the verses within individual psalms. Most psalms have what is called a "title" or short directive as to authorship and style of singing (for instance, melody or musical instrument or attitude or day of the week). Referring back to Psalm 51, one notes that the title of Psalm 51 reads: "To the leader. A Psalm of David, when the prophet Nathan the prophet came to him, after he had gone in to Bathsheba." The NAB conforms with the Hebrew in numbering the title verses 1-2; the psalm proper begins with verse 3, "Have mercy on me, O God, in your goodness . . . ."

The Hebrew prints the title in a type size equal to the rest of the psalm. Rabbis, in commenting on the psalm, spend equal, if not more, time on the title. Without a doubt, Jewish people venerated the title as an integral part of the inspired Holy Scripture. The NAB is not quite sure, for while it prints the title of Psalm 51 as verses 1-2, it also reduces the size of the lettering. NRSV and NJB print the titles but also in small letters and outside the numbering. The ancient Latin translation, called the Vulgate, similarly leaves the title without numbers. These two traditions can each be traced back to a liturgical reason. Because the titles were never used in prayer and worship, the Vulgate, which reflects the liturgical texts and practices of the Western church, omitted the numbers to the title. The Hebrew tradition kept the number because the title frequently describes how the psalm is to be sung or used during liturgy.

All this convoluted data about numbering psalms and their individual verses may seem of interest only to scholars and other antiquarian-minded people, but such a statement is not true for the following reason that is based upon the Hebrew tradition. Again the title of Psalm 51, quoted above, serves as a working example. "To the leader," refers to the master of the ceremony or choir director, and alerts this person to the fact that the following psalm requires special attention. The phrase, "A Psalm of David," does not so much intend to certify the authorship by King David himself, as to copyright the psalm for a guild of psalm writers under the patronage of King David and possibly founded by him. Most scholars hesitate about the immediate composition by David because the psalm shows the influence of Second and Third Isaiah (Isaiah 40–55 and 56–66) as well as of Ezekiel. These prophets lived some four or five hundred years after King David (1000–965 B.C.E.) during and at the end of the Babylonian exile (587–539 B.C.E.). Compare Ps 51:3-4 with Isa 59:12-13 or Ps 51:6-10 with Ezek 36:25-26.

Because the titles to the psalms invoke a spirit to accompany the psalm, they evoke a very important conclusion. How one recites, prays, or sings a psalm becomes an integral part of the psalm. As noted earlier, the Isaian tradition kept alive the message of First Isaiah and also adapted it to later ages. The book of Isaiah represents as much an inspired tradition over several centuries, a Second and a Third Isaiah, as it does an individual inspired author, First Isaiah, at the beginning. The psalms absorb their prayers into an inspired psalm tradition. One's attitudes and applications may never be added to the Bible like the titles were, nor like the Second and Third Isaiahs. Yet, the psalms affirm people with a style that is genuinely biblical. The psalms, besides being inspired, are also canonical: they are an authentic witness and norm of faith for all generations and, therefore, they are entitled to a place in the Bible.

This explanation brings up an important theological position specific to the Catholic Church, namely, that the Bible is to be read and interpreted within the faith of the community. The movements of liturgical worship, of justice and compassion—the heartbeat of Catholic life and the bonding within a world church which shares its insights and unique religious movements—this setting of a community alive in its prayer, study, teaching, and work leads one to new perceptions and applications while reciting or singing the psalms. Important moments in the Liturgical Year like Easter and Pentecost, new as well as ancient feasts, suggest "antiphons" or short prayerful statements before and after the psalms, plus a special prayer at the end. In all these ways readers are led to interpret the psalms and the entire Bible within the context of a community of faith. Much progress has been made in light of the titles to the psalms. Yet, the way is continuous, so that the tradition and purpose of titles live on within the antiphons in prayer books, and within the larger setting of the believing community.

This chapter opened with the Gospel writer Luke portraying Jesus instructing his eleven apostles: "Then he said to them, 'These are my words that I spoke to you while I was still with you—that everything written about me in the law of Moses, the prophets, and the psalms must be fulfilled'" (Luke 24:44). Immediately afterward, Luke adds: "Then he opened their minds to understand the scriptures" (Luke 24:45). The text suggests that Jesus' disciples were empowered to look into the Scripture with a new depth of meaning. People today, through their faith in Jesus as Lord and Savior, continue to perceive new insights and applications. Jesus lives within the body of the Christian community (1 Cor 12:27-30), where the Holy Spirit not only bestows various gifts and ministries (1 Cor 12:4-11; Eph 4:1-16) but also, through these gifts, leads to diverse, complementary perceptions and applications (1 Cor 3:5-15; 9:19-23; Gal 1:12; 2:7-10).

The book of Psalms, even from only a quick walk through its pages, manifests many signs of growth and development. This one book is actually a collection of five books. After one of the books was completed, new psalms began to cluster together and soon became a book all their own. Growth such as this never repeated the past but adapted earlier traditions for prayer and worship to later, different circumstances. Psalm 108 made something new, even if it consists of one-half from Psalm 57 and the other half from Psalm 60. The titles were added to the psalms in order to instruct the community, as evidenced by Psalm 51. Even the different ways of numbering the psalms and the verses within individual psalms mirror liturgical traditions. How the psalms were used in the liturgy affected the final canonical shape of the psalms in the Bible.

Contemporary believing communities are inheritors of the faith and traditions of the biblical people. The psalms not only offer guidance but also are seen in new forms. Just as Psalm 108 reached something new, likewise readers and hearers of the psalms can arrive at new insights, in continuity with the biblical ancestors in the faith yet beyond their clear knowledge of what the psalm is saying.

In summary, unfathomable riches of the psalms, hidden for all ages in God, the Creator, enlighten people today. God's manifold wisdom is made known in the life and work of the community in accord with God's age-old purpose in Christ Jesus our Lord (cf. Eph 3:8-12).

Chapter Two

Methods for Studying
and Praying the Psalms

"O that today you would listen to his voice!" (Ps 95:7).

Chapter 1 discussed various aspects of the book of Psalms, mostly external details about the sweep of the 150 psalms in the Bible, such as the different systems for numbering the psalms and their verses, as well as the question of "titles." Chapter 2 draws closer to the texts of the individual psalms, with particular attention given to Psalm 95, in order to clarify some helpful methods for studying each and every psalm. What follows is a series of seven guiding "principles" that can help readers to become fully engaged in the psalms not only as historical and literary documents but more specifically as expressions of prayer.

First Principle: "Today" Has Its Own Grace

Psalm 95 is an example with which to begin a discussion not only because it reflects enough structure and variety to apply its principles to other psalms but also because Psalm 95 is the traditional "invitatory psalm" of the divine office or official prayer of the Church. For many centuries, Psalm 95 invited the monks, nuns, and congregations to prayer at the early dawn of each new day. While the psalm itself was chanted by a special choir or by a solo voice, the congregation intervened about every four lines with an "antiphon."

The "antiphon" consisted of a refrain linked with the feast for the day or with the liturgical cycle. It often included the word "today" from verse 7 of Psalm 95: "O that today you would listen to his voice!" The word "today" of Psalm 95, typical of the book of Deuteronomy, made the ancient mystery of Christ's birth or Pentecost happen again in the moment of prayer and worship. An example of this theology of "actualization," actualizing now what happened then, occurs frequently in Deuteronomy. For example:

> Hear, O Israel, the statutes and ordinances that I am addressing to you today; you shall learn them and observe them diligently. The LORD our God made a covenant with us at Horeb. Not with our ancestors did the LORD make this covenant, but with us, who are all of us here alive today. The LORD spoke with you face to face at the mountain, out of the fire (Deut 5:1-4).

See as well Deut 6:20-25 with its repetition of "us," not "them." This theme of "today" recurs frequently in Deuteronomy (e.g., Deut 4:4, 8; 6:6; 7:11; 11:8, 13, 27, 28, 32; 13:18; 29:12, 15; 30:2, 8, 11, 16, 18, 19). The book of Deuteronomy recasts the instruction and laws of Moses in the form of great sermons (like the Gospel of Matthew does in depicting Jesus as one who preaches and teaches) so that later generations re-experience, spiritually or liturgically, in new and different circumstances, what God accomplished for their ancestors in the days of Moses.

There are other similarities besides "today" between Psalm 95 and Deuteronomy. (Although Psalm 95 has been influenced by other parts of the Bible, like Isaiah 40–55, here the concentration is upon its relation with Deuteronomy.) Like Psalm 95, this fifth book of the Torah frequently warns the people against temptation (e.g., Deut 6:10-15; 8:6-20). Very similar to Ps 95:8 is the passage: "Do not put the LORD your God to the test, as you tested him at Massah" (Deut 6:16). Deuteronomy, like Psalm 95, alludes to the anger of the Lord against sinful Israel (Ps 95:11; Deut 6:15; 9:16-22), to the wonders which Israel witnessed (Ps 95:9; Deut 6:22; 10:21; 11:1-9), and to the promised rest (Ps 95:11; Deut 12:10). Indeed, to appreciate the movement of thought in Psalm 95, especially in verses 7b-11, one needs to glance over the first ten or twelve chapters of Deuteronomy.

Further attention will be given to Deuteronomy in order to understand better the seemingly abrupt transition in Psalm 95 from verse 7a to 7b. (In the second half of verse 7 the joy of an exuberant hymn quickly switches to a prophetic warning.) Here, however, the focus has been on Deuteronomy in order to gain a sense of the forcefulness of the word "today." This new day—a day with its own set of hopes and problems, of feasts and liturgical seasons—has its own special graces and inspiration.

The first recommendation for a method in reading the psalms intelligently and profitably is to believe firmly that God has a special grace for all creation this day in the psalms. This unique grace repeats what has been given to God's ancient people, yet the repetition comes new as though for the first time. It answers the needs and hopes of "today."

Second Principle: Read the Text of the Psalm

It may seem strange to repeat the obvious: one needs to read the text, the actual words of the psalm that are intended for study and prayer. Perhaps what this second principle is stressing is the need to read the psalm slowly and reverently. Savor each word. Read with the faith that God is speaking each word as though for the first time.

Psalm 95 reads according to a new translation, proposed by a subcommittee of the International Commission for English in the Liturgy (ICEL):

> Come, sing with joy to God,
> shout to our savior, our rock.
> Enter God's presence with praise,
> enter with shouting and song.
>
> A great God is the Lord,
> over the gods like a king.
> God cradles the depths of the earth,
> holds fast the mountain peaks.
> God shaped the ocean and owns it,
> formed the earth by hand.
>
> Come, bow down and worship,
> kneel to the Lord our maker.
> This is our God, our shepherd,
> we are the flock led with care.
>
> Listen today to God's voice:
> "Harden no heart as at Meribah,
> on that day in the desert at Massah.
> There your people tried me,
> though they had seen my work.
>
> "Forty years with that lot!
> I said: They are perverse,
> they do not accept my ways.
> So I swore in my anger:
> They shall not enter my rest."

This translates the Bible according to the principle of dynamic equivalence. According to this norm, the Hebrew text is not rendered word for word (formal equivalence) but, rather, its words are communicated with the intention of dynamically involving the reader or listener, the one at prayer or at worship, in the message of the Bible.

The second principle also invites readers, ideally at least, to read the psalms according to many, or at least more than one, translation. One needs to read with an eye to difference, and ask "Why?" or "What new insight can be gained?" A person may want to compare the following, somewhat literal translation with the one above, which is a dynamic equivalent to what follows:

Part One

-a-

1. Step forward! Ring out [your joy] to the Lord!
       Let us sing aloud [literally: shout] to the Rock, our Savior!
2. Gratefully, let us approach God's presence [literally: face].
       With music[al instruments] let us sing aloud [literally: shout]
          to God.

-b-

3. What a great God is the Lord,
       a great king over all gods.
4. In his hand the depths of the earth,
       and the mountain peaks.
5. The sea belongs to its Maker,
       the dry land too, formed by God's hand.

-c-

6. Come! Let us worship! Let us bow profoundly!
       Let us kneel in the presence [literally: before the face] of the
          Lord [now] creating us.
7a. The Lord, indeed, is our God,
       while we are the people of God's shepherding,
          the flock in God's hands.

Part Two

-a-

7b. Oh, that today you hear God's voice!

-b-

8. Do not let your heart be hardened as [happened] at Meribah
       [or place of Dispute],
          as on that wilderness day at Massah [or, at Testing Place].
9. There your ancestors tested me,
       they tempted me, though they had seen my wonders.

-c-

10. For forty years how I loathed that generation,
    I declared them a people with erring heart,
        wandering off from my way [literally: not experiencing my way].
11. Angrily I swear:
    [thus] they can never be at rest with me [literally: enter into my rest].

A slow, prayerful, and studious reading of the text, comparing translations if one has access to the Hebrew poetry, should do more than acquaint readers with the text of the Bible. Hopefully it will revive memories of other times at prayer when this psalm had impressed its readers and hearers, and had communicated secret, penetrating messages from God. Perhaps this or another psalm being studied was sung at a wedding or a religious profession of vows or at the funeral of a dear one. Such a remembrance draws listeners and readers into a company of saints, or what the epistle to the Hebrews calls a "great . . . cloud of witnesses" (Heb 12:1).

A careful yet informed and critical reading of the text of the Bible, and specifically, the text of the psalms, can draw someone into a sacred company of saints and memories. Together hearers listen reverently and gratefully, carefully and delicately to God's word handed down to the community of believers by the community's ancient ancestors whose lives and experiences reflected in the psalms can offer people hope and consolation, and a glimmer into the divine ways of God.

Third Principle: Read the Text with Imagination

Very few parts of the Bible originated in mystic isolation, separated from us in opaque silence. The Bible generally unravels in stories, teeming with conversation and movement, color and sound. We need to read and listen with imagination. Yet, as the psalms ritually reenact these stories of salvation, they blend silent adoration with singing and procession. Imagination never excludes ecstatic prayer.

Before returning to Psalm 95 to exemplify this third principle or method for reading and praying with the Bible with imagination, a few incidents in the career of Moses, the founder of Israel's religion and its great lawgiver, need consideration because the second part of Psalm 95 reminisces about the days with Moses at Meribah and Massah in the Sinai desert.

When Moses first ascended Mount Sinai, "there was thunder and lightning, as well as a thick cloud on the mountain, and a blast of a trumpet so loud that all the people who were in the camp trembled" (Exod 19:16). This same chapter, if reread carefully, records Moses' frequent return trips to the people before again reentering the cloud, smoke, and thunder of God's presence. Notice, for instance, the trips up and down the mountain in verses 3, 14, 20, 24-25.

Moses was even to spend forty days and forty nights, without eating any food or drinking any water: "he neither ate bread nor drank water" (Exod 34:28; see also Exod 24:18). When Moses returned to the people, "the skin of his face shone because he had been talking with God. When Aaron and all the Israelites saw Moses, the skin of his face was shining, and they were afraid to come near him" (Exod 34:29-30). As a result, except when conversing with God, Moses "put a veil on his face" (34:33). Moses' actions, up and down the mountain, in and out of the meeting tent, as well as his drawing and withdrawing a veil over his face, radiate with light—everything involves the imagination if listeners and readers are to feel the impact of the biblical account.

Likewise, Psalm 95 invites its audience into a liturgical procession with sound and sight, until the audience is at the sanctuary and filled with awe. There is much for the imagination. The psalm invites those assembled to "come into [God's] presence" (v. 2a). The people encourage one another to "make a joyful noise to [God] with songs of praise!" (v. 2b). Verse 4 addresses "the depths of the heights of the mountains," possibly those that flank the Kidron Valley that separates Mount Zion on the west and the three mounts of temptation, evil counsel, and olives on the east. The appeal to the imagination invites listeners and readers to reach out to glimpse the desert farther to the east and the Mediterranean Sea which guards Israel on the far west. The psalmist continues to proclaim: "The sea is his, for he made it, / And the dry land, which his hands have formed."

One's imagination continues with the procession through the Kidron Valley until it arrives at the base of the temple. Here it ascends, passes through the outer gate, and leads the people into the courtyard immediately before the Holy Place and the Holy of Holies (cf. Exod 26:31-37; 40:16-33). In this open area, which included the altar of holocaust, the people were invited to "bow down" and "kneel before the LORD" (v. 6). Awesome silence settles over the congregation. Picturing the people grouped together, one then hears the cantor sing: "We are the people of his pasture, / and the sheep of his hand" (Ps 95:7a).

One's imagination, in fact one's whole attitude of joyful singing with musical instruments, can easily picture different groups of people. While the entire congregation sings the two refrains (vv. 1-2, 6), a special choir intones more elaborately the motivation for processing to the sanctuary (vv. 3-5) and prostrating before the Holy Place (v. 7a). One can spot as well the different musicians. No doubt, children are running along and shouting as they did in Jesus' day (see Matt 21:15-16).

Finally, Psalm 95 causes one to experience a jolt caused by the sudden change to a prophetic threat against false, formalistic worship:

> O that today you would listen to his voice!
>   Do not harden your hearts, as at Meribah,
>   as on the day at Massah in the wilderness (Ps 95:7b-8).

If one has been picturing and resonating with the intense, joyful scene, then one needs a further explanation. If one recalls the earlier discussion of the first principle about today having its own grace and the influence of the book of Deuteronomy on the composer of this psalm, then one can picture an action between verse 7a and verse 7b. In the spirit and style of Deuteronomy, a Levite comes forward to proclaim the sacred Scripture or Tradition and then to preach about its meaning and application. See, for instance, Deut 31:9-13, 24-29 or a later, very similar instance during the reform of Ezra the scribe: "Then Ezra blessed the LORD, the great God, and all the people answered, 'Amen, Amen,' lifting up their hands. . . . So they read from the book, from the law of God, with interpretation. They gave the sense, so that the people understood the reading" (Neh 8:6, 8).

Moreover, in the pronouncement of Ezra and Nehemiah to the people who are fearful about their sinfulness: "This day is holy to the LORD your God; do not mourn or weep" (Neh 8:9), there is yet another parallel that illuminates the seeming disjuncture of verse 7a-b.

Imaginative, reverent, and attentive involvement in the stages of action in Psalm 95 could enable hearers and readers to supplement the psalm with the proclamation of Scripture and a sermon between verse 7a and verse 7b. The prophetic threat then in verses 7b-11, in the spirit of the previous passage from Nehemiah 8–9 or again from Deuteronomy 31, becomes the solemn closing of the sacred service in Psalm 95. As the people leave the sanctuary and return home, they must not imitate the disobedience and insolence of their ancestors in the wilderness with Moses. Otherwise, they will not enter into God's rest.

Fourth Principle: Read the Psalms According to Its Key Words

Hebrew, like other ancient, Semitic languages, was primarily an oral language and only secondarily a written language. References to writing down the inspired word, or reading it from a written text, do not become frequent and dominant until the time of Isaiah (740–696 B.C.E.; see Isa 8:16; 30:8) and Jeremiah (627–587 B.C.E.; see Jeremiah 36), some five or six hundred years after Moses. Even the Hebrew words for scroll or book did not mean in their original or primary sense "to write down." "Scroll" comes from a Hebrew word meaning "to roll"; "book" derives from a Hebrew word meaning "to proclaim" or "to announce."

In any oral culture and, for that matter, even in a written culture, when people speak conversationally and especially when they orate publicly, the sound of words, their rhythm, and their repetition take on a unique significance. Music and poetry move on a momentum of sound and refrain.

The psalms belong to Israel's oral culture. In order to perceive properly what the inspired poet is communicating, one needs to attend to key words. These are words that are repeated or that occur in strategic places as at the beginning, middle, or end, or at important transitions. Dependent upon one's knowledge of the Hebrew language, key words can be recognized when they share very similar sounds or else are identical in sound but actually are to be translated differently in English.

Two examples, dependent on the Hebrew, come into focus in Psalm 8. "Your name" (v. 1), "your heavens" (v. 3), or simply "heavens" sound almost the same in Hebrew: *shemeka, shamêka,* and *shamayim.* The heavens, accordingly, proclaim the name of the Lord and surround the earth with what the name signifies: an intimate, personal presence or, even more pointedly, a special "vocation" or "calling." The heavens with its stars, moon, and sun spell out the name of the Lord, our Savior and our God. A second example, the interrogative particle in "*how* majestic" and "*what* are human beings" (Ps 8:1, 4), is the same in both cases: *mah.* The use of a single word unites the two exclamations (for that is what they are, rather than a question): How splendid or glorious is God's name! What then must be the wonder of a human being—even if this human being at first appears so tiny and unimportant compared to the expanse of sky with its heavenly bodies? Thus, key words center the cosmos first around man and woman and, ultimately, around the Lord God. God, of course, is first and foremost, but God, as the text suggests, lays the world at the feet of man and woman, crowning them with glory and splendor.

The key words in Psalm 95—and there are quite a few of them—are immediately evident to a non-Hebrew reader. Most frequent are the words for "come" or "step forward," "process," "move onward." These words in part one, then, become a motif in the second part that deals with Israel's journey through the wilderness with Moses. Another key word, "his hand" or "hand of God," is found three times:

> v. 4: In his hand are the depths of the earth;
>   the heights of the mountains are his also.
> v. 5: The sea is his, for he made it,
>   and the dry land, which his hands have formed.

v. 7a: For he is our God,
>> and we are the people of his pasture,
>> and the sheep of his hand.

Because of their central, pivotal places in the psalm, the words "today" and "rest" also deserve to be recognized as key words.

As the phrase "key word" declares, each word acts as a key to open up new treasures and to communicate an otherwise hidden or mysterious meaning. Key words function this way both for the psalm and for the reader or community. A curious and very revelatory experience occurs when a group of people, studying a psalm, are asked to pick out their key word. The word should be truly key or truly significant in the psalm, but in this case, there are at least three key words. Different persons in the group will usually choose different words. Why?—because of personal insights or problems or experiences, unique to themselves. In this case, a study of the psalm from the vantage of a key word brings to light hidden aspects of the psalm that, in turn, can throw light upon the person choosing the word.

One such example is the key word (or, perhaps better here, the single key idea) of "come," "step forward," "move onward," "stay on pilgrimage":

> vv. 1-2: Only if people continuously move onward, not alone but as a community in worship, can they come into God's presence.
> v. 4: At times one may reach exalted moments, and one's mountain peaks; at other times the person may feel depressed in the depth of the earth. Come—move onward! Neither experience lasts forever; it will pass. Reality is more in change than in inertia.
> v. 6: Even ecstatic moments of prayer will pass away, and a person then needs to move onward, back to monotonous routine.
> vv. 9-10: The goal is for all people to move onward, realizing that no one is ever destroyed by sin and guilt. As for Israel, so for God's people, these negative experiences are all anticipated, so that they can learn to struggle and to assist others in their struggle and move onward to peace.
> v. 11: Even God's anger and oath are passing. As in the days of Moses (see Exod 32:14), so now God moves onward. God relents, as the prophet pleads so eloquently in Isa 63:7–64:11.

Most of all, perhaps, the key idea to "come" and "move onward" lies in what is most essential in any journey, whether Israel's in the wilderness, the community's toward the sanctuary, or one's own in his or her ethical striving. Only at the end is there any hope of rest—the last word in Psalm 95. This example shows how a psalm takes on new meaning or reflects hidden karats of beauty by rereading the psalm from the focus of one of its key words.

Fifth Principle: Read the Psalm with Other Parallel Passages

Key or identical words also show up in another way, namely, when phrases or lines of a psalm are quoted elsewhere in the Bible. Often this is a matter of New Testament writers using an Old Testament passage, but not always. Job 7:17 seems to be alluding to Ps 8:4; another link occurs between Jer 1:5 and Ps 22:9-10 as well as between Ps 51:3-4 and Isa 59:12-13. In fact, some psalms, like Psalm 143, are filigrees of biblical passages. As already noted in Chapter 1 of this book, more psalms are repeated in part or in their entirety elsewhere in the book of psalms: Psalms 14 and 53 are almost identical; Psalm 70 is repeated at the end of Psalm 40; Psalm 108 consists of Pss 57:7-10 and 60:6-12. This is not a matter of repetition, however, as a new setting is always provided. Another word for this phenomenon, instead of repetition, is "parallel places." That phrase provides readers and listeners with the rubric in this study of the fifth principle for interpreting psalms.

Most English translations of the Bible supply cross-references to other parts of the Bible—as the *New Jerusalem Bible* does handily in the margins or the *New American Bible* does toward the bottom of each page. These citations draw attention to the way that the Bible interprets the Bible.

In quoting an earlier part of the Bible, the new inspired author is not a literalist or a modern scholar of critical-historical bent. In fact, when Eph 4:8 reads a passage from Ps 68:18, the author goes so far as to reverse the meaning, as the following lines manifest:

Ps 68:18	Eph 4:8
You ascended the high mount, leading captives in your train, and receiving gifts from people.	When he ascended on high he made captivity itself a captive; he gave gifts to his people.

While the author of Ps 68:18 was most probably referring to King David who, returning victoriously to Jerusalem after subduing a revolt somewhere in his extensive empire (cf. 2 Sam 12:26-31), assigned some of the captives as temple slaves (cf. Josh 9:23, 27; Neh 7:22), such a situation gradually became religiously intolerable for later rabbis. Their problem was not so much over slavery, unfortunately taken for granted as also in the New Testament, but over the bold and blunt statement that men and women gave gifts to God. As Psalm 50 declared in God's name:

> If I were hungry, I would not tell you,
>   for the world and all that is in it is mine.
> Do I eat the flesh of bulls,
>   or drink the blood of goats?

Offer to God a sacrifice of thanksgiving
and pay your vows to the Most High (Ps 50:12-14).

In the ancient Israelite worldview, God was seen as being supremely independent. Lest the sovereignty of God be misunderstood and compromised, teachers of a later age read the psalm similarly to the New Testament—only with a different interpretation. The rabbis explained that Moses was the one who "ascended on high," namely Mount Sinai, where God gave him the gift of the Law and covenant. The epistle to the Ephesians develops the application still further, this time about Jesus who died, was buried, rose to God, and sent the gift of the Holy Spirit. This same Holy Spirit lavished upon the Church the many ministries for service:

([Christ] who descended is the same one who ascended far above all the heavens, so that he might fill all with things.) The gifts he gave were that some would be apostles, some prophets, some evangelists, some pastors and teachers, to equip the saints for the work of ministry, for building up the body of Christ" (Eph 4:10-12).

The Bible, even when written down, never remained a dead letter but lived with the growing religious sense and the pastoral needs of the people of God. It was being interpreted within a living tradition. This brief study of Ps 68:18 and Eph 4:8 exemplifies what Christians mean in stating that the Bible is to be interpreted within the believing community. It is not that the community members declare the Bible to be incorrect and so change it. Rather, like the rabbis of pre-Christian times, there is a recognition that a text can give a wrong meaning or be misinterpreted in the new setting of a later age. The Bible is always in need of elucidation through prayer, research, study, and teaching. This short diversion with Psalm 68, with its radical change of meaning in the rabbis and in the New Testament, helps illustrate the principle of interpretation being discussed.

Returning now to Psalm 95, one discovers that verses 7b-11 enrich the epistle to the Hebrews. The author of this heavily theological document—also a liturgical work of art—draws upon many Old Testament passages to show how Jesus, like ancient Israel, followed a long journey. Jesus, the eternal word, came from heaven to earth and returned to heaven in magnificent glory (ch. 1). Jesus came on earth as a compassionate high priest, and calls us to be with him and so enter with him into our eternal rest (chs. 2–4). Jesus, priest according to the eternal order of Melchizedek, enters the heavenly sanctuary to bring about the perfection of the old in the glory of the new covenant and to purify all people by his blood in a new feast of Yom Kippur or Atonement (chs. 5–10). The epistle ends with a journey across the Old Testament in the company of its saints and heroes (chs.

11–12), ending with the final journey of Jesus whom God brought from death into glory (ch. 13).

Journey, then, is the major motif in both Psalm 95 and the epistle to the Hebrews. Psalm 95 blends a liturgical journey (vv. 1-7a) with Israel's journey through the wilderness as they murmur and dispute with God. The epistle to the Hebrews does the same. With many liturgical references, for instance that of the Jewish High Priest entering into the Holy of Holies on the feast of Yom Kippur or Day of Atonement (Heb 9:11-14) or Moses' journey up Mount Sinai to solemnize the ritual of the covenant (Heb 9:15-22), the New Testament author is also continually calling for obedience, perseverance, and compassion. By these virtues one is led on a journey toward peace and holiness.

The epistle to the Hebrews is quite dense; it compresses rich biblical allusions in every single section. Typical too of a classical rabbinical style, the author of the book of Hebrews joins distant biblical passages because of a word like "today" and "rest" (Hebrews 3–4). Just as God rested on the seventh day after creating the universe, all creation is being called to enter into a heavenly rest today. No previous moment of rest adequately fulfilled God's plans, not even, says Hebrews, when Joshua led Israel into the Promised Land (Josh 22:1-6). Joshua realized that Israel might sin and be driven off the land (Josh 23:14-16). The epistle focuses on our eternal rest with Jesus, in God:

> . . . Again he sets a certain day—"today"—saying through David much later, in the words already quoted,
> "Today, if you hear his voice,
> do not harden your hearts."
>
> So then, a sabbath rest still remains for the people of God; for those who enter God's rest also cease from their labors as God did from his. Let us therefore make every effort to enter that rest, so that no one may fall through such disobedience as theirs (Heb 4:7, 9-11).

The New Testament work, as the text suggests, dwelt long on two key words in Psalm 95, namely "today" and "rest." It drew listeners and readers far along in their journey with Jesus, the compassionate high priest, through the struggles of this life, even death, into our heavenly rest. One cannot absorb such teaching quickly. Just as the text of the psalm—according to our second principle—requires an attentive, prayerful reading, so does a New Testament work like the epistle to the Hebrews.

Sixth Principle: Read the Psalms according to the Liturgy and Classic Spiritual Writers

First in Israel and then in the Christian community, certain psalms gravitated toward special feasts. On these feasts, various psalms were clustered with readings, prayers, and short antiphons. Preferences for some psalms over others and, similarly, for some books of the Bible over others, is noticeable among classic spiritual authors like the Fathers of the Church, the Helfta mystics such as Gertrude the Great, influential monastic teachers of the Middle Ages, and well-known contemporary religious writers like Thomas Merton. Major documents of ecumenical councils, particularly Vatican II, and of recent popes, as well as the pastoral letters of the U.S. bishops, each tend to highlight unique biblical sources.

A phrase was coined for these works: each favors its own canon within the canon. "Canon" refers to the list of books within the Bible. Almost all important documents and vigorous thinkers prefer some books to other ones. Even New Testament writers and Jesus himself had their favorites. Paul seemed to have liked the prophet Isaiah most of all, especially the second and third parts (chs. 40–55; 56–66), judging from the number and comparison of Old Testament quotations and references. The Gospel writers depict Jesus turning to the book of Psalms, Deuteronomy, and Jeremiah. Thus, one could say that they each had their own personal canon. What constitutes this canon within the canon reveals major emphasis and main lines of spirituality.

To pursue this principle in studying the psalms, the first requirement is to read the document carefully. At times biblical phrases are woven into the fabric of someone's words, perhaps subconsciously, without explicit citations. In contemporary works, authors are generally careful to mention their source, at least in footnotes. Liturgical documents, prayers, readings, and antiphons normally, though by no means always, include in parenthesis the name of the biblical book, its chapter and verse.

Psalms supply most frequently the biblical quotations in the liturgy, whether for the Eucharist, for the Liturgy of the Hours (Prayer for Christians), or for administering the sacraments.

For feasts of Mary, one generally finds Psalms 8; 15; 19; 24; 46; 87; 113; 147. These psalms, for the most part, fall into two categories. They are hymns of praise glorifying God, either for the wonders of creation or for the divine presence in the Jerusalem Temple. Creation stretches out before us in translucent majesty, pure and clean as on the first day of its existence. Sin or chaos are mentioned, only to have been overcome and driven away by babes and sucklings in Psalm 8. Jerusalem stands firm and undisturbed according to Psalm 46, with God enthroned in its holy Temple. From the association of these psalms with the feasts of Mary in the earliest church, several Catholic doctrines gradually evolved ever more clearly in the piety of the faithful. These psalms of Jerusalem, all pure, and creation, brilliant in its splendor, drew out of tradition an appreciation of Mary as one who is holy, even from the moment of her conception. Jerusalem, unshakable and permanently in place, never subject to destruction, provided the setting in which the Church celebrated the glorious "sleep" or assumption into heavenly glory. Her body, like Jerusalem, was never to be destroyed.

With liturgical books, or the Fathers of the Church, or the great spiritual classics at one's elbow, a person can spend many hours, for great religious benefit, studying the major psalms and their relation to our readings and antiphons. Toward the beginning of this section presenting the sixth principle for studying the psalms, the maxim of a "canon within a canon" was cited, that is, one's favorite books or prized psalms. At the end there is a reference to still another maxim, *lex orandi, lex credendi:* the law or practice of praying becomes the law or practice of professing one's faith. Within the Christian community at prayer with the psalms, there developed the main lines of the community's theology and spirituality.

Seventh Principle: Consult Commentaries

If a person is studying the psalms primarily for prayer and work among God's people, then the ambiance is first the presence of God. God, such a person believes with conviction, is communicating a personal message. This message has resonated through the centuries; each century added its own accent or coloration to the word, and so does the background of the person of faith today. After one has listened to the words of a psalm, reflected on the psalm in relation to the life of Israel and one's own personal life experience, the next step is to consult recent commentaries on the psalms.

Commentaries add many details; for instance, the meaning of Hebrew words, the original setting in Israel and a hypothesis about the psalm's role in Israel's annual liturgy, or the relation of one psalm with others in the Psalter and with poems elsewhere in the Bible. Commentaries alert readers to aspects of archaeology: the structure of houses and temples, the number of inhabitants, their life-style, diet, and social practices, the kinds of musical instruments and religious symbols. So far as information is available, readers learn from commentaries about the religious and civil leaders in Israel, their function in worship and instruction, the evolution and changes in their roles. Commentaries reconstruct ancient services or rituals in which psalms played a part.

Commentaries contain important information. Were there different ways of translating Hebrew words in other ancient languages? What new insights come from the early Greek translation, called the Septuagint? How have culture, worldviews, and certain religious beliefs influenced the writing of the psalms and their message?

If the principle norm for interpreting the psalms rested with what the original writer intended to say, then one needs to reverse the process and turn the final principle, the use of commentaries, into the first principle. Pope Pius XII in the famous encyclical, the "magna carta" of modern biblical studies in the Roman Catholic Church, named from the opening Latin words, *Divino Afflante Spiritu* (the Divine or Holy Inspiring Spirit), wrote:

> What is the literal sense of a passage is not always as obvious in the speeches and writings of the ancient authors of the East, as it is in the works of our own time. For what they wished to express is not to be determined by the rules of grammar and philology alone, nor solely by the context; the interpreter must, as it were, go back wholly in spirit to those remote centuries of the East and with the aid of history, archaeology, ethnology, and other sciences, accurately determine what modes of writing, so to speak, the authors of that ancient period would be likely to use, and in fact did use (§35).

Pius XII, however, had to defend the critical, historical method for studying the Bible, under attack from several reactionary sources. He never intended this method to be the final word, nor the advances of his age the definitive expression. He not only insists upon the religious meaning of faith, but he also states that every age has its own contribution to make for plumbing the inexhaustible riches of Scripture. Other abstracts from the encyclical include:

> Wherefore the exegete, just as he must search out and expound the literal meaning of the words, intended and expressed by the sacred writer, so also must he do likewise for the spiritual sense, provided it is clearly intended by God (§26).

> Moreover we may rightly and deservedly hope that our time also can contribute something towards the deeper and more accurate interpretation of Sacred Scripture. For not a few things, especially in matters pertaining to history, were scarcely at all or not fully explained by the commentators of past ages, since they lacked almost all the information which was needed for their clearer exposition (§31).

Because the historical-critical method is firmly established in various church circles, one can and should have recourse to that method, as well as other and newer methods, in the study of the psalms from commentaries. Only after one has come to understand the Bible as a document that reflects ancient Israel's experience, and a story conditioned by history, culture, and various theological perspectives, heard and proclaimed over the centuries within Israel, various believing communities, and today within not only the context of contemporary faith communities but also within the temple of one's heart, can one then further enrich its meaning by having recourse to its origins and first use in Israel. Fortunately, many scholars begin with this seventh principle so that they delve into the task with fresh energy and high hopes.

Chapter Three

Hymns of Praise

Praise the LORD!
Praise the LORD from the heavens;
  praise him in the heights!
Praise him, all his angels;
  praise him, all his host!
Praise the LORD from the earth,
  you sea monsters and all deeps,
Mountains and all hills,
  fruit trees and all cedars!
Wild animals and all cattle,
  creeping things and flying birds! (Ps 148:1-2, 7, 9-10).

Part One
Praise from Sky and Earth

In its origins with Moses and the covenant at Mount Sinai, Israel's religion did not so much resound with praise from the heavens and the earth as it did with victory songs over oppression and slavery. Foremost in the people's praise of God was God's wonders in their history. For Israel (and modern Judaism) the first of the Ten Commandments is the basic confession of faith: "I am the LORD your God, who brought you out of the land of Egypt, out of the house of slavery" (Exod 20:2). Among Christians, Catholics unite this statement of faith with the prohibition of other gods (v. 3) and of idols (vv. 4-6). For Protestants, however, the first commandment extends only to verse 3; they consider verses 4-6 their second commandment. And since all three—Catholics, Protestants, and Jews—must end up with ten commandments (cf. Exod 34:28), the latter unite the ninth and tenth commandments of the Catholic enumeration against coveting a neighbor's wife or goods. However, having noted these differences in the numbering of the Commandments (there are also different systems for numbering the psalms and their verses), the Israelites' foundational perception of God as Savior from slavery now comes into focus.

The story of creation in the opening book of the Bible—in fact, in its very first chapter—may seem to contradict this statement focusing on God as liberator, but not if one considers it within the liturgical cycle of Israel's annual reading of the Torah (the five Books of Moses). When the lector came to the final chapter thirty-four of Deuteronomy, without a pause the reader would then begin at once with Genesis chapter one. The day itself became a major feast, called *simhat hattôrah,* the "Joy of the Torah." Israel rejoices that the study of the Torah never ends but always begins again. The rabbis, following the lead of the Wisdom literature (Prov 8:22-33; Sirach 24), explained that God begins to create in Genesis with the beauty and wisdom of the Torah (the five Books of Moses) in mind.

Essential to the Torah is God's liberation of the chosen people from Egyptian slavery. Creation, therefore, is to be seen within the context of redemption. Or, to repeat this truth somewhat differently, redemption reaches its fullest expression in God's creating new heavens and a new earth (see Isa 65:17; 66:22). Creation, accordingly, looks principally to the last days when God renews and transforms the universe. With this in mind, another tradition is left aside, namely, that the heavens and the earth will explode in chaos at the end (Mark 13:24-27), different but not irreconcilable with the previous reference to Isaiah.

Early Traditions: Canaanite and Polytheistic

The book of Psalms seems to reverse this conclusion. In particular the earliest psalms, which were under strong foreign influence, do not reflect the cycle of Israel's three major feasts celebrating such redemptive acts as the Passover from Egypt, the Giving of the Law, and the Settlement in the Land/Protection in the Wilderness (see Leviticus 23; Deuteronomy 16). One even detects in them vestigial remains of polytheism as when Ps 8:5 refers to "gods," a passage which the ancient Greek and the NAB translate as "angels," or when Ps 29:1 refers to the "sons" or "children of the gods" with a Hebrew phrase commonly used by the Canaanites for lesser gods around the throne of God. Additionally, some tutelary gods are called "holy ones" in Ps 89:7 (NRSV). All these references occur in passages about creation. Israel's primary concern with God as Redeemer rather than Creator separated Israel very significantly from its neighbors.

The simplest explanation for the difference may be the truest. Upon entering the land and settling in under Joshua and the Judges, Israel depended heavily upon the local Canaanites for survival and cultural advance. The Canaanites instructed these people, for generations slaves in Egypt and wanderers in the wilderness, how to farm and how to build homes and sanctuaries. Israel's alphabet derived from these same people, as did Israel's dialect of a Semitic language, called Hebrew. In absorbing Canaanite culture Israel learned about musical instruments and poetry. In fact, so complete was this process of "Canaanization" that almost the whole fabric of expressing faith and religion came from Israel's culturally advanced neighbors.

The fabric was Canaanite, as were some of the early designs which spoke of God as Creator. Yet the intuition of God as Savior and Redeemer, dominant in the Torah (the five Books of Moses), not only persisted but emerged as a central concept. Marvelous moments, inspired by Israel's history, began to control the psalms and there was even a subtle—or not so subtle—tendency to make theological corrections in earlier psalms. An example is a comparison between Psalm 29 and 96:

Ps 29:1-2	Ps 96:7-9a
Ascribe to the LORD, O heavenly beings,	Ascribe to the LORD, O families of the peoples,
ascribe to the LORD glory and strength.	ascribe to the LORD glory and strength.
Ascribe to the LORD the glory of his name;	Ascribe to the LORD the glory due his name; bring an offering, and come into his courts.
worship the LORD in holy splendor.	Worship the LORD in holy splendor.

The much later Psalm 96 not only adapts the lines to include actions within the sanctuary ("bring an offering, and come into his courts"), but unabashedly changes "sons of the gods" to read "families of the peoples." The most serious question is not why later psalm writers dared to correct earlier, inspired text, but rather: Why did God tolerate these expressions of polytheism, small in number as they are? The second question will be addressed later in this chapter.

Praise!—What Is It?

Praise? Is that what we, following the example of ancient Israel, give to God in our songs and prayers, complimenting God for bestowing many gifts and working many wonders in our midst? The translation of Psalm 29 seems to affirm this explanation.

Ascribe to the LORD, O heavenly beings,
ascribe to the LORD glory and strength.

> Ascribe to the LORD the glory of his name;
>> worship the LORD in holy splendor (Ps 29:1-2).

At once some serious problems face us with this explanation of praise as happily giving to God. Do people really give anything to God? Prophets like Amos and Jeremiah lashed out at this smug idea, for it includes an attitude of bribing God, or cajoling God to look away from one's sins. Psalm 50, composed under strong prophetic influence, lashes out at this ridiculous but dangerous and prevalent mentality:

> Not for your sacrifices do I rebuke you;
>> your burnt offerings are continually before me.
> I will not accept a bull from your house,
>> or goats from your folds.
> For every wild animal of the forest is mine,
>> the cattle on a thousand hills.
> I know all the birds of the air,
>> and all that moves in the field is mine.
> If I were hungry, I would not tell you,
>> for the world and all that is in it is mine (Ps 50:8-12).

Holocausts and sacrifices give nothing to God that God does not already possess: "every wild animal of the forest is mine." Neither does praise give anything to God that does not belong to God.

What is praise then? What does one do in praising God? Praise, we propose, is a wondrous, joyful way of recognizing the wonders of God's powerful love in our regard. Praise contagiously draws others into this happy rhythm. Praise is a public community act by which people are absorbed into a cycle like rain and snow. These come from the heavens and, once soaking the earth, return to the heavens in the form of trees, vegetables, and flowers. Such, in fact, is the metaphor used by the prophet Isaiah to describe the word of God (Isa 55:10-11).

In the psalms of praise God's wonders can penetrate our hearts and minds—wonders that have become memories and traditions of what God did for the Israelites, wonders that reach across the universe in bursts of splendor from distant stars:

> When I look at your heavens, the work of your fingers,
>> the moon and the stars that you have established;
> what are human beings that you are mindful of them,
>> mortals that you care for them? (Ps 8:3-4).

When someone is lost, even overwhelmed by surrounding wonders, the psalms of praise can lift up that person with joyful dignity before God. "You have given them dominion over the works of your hands; / you have put all things under their feet" (Ps 8:6). Praise enables the awesome, mysterious though silent universe to resound with music and reach in new, marvelous ways toward God.

When hymns of praise put joyful words to Israel's memory of God's marvelous, redemptive deeds in its history, God continues to accomplish with each new generation what God had done for the ancestors. Praise transforms history from being a "once for all" into an "ever new for all." Memory, the stuff of God's great interventions, activates the faith of a later generation that, in song and hope, anticipates a renewal of the past deeds of God. God is always the one who takes the initiative. Praise surges forward from the memory of God's action and from the faith that such a God is always present with the chosen people.

Not only in the psalms, but especially there, past and future merge in the wonder of the present. What God has done, for instance in bringing Israel out of Egypt, God continues to do in a moment of worship that prepares the future. Yet the present moment is so wonderful in its praise that worshipers are stunned into ecstatic silence, absorbing the rhythm of the music. All of this description of praise turns from theoretical statements into vibrant action in a psalm supposedly sung by Jesus and the disciples at the Last Supper, as it was by all Israelites celebrating the three great pilgrimage feasts at Jerusalem:

> When Israel went out from Egypt,
> > the house of Jacob from a people of strange language,
> Judah became God's sanctuary,
> > Israel his dominion.
>
> The sea looked and fled;
> > Jordan turned back.
> The mountains skipped like rams,
> > the hills like lambs.
>
> Why is it , O sea, that you flee?
> > O Jordan, that you turn back?
> O mountains, that you skip like rams?
> > O hills, like lambs?
>
> Tremble, O earth, at the presence of the LORD,
> > at the presence of the God of Jacob,
> who turns the rock into a pool of water,
> > the flint into a spring of water (Psalm 114).

This poetic gem bursts with excitement and silence, reflecting the liturgy. It ends with sprinkling water on the altar and on the people who also drink its fresh taste. Events in the Sinai desert turn into happy moments of life (Exod 17:1-7; Num 20:6b-13). The psalm blends the Exodus out of Egypt, where there were no mountains, with the mountain seen from the river Jordan. The psalm transforms the liturgy from the ancient sanctuary of Gilgal, near the place where the river Jordan empties its water into the Dead Sea, to the central sanctuary of the Jerusalem Temple. Little wonder the worshipers and the earth on which they prostrate tremble. The people tremble "before the Lord." Events are really not events but the Lord who is present in marvelous ways. "Tremble . . . at the presence of the God of Jacob."

The mountains and hills probably did not skip like rams and lambs. They might have seemed to move, however, in the shimmering light of the desert as hot air from the earth is sucked into the upper reaches of the cold sky. Yet, their skipping came alive in the music and dance of the people:

> Your solemn processions are seen, O God,
>   the processions of my God, my King, into the sanctuary—
> the singers in front, the musicians last,
>   between them girls playing tambourines (Ps 68:24-25).

> They shall come and sing aloud on the height of Zion . . .
> Then shall the young women rejoice in the dance,
>   and the young men and the old shall be merry (Jer 31:12-13).

As memories of God's great deeds strike fire in Israel's faith, and this faith rings out in song and dance, God renews the great wonders of the past. Praise, then, is the wondrous acclamation of God, and of what God has done and continues to do in the lives of people of faith. These people are truly alive, and so the hymns of praise teem with activity. People are summoned to sing (Psalm 98), clap their hands (Psalm 98), bow down (Psalm 95), dance (Psalm 150), play musical instruments (Psalm 150). They question one another, almost in disbelief (Psalm 8). Thus, praise is wondrous acclamation—full-bodied acclamation.

Finally, there is the simple, effective literary style of a hymn of praise. This type of psalm begins with a call or summons: "Sing to the Lord" (Psalm 96) or "Come, let us . . ." (Psalm 95). This invitation may be a community refrain (Ps 8:2, 10). This initial movement may not be repeated only at the beginning and end, but may possibly be sung continuously, *sotto voce,* by the entire congregation. The central part of the psalm, frequently introduced by the Hebrew particle *kî,* does not give the reason but the motivation for praising God. Although *kî* can mean "because" or "for" and provide a reason or cause, its original sense was an exclamation of wonder, something like "Indeed!" or "Lord!" Praise results not so much from one's reasoning about God's glories, but rather, the initiative for praise comes from God.

Spontaneity and Discipline

The hymns of praise, especially the early ones that draw their motivation from God the Creator's manifestation in the heavens and across the earth, introduce listeners and readers to a carefully structured and highly disciplined poet. Having already touched upon the literary structure and form of these poems, there is more to say about this aspect of the hymns. First, however, one needs to realize that an initial reading can give the opposite impression, one of spontaneity, or even free and uninhibited movement. This occurs in the mounting repetition, as in Psalm 93:

> The floods have lifted up, O LORD,
>> the floods have lifted up their voice;
>> the floods have lifted up their roaring,
> More majestic that the thunders of mighty waters,
>> more majestic than the waves of the sea,
>> majestic on high is the LORD! (Ps 93:3-5; see also Psalms 29 and 96);

or in the cascade of musical instruments, as in Psalm 150:

> Praise him with trumpet sound;
>> praise him with lyre and harp!
> Praise him with tambourine and dance;
>> praise him with strings and pipe!
> Praise him with clanging cymbals;
>> praise him with loud clashing cymbals!
> Let everything that breathes
>> praise the LORD! (Ps 150:3-6).

This free movement in changes in time and style is found in Psalm 68. Notice its two opening hymns: (vv. 1-3, 4-6) a motivation that moves, at times, backward and then forward through Israel's history (vv. 7-10, 11-14, 15-18, 19-23); and its temple procession (vv. 24-27) completed by petitions (vv. 28-35). The repetition of two ceremonies in Psalm 80 provides yet another example: one addresses Israel in the first person (vv. 6-7, 18-19) and the other speaks about Israel in the third person (vv. 8-17).

However, a closer study of each of these psalms detects more order than disorder. The two ceremonies in Psalm 81, for instance, each proceed from a prophetic warning to some kind of sacred meal, indicated by the phrases: "open your mouth wide and I will fill it" (v. 10b), and "with honey from the rock I would satisfy you" (v. 16). Psalm 95, with its similarity to Psalm 81, provides an alternate form for the same liturgy.

Another example is Psalm 29, one of the most spontaneous yet beautifully structured hymns. The repetition of words sets up a pattern of development. Locked into the repetition, the development is assured. The pattern is as follows:

	a	b	c	d	e
v. 1	Ascribe	to the LORD	O heavenly beings	—	—
	Ascribe	to the LORD	—	glory and strength	—
v. 2	Ascribe	to the LORD	—	the glory	of his name
v. 3	The voice of the LORD	is over the waters	—	—	—
	The LORD	over waters	mighty	—	—
v. 4	The voice of the LORD	—	is powerful	—	—
	The voice of the LORD	—	—	is full of majesty	—
v. 5	The voice of the LORD	breaks	the cedars		
	The LORD	breaks	the cedars	of Lebanon	

The momentum gathers as each line builds on the preceding line. Notice, too, that in the opening verse the people give to the Lord "glory and strength" (v. 1b), while in the final verse the Lord imparts strength to the people. The original gift returns divinized. This repetition of a word from the first verse again at the end goes under the technical title of *inclusio*. The whole psalm is thus wrapped up and included within an envelope. The repetition of the refrain in verses 1 and 9 of Psalm 8 constitutes another *inclusio*.

This same movement of repetition and development generally characterizes all Hebrew poetry, even if it is a case of similar ideas and not identical words. This characteristic is called "parallelism." The second line can repeat the thought: "Be a rock of refuge for me, / a strong fortress to save me" (Ps 31:2b). Or, it may reverse the thought: "In you, O LORD, I seek refuge; / Do not let me ever be put to shame" (Ps 31:1). Or the second line may develop one or more words or aspects of the preceding line as in Psalm 31 where the conniving "whispers of the crowd" are portrayed in greater detail:

> For I hear the whispering of many—
> > terror all around!—
> as they scheme together against me,
> > as they plot to take my life (Ps 31:13).

In a later verse, the second part develops two words in the first, one negatively ("shame" . . . "shame") and the other positively ("call" . . . "dumbfounded"):

> Do not let me not be put to shame, O LORD,
> > for I call on you;
> let the wicked be put to shame;
> > let them go dumbfounded to Sheol (Ps 31:17).

While Psalm 29 clearly showed how parallelism is enhanced through the skillful repetition of identical or new words, there is still another literary device used in the psalm. It is called a chiasm. The word derives from the letter of the Greek alphabet, chi, formed as a capital "X." Words in a line, a series of lines, or even a series of chapters form the letter chi or "X" by returning in the opposite direction as the downward stroke: a-b-c, c-b-a or:

a		c
	b	
a		c

Elaborate chiasm, as in Amos 5:4-6, proceeds as follows: a-b-c-d-c-b-a. Still more complicated is the relation of the chapters in Isaiah 56–66. The center of Third Isaiah occurs in chapters 60–62, the heart of which is Isa 61:1-3 (the anointing of the servant). The beginning and end of Third Isaiah concern themselves with outsiders worshiping at the Temple (Isa 56:1-8; 66:17-24). The material leading to and from the center describes the sorrows and comforts, struggles and controversies facing the returned exiles.

An effective use of chiasm occurs at the beginning of Psalm 19, most noticeable in the arrangement of Hebrew words. The downward stroke of part one is revised in the upward stroke of part two:

a	The heavens	the firmament	a
b	are telling	proclaims	b
c	the glory of God	his handiwork	c

The center phrases complement each other. "The glory of God" stresses the might of God's majesty; "glory" comes from a Hebrew word meaning "to be heavy." Glory is always awesome, even fearful, as in Isaiah's vision (Isaiah 6). The parallel word, "handiwork," carries a personal, even intimate signature—as does all handcraft. As in Psalm 8, where it is said that the heavens are created by God's fingers, so here God is personally and care-fully attending to the vault of the sky over earth and the human family.

Several times the psalms display a care for structure and discipline. Psalm 33:3 uses a common thought, "be good at it," translated more styl-ishly by the NRSV as "play skillfully on the strings." Psalm 47:7 introduces a different Hebrew word, common enough with Wisdom literature, tech-nically meaning "the wise": "Sing praises with a psalm."

This blend of spontaneity and discipline offers good advice for tem-pering one's passion for excitement and the drive for initiative with a healthy dose of structure. This advice is made all the more pertinent by re-calling that hymns of praise are intended for public liturgy and commu-nity participation. As people share their joys and gifts with others, they do not want them to be bystanders but instead to sing and dance and partici-pate in God's goodness and grace. Furthermore, care for the common good keeps alive spontaneity and enthusiasm. Community singing and a balanced community life can lose their spirit of joy if the common good is forgotten.

Before proceeding to another aspect of the hymns of praise, one needs to acknowledge that every inspired poem is not a masterpiece. God could and did invite a wide range of personalities and gifts. Psalm 70 may be one of the most carefully crafted poems in the Psalter and exceptionally sincere, but this psalm of lament lacks the agony and pathos of Psalm 12 or Psalm 22. As hymns of praise, Psalms 96–97 are too dependent on other psalms to pulse with the verbs and strength of Psalm 93. Psalm 141 was so poorly transmitted that verses 5-7 are practically meaningless. The Jerusa-lem Bible, in four successive editions, rendered the lines differently each time. The terse remark of John Chrysostom sums it up: "obscure psalm, which all the world chants without comprehending it!" This psalm has that most popular verse: "Let my prayer be counted as incense before you, / and the lifting up of my hands as an evening sacrifice" (v. 2).

Polytheism—Contradictions and a Sense of Mystery

A far more serious problem arises from the question of polytheism or contradictions in corrections in the psalms. One example appears in the rendering of "the gods" in Psalm 8 (Heb., v. 6) as "angels" in the ancient Greek translation. While the Torah (the five Books of Moses) treats this question of gods or spirit world very cautiously (see Deut 18:9-14 but also Deut 4:19; 29:26; 32:8-9), the book of Psalms appears more relaxed and tolerant of the spirit world. Psalm 91, a prayer of confidence close in some ways to the hymns, refers extensively to evil spirits or their curses. The psalmist professes confidence in God as a shield against deadly pestilence, the terror of the night, arrows by day, destruction, the lion, the adder, and the serpent. The superstitious tendency of this psalm continued into the Christian practice of copying verses from the psalm onto sacred parchment to be attached to one's clothing for protection. The early Church recited this psalm in an exorcism ceremony to drive demons out of a person. Popular piety in biblical times and today takes seriously the spirit world of superhuman beings.

This piety shows up in the acclamation to the sun in Psalm 19. The text is irregular, especially at the start, due perhaps to the ragged edge where the verses were attached to the psalm. Translated from the Hebrew literally, verses 5c-6 read:

> To the sun there is a tent among them.
> He indeed goes forth like a groom from his bridal chamber,
> like a warrior he joyfully runs his course.
> From one end of the heavens his going forth,
> his full course to its other end.
> No one escapes his heat.

Comparison with ancient religious texts from Egypt and especially Babylon leads some to the conclusion that the poet or editor incorporates a heavy dose of polytheism. Scholars are undecided whether Psalm 19 was originally composed in its entirety by a single poet or whether an editor stitched together two independent poems (vv. 2-5b and vv. 8-13, Heb.), uniting them, a bit irregularly, by the polytheistic segment from a third poem (vv. 5c-7).

The first major section (vv. 2-5b) exults in the mysterious wonder of the heavens. Moon and stars at night and sun during the day glorify God, yet silently wait for a chosen people to compose words and music for their praise. Just as the heavens span the earth from one end to the other, the earth reaches out with a universal message, too overwhelming and magnificent ever to be restricted within the bounds of words and sentences, yet so loud and clear as to reach the utmost bounds of the earth. The poet, if the phrases are translated literally, writes with lyric resonance and mystic intuition, structured within paradox and seeming contradiction. What verse 3 affirms, verse 4 denies, only for verse 5 to reaffirm "to the ends of the world." Drawing directly from the Hebrew, one reads:

> v. 3: Day unto day is gurgling the sound,
>   night unto night breathes the experience.
> v. 4: Yet, there is no sound, no words,
>   their voice is never heard.

> v. 5: Throughout the earth their voice goes forth,
>   to the ends of the world their fullness.

What verse 3 mystically perceives and secretly hears—the gurgling sound of water bubbling from a rocky spring and the pulse of breathing at night—verse 4 can deny. It is heard only in the undistracted stance of faith. Yet, from faith comes a transfer of sound into a message of salvation. The stronger the faith, the fuller and more profound the message.

The third verse of this triad becomes the climax in Paul's and the Church's commission to bring gospel salvation to all men and women. He wrote in the most theological of all his epistles, that to the Romans:

> But how are they to call on one in whom they have not believed? And how are they to believe in one of whom they have never heard? And how are they to hear without someone to proclaim him? And how are they to proclaim him unless they are sent? As it is written, "How beautiful are the feet of those who bring good news!" But not all have obeyed the good news; for Isaiah says, "Lord, who has believed our message?" So faith comes from what is heard, and what is heard comes through the word of Christ.
> But I ask, have they not heard? Indeed they have; for
> "Their voice has gone out to all the earth,
>   and their words to the ends of the world" (Rom 10:14-18).

From Isa 52:7, Paul begins with the footprints of the Gospel, left behind by one of God's earlier messengers, the prophet Isaiah:

> How beautiful upon the mountains
>   are the feet of the messenger who announces peace,
> who brings good news,
>   who announces salvation,
>   who says to Zion, "Your God reigns."

Drawing again from his favorite book, Second Isaiah (Isaiah 40–55), this time from a most favorite part, the song of the Suffering Servant, Paul comments: "But not all have obeyed the good news; for Isaiah says, 'Lord, who has believed our message?'" (Rom 10:16; see Isa 53:1). Faith is necessary to hear the secret message of salvation, "the word of Christ." Faith also comes from hearing because the word reaches deeply and enlivens what has become a faded memory of God's presence, "footprints" over the mountain peaks. Because of faith, Paul can conclude with a thought adapted from Ps 19:5: "Their voice has gone out to all the earth, / And their words to the ends of the world."

It seems that the incorporation of polytheistic elements in verses 5c-7 (Heb.) enabled the psalmist to reach beyond the status of a nature-preserver or nature-enthusiast, beyond the status of a deist who believes in a distant, awesome and unknowable deity, to a person of faith. For an Israelite, faith called for the sense of a personal, compassionate God who revealed the divine presence to Moses: "I have observed the misery of my people who are in Egypt; I have heard their cry on account of their taskmasters. Indeed, I know their sufferings" (Exod 3:7). Israelite faith, with Moses on Mount Sinai, hears God's self-identification as:

> The LORD, the LORD,
> A God merciful and gracious,
> slow to anger,
> and abounding in steadfast love and faithfulness,
> keeping steadfast love for the thousandth generation,
> forgiving iniquity and transgression and sin,
> yet by no means clearing the guilty (Exod 34:6-7).

It is not the case at all that the mythological or polytheistic acclamation to the pagan sun-god in verses 5c-7 accomplished all this. What it did ensure, however, was a sense of divine presence, wondrous and incomprehensible, across the universe, which Israel's traditional faith identified as YHWH, a God unique, compassionate, and personal. Just as Paul presumed faith in Jesus as Savior of the world, the psalmist proceeds from the basis of Moses' intuition and experience of a personal, merciful God. While the Mosaic tradition, as mentioned earlier in this chapter, restricted YHWH's presence to Israel and within Israel's history, the polytheistic religion of outsiders provided a means of seeing YHWH's presence across creation in the wonder of heaven and earth.

Verses 5c-7 bind together the two main sections, verses 2-5b and 8-15, thereby strengthening the presence of YHWH, the lawgiver of Mount Sinai, within the created universe. Particularly in Babylonian religion, the sun was venerated as creator of law and the order of the universe. The perception comes, of course, from the role of the sun, its cycles, "rotation," and influence upon the seasons of the year. The famous stone tablet of Hammurabi's law code, now in the Louvre Museum at Paris, shows at its top the sun-god, giving the laws to the Babylonian king through an intermediary deity.

Through verses 5c-7, the brilliance and wonder of the universe are linked with Israel's Law, also divinely created. Just as the universe helps one to appreciate the wisdom and even the sweetness of the Law of the Lord, these laws enable Israel to identify who is truly the Creator-God—not the sun-god but YHWH. As just mentioned, Israel's faith in YHWH added a liturgy of sweetness, gentleness, and rejoicing to what, in other religions, was simply a litany of distant wonder and stern discipline. The Law of YHWH revealed on Mount Sinai embodies the attributes of YHWH, the true Creator-God:

> The law of the LORD is perfect,
>> reviving the soul;
> the decrees of the LORD are sure,
>> making wise the simple;
> the precepts of the LORD are right,
>> rejoicing the heart;
> the commandment of the LORD is clear,
>> enlightening the eyes;
> the fear of the LORD is pure,
>> enduring forever;
> the ordinances of the LORD are true
>> and righteous altogether.
> More to be desired are they than gold;
>> even much fine gold;
> sweeter also than honey,
>> and drippings of the honeycomb (Ps 19:7-10).

With such a law, the psalmist proclaims further:

> Let the words of my mouth and the meditation of my heart
>> be acceptable to you,
>> O LORD, my rock and my redeemer (Ps 19:14).

In the Hebrew language, "redeemer" catches the tribal background of a blood bond, intimate and demanding.

With this transformation of pagan mythology, can one properly refer to polytheism in Psalm 19? Yes, one can if verses 2-7 are read by themselves. While God has the common Semite name of 'El in verse 2 and seems related to the sun-god in verses 5c-7, only in verses 8-15 is God addressed by Israel's unique and proper name of Lord or YHWH. Yet, because the most mythological section (vv. 5c-7) closely unites verses 8-15 with verses 2-5b, the entire psalm becomes integrally bound to YHWH, now venerated as Creator. And as Creator, YHWH is redeemer of all creation.

This last important insight, namely that YHWH was the redeemer of all creation, was difficult for Israel to accept. This implication, a contribution of nature religion, seemed almost impossible to harmonize with Israel as the elect, chosen people of the Lord. All other people must be non-elect and non-chosen. What the prophecy of Isaiah struggled to express—in such passages as 49:6; 56:1-8; 66:18-21, Paul makes so explicit as to be a major plank in his "gospel." Paul, through this, shows his gratitude for a thought originally due to a polytheistic, creation-centered religion.

From Psalms to Other Biblical Passages

One of the principles for interpreting the psalms is to chart the presence of key lines or verses elsewhere in the Bible. Paul's use of Ps 19:5 became an important link to its use in a chain of passages, concluding in universal salvation. Chapter 2 of this study showed how the Bible, in quoting the Bible, can even go so far as to reverse Scripture's own meaning. The case at point is exemplified in the way that Eph 4:8 quotes Ps 68:18. From another example, one can see how a later passage again reverses the sense of this psalm and how the psalm in its main ideas controls the development of thought in an important New Testament story. Another hymn of praise from nature, Psalm 8, became a popular prayer and a goad for reflection. The important line is: "What are human beings that you are mindful of them, / mortals that you care for them?" (Ps 8:4). The passage occurs again in Ps 144:3, in this case, in the midst of lament over sorrow, a theme totally absent from Psalm 8. Psalm 144 has joined many different parts together: royal titles and images from Psalm 18 in verses 1-11; eschatological hopes for a dramatically new age in verses 5-8; a style commonly associated in Wisdom psalms with blessings upon the just person in verses 12-15. Thus, the ancient biblical writers freely used and adapted material from the Bible itself, and references then took on new meanings and nuances that differed from their original sense once in their new settings.

Such a new situation occurs in Job 7:17-21. Here the setting is given to us in the thoroughly discouraged, mistreated, and contentious Job. While Psalm 8 answers its own question, "What are human beings?" with God's tender regard and glorious gifts, Job thinks differently:

> What are human beings, that you make so much of them,
>   that you set your mind on them,
> visit them every morning,
>   test them every moment?
> Will you not look away from me for a while,
>   let me alone until I swallow my spittle? (Job 7:17-19).

Job argues in a way that mixes sarcasm and distress, tender plea and abject helplessness—as if to say: if I am so insignificant, why must you hound me at each moment and study each move under a divine microscope? Why? I am not alone long enough even to swallow my spittle! Job has stepped far away from the spirit and response of Psalm 8.

A New Testament passage—Matt 21:1-11—on the contrary, almost seems to be constructed according to the main ideas or stages of Psalm 8. A quick review of the psalm reveals:

- *sign of royalty,* one perhaps granted to the Davidic kings: "Yet you have made them a little lower than God, / and crowned them with glory and honor. / You have given them dominion over the works of your hands; / you have put all things under their feet" (vv. 5-6);
- *signs of struggle,* yet with a quick victory: "Out of the mouths of babes and infants / you have founded a bulwark because of your foes, / to silence the enemy and the avenger" (v. 2);
- *the question:* "What are human beings?" (v. 4);
- *the wonder of a new creation:* "How majestic is your name in all the earth!" (v. 9).

Matthew develops the account of Jesus' triumphant entry into Jerusalem on Palm Sunday along these same lines, to end with an explicit quotation from Psalm 8:

- the crowds acclaim Jesus as a royal offspring from David's house: "Hosanna to the Son of David! / Blessed is the one who comes in the name of the Lord!" (Matt 21:9);
- *the question* as "the whole city was in turmoil, asking, 'Who is this?'" (Matt 21:10);
- *the struggle* when "Jesus entered the temple and drove out all who were selling and buying" (Matt 21:12);
- *the new creation,* as Jesus cured "the blind and the lame" (Matt 21:14);
- *again the struggle,* when "the chief priests and the scribes saw the amazing things that he did, and heard the children crying out in the temple . . . they became angry and said to him, 'Do you hear what these are saying?'" (Matt 21:15-16a).

The account closes with Jesus' response to the chief priests and scribes from Ps 8:2: "Out of the mouths of babes and infants you have founded a bulwark."

Typical of rabbinical, midrashic style, an earlier biblical passage is quoted, not so much to supply the principal, new teaching as to locate the setting for the latter. The larger context of the earlier passage then leads us forward in such a way that the new surpasses the old or at least builds on it. Another example of this occurs in Matt 2:13-23. There the larger setting of Jer 31:15-17 (even though only v. 15 is quoted) gives us a new, larger view of the meaning of Joseph, Mary, and Jesus' flight into Egypt and return to Nazareth. Jeremiah casts the story into an image of Israel's lost tribes coming back to life, while Matthew gives hope to all persecuted and lost followers of Jesus that they will rise to a new and peaceful life.

Tracing the path of the psalms in the Old and New Testaments requires that one do more than match verse by verse, more than seek fulfillment of prophecy. Sometimes, as one saw in the case of Psalm 144 and Job 7, the later passage may go its own independent way. Yet, in other cases, the larger context of the psalm leads us to new depths of appreciation of the New Testament passage.

Chapter Four

Hymns of Praise

Seek the LORD *and his strength,*
seek his presence continually.
Remember the wonderful works he has done,
his miracles, and the judgments he uttered (Ps 105:4-5).

Part Two
Praise from Time and Place

A selection from a psalm, which is not properly a hymn of praise but an expression of thanksgiving, introduces this chapter. Yet thanksgiving does not ring out clearly and distinctly in the Bible; it easily merges with praise. In fact, the Hebrew word commonly translated "to thank" can also be understood as: "offer to God a sacrifice of thanksgiving." Thanksgiving is a conscious and personal response that reaches out to God in a full-bodied way. This chapter opens with a quote from Psalm 105. The verses center on (1) the memory of God's marvelous deeds in Israel's history and (2) the sanctuary or temple where they are reenacted and re-experienced.

Seeking the Face of the Lord

The verses from Psalm 105 speak of seeking God's face. This phrase was taken from the Canaanites. In going up to the sanctuary they looked upon the statues or "faces" of their gods and goddesses. While Israel had no statues of YHWH, nonetheless they continued to speak of going to the sanctuary as seeking the face of God:

> My soul thirsts for God,
>   for the living God.
> When shall I come and behold
>   the face of God?

My tears have been my food
    day and night,
while people say to me continually,
    "Where is your God?"

These things I remember,
    as I pour out my soul:
how I went with the throng,
    and led them in procession to the house of God,
with glad shouts and songs of thanksgiving,
    a multitude keeping festival (Ps 42:2-4).

Through the phrase and movement of "seeking the face of God" in pilgrimage to the Temple, one is brought to the realization in Ps 105:4-5 that Israel fulfilled this hope not by looking upon statues like the Canaanites did, but by liturgically remembering, that is, by reenacting and re-experiencing "God's marvelous deeds" from their history. Psalm 105 proceeds to recount this history from the time of the patriarchs to their settlement in the land. Psalm 68, another "thanksgiving" psalm, retells most of the same story in ritual.

In this chapter there will be a brief excursus on the important role of ritual or liturgy in forming the "sacred history" of Israel, a history that told of God's marvelous deeds in fulfillment of earlier promises (recall Ps 105:5). After this excursus on the peculiar nature of history in the Bible, several groups of psalms that celebrate Israel's history associated with the Temple will be considered. The first is the "Great Hallel" or "Great Praise" Psalm (Psalm 136), the Jewish predecessor of the Christian song of joyful thanksgiving, *Te Deum Laudamus* ("We praise you, O God"). Sung every Sabbath morning but one, as well as on the feast of Passover, the Hallel recounts each step of Israel's history, always with the refrain, "God's loving kindness [lasts] for ever!" The major place, the most sacred of all, specially chosen by God for celebrating this wonderful history (Deut 12:1-4), the sanctuary eventually to absorb all others, became the Jerusalem Temple. A look at Psalm 46 offers insight into the meaning of this temple for Israel.

Finally, several pilgrimage or entrance psalms, composed for Israelites either coming from some distance (Psalms 120–134), circling the holy city in solemn procession (Psalm 68), or fulfilling a ceremony at the Temple gate (Psalms 15 and 24) are examined. Thus, the hope is to cover not only the span of Israel's marvelous history but also its celebrations over the centuries at the Jerusalem Temple.

History Liturgically in the Making

No matter where a person stands on the controversial issue of history and history-writing in the Bible, all, perhaps, would agree that the Bible writes its own unique kind of history. This fact continues into the New Testament, where the Gospels have no close parallel in the world's ancient literature. The question of history in the Old Testament will be dealt with principally from the light cast by the psalms. As will be shown, the psalms and their role in Israel's temple liturgy are essential ingredients in forming Old Testament history.

Several transitions or movements took place before events took on their life in the Bible: (1) secular events came to be seen as sacred, because Israel recognized the active presence of God within them; (2) insignificant events took on mighty proportions, now sacred as the act of God, because of their impact upon later generations of Israelites at study, prayer, or temple worship; (3) the events were retold, not just as they happened long ago but as stimulants to the people's faith—faith in God's continuous action now; (4) retold in such a way, liturgical stories absorbed later details, somewhat the way a good sermon blends the biblical account with people's daily life; (5) the retelling and re-enactment of the story within the liturgy, influencing new generations of Israelites and of outsiders, ensured a strong impact upon later generations and in this way enshrined the early events in Israel's sacred or salvation history.

This process of history liturgically in the making is reducible to three vital stages.[1] In the first stage, an event would have seemed secular to any observer, possibly insignificant as well, even if one or several persons in places of leadership were convinced that God was summoning them and accomplishing it for the people Israel. The second stage celebrated the success of the initial event, again mostly a-religious or secular in appearance. The larger majority may have attributed the success to the weather, prudent or courageous decisions, mistakes on the part of the adversary, good timing, or just good luck—or a combination of factors. Always, however, there are a few persons with the insight of faith, gratefully recognizing God's effective presence. The third stage is set by the new generation who remembered the early event for what it really was, an act of God. Many of the secular details became unimportant. What was stressed, instead, was the role of God who will do the same for each new generation. In order to affirm such faith and to afford further examples of it, stories of later ages were blended with those of earlier times—always with the intention of edifying the worshipers. Recall, if you can, the earlier discussion in Chapter 2 of this book. "Today" continued as a key motif in the liturgy. Each new day became its own "today."

---

[1] See Donald Senior and Carroll Stuhlmueller, *Biblical Foundations for Mission* (Maryknoll, N.Y.: Orbis Books, 1983) 13.

Liturgical ceremonies in their splendor and song allowed the original event to be seen visibly as the *mirabilia Dei,* God's wonderful way of saving the chosen people. The strong, long impact of the liturgy ensured a place in history for that which, by itself, would never have been remembered—and so would never have made history. History requires more than that an event happen. It must also be memorable because of its influence on many people across a long period of time. Each group of people has every right to decide what aspect of the event should be remembered, how, and why. Israel stressed God's part. "How?": by liturgical ceremonies. "Why?": to influence later generations in a context of worshiping God. It was their privilege—as well as that of contemporary readers—to disagree with the point that history writing did not have to correspond in all its details to the original event.

One example is the Exodus out of Egypt. On giving consideration to this event, it is better to begin with a more realistic, secular description: the flight for freedom by a motley group of Asiatic slaves. As to be expected in the case of slavery and oppression, these people were slipping out of Egypt at different times and in different ways. In some places the Bible leaves the impression that they were expelled and left in broad daylight: "Then the LORD said to Moses, 'Now you shall see what I will do to Pharaoh: Indeed, by a mighty hand he will let them go; by a mighty hand he will drive them out of his land'" (Exod 6:1; see also 11:1; 12:31-39). Again another series of passages implies that Pharaoh refused and they were forced to flee secretly: "But the LORD hardened Pharaoh's heart, and he was unwilling to let them go. Then Pharaoh said to him, 'Get away from me! Take care that you do not see my face again, for on the day you see my face you shall die'" (Exod 10:27-28). The Bible is not contradicting itself. Furthermore, its editors were not concerned with external details, but with writing a liturgical document to inspire later generations. They deliberately combined various accounts, each with its own specific religious message. Further indication that the various flights, some by stealth and others because of open expulsion, were not "history" in the Egyptian eyes comes from Egyptian sources. From reading the Bible, one could assume that every aspect of Egyptian life was turned upside down: death of all firstborn, even the heir to the throne; decimation of livestock and agriculture; total pollution of all the water; and the humiliating debasement of religion. Yet in all the Egyptian inscriptions of this period—and they are somewhat staggering in their details in such places as the monumental temples at Karnak in southern Egypt—there is not a whisper of a reflection on Israel's departure.

When Israel began to celebrate the Exodus liturgically, two tendencies, as already mentioned, showed up: one, to focus ever more exclusively on God as actor; two, to adapt for later circumstances. Chapter 3 of this book already examined Psalm 114, an eloquent, moving liturgy that blends the crossing of the Red Sea with the passage through the River Jordan. Psalm 114 also calls for silent adoration in God's presence. Another example of aggrandizing the role of God, so that people became ever more God-minded, occurs in the story of the plagues in Egypt. Here we reach beyond hymns of praise and even beyond the psalms. Moreover, these texts also provide a convenient way to appreciate the biblical process of keeping ancient traditions up to date.

The story of the first plague in Egypt, that which turned water into blood, combines two accounts. The account that is more secular and entertaining, closer to reality, is called the Yahwist or "J" ("J" from the German spelling for Yhwh). The account that is more religious and demanding, closer to liturgical services, is called the Priestly or "P." Below is a segment of the two accounts side by side:

"J"—Exod 7:17-18, 24	"P"—Exod 7:19, 21b
"Thus says the Lord, 'By this you shall know that I am the Lord.' See, with the staff that is in my hand I will strike the water that is the Nile, and it shall be turned to blood. The fish in the river shall die, the river itself shall stink, and the Egyptians will be unable to drink water from the Nile." And all the Egyptians had to dig along the Nile for water to drink, for they could not drink the water of the river.	The Lord said to Moses, "Say to Aaron, 'Take your staff and stretch out your hand over the waters of Egypt—over its rivers, its canals, and its ponds, and all its pools of water—so that they may become blood; and there shall be blood throughout the whole land of Egypt, even in vessels of wood and in vessels of stone.'" The river stank so that the Egyptians could not drink its water, and there was blood throughout the whole land of Egypt.

Rather than conclude that the "P" tradition falsifies the account or, at best, exaggerates beyond the bounds of truth, readers would do better to realize that the "P" tradition is adapting the story to later liturgical instruction. It makes the suggestion that everything that a selfish or stubborn person touches turns to "blood." Whatever is touched becomes contaminated and harmful. In this case, the plagues did not happen but once against the Egyptians, but what took place is a warning of what can afflict sinful people, whoever and wherever they are. Such Israelites, as the prophet Hosea declares, symbolically "shall return to the land of Egypt" (Hos 11:5) because they refused to return to Yhwh.

Several psalms made the application to the land and later lives of the Israelites all the more forcefully. Again a series of three accounts will show the evolution. In each case the biblical passage is mentioning the plagues:

Exod 9:31-32	Ps 78:47	Ps 105:33
(Now the flax and the barley were ruined, for the barley was in the ear and the flax was in bud. But the wheat and the spelt were not ruined, for they are late in coming up.)	He destroyed their vines with hail, and their sycamores with frost	He struck their vines and fig trees, and shattered the trees of their country.

Flax and barley were Egyptian crops; in Israel, on the contrary, fig trees were more normal. If Israel sinned, symbolically the people were again not only in Egypt but in the place of the Egyptians.

One can see, then, that the major question was not so much were the Egyptians struck by plagues in punishment for their sins, but rather how the Israelites would be continually punished if they sinned. The liturgy and its instructions kept the religious meaning alive and, in doing so, the liturgy made sure that the Egyptian experience was remembered with a strong impact. Thus it made its mark in history.

The Great Hallel or Praise

On each Sabbath, except the one before the New Year, as well as on the feast of Passover, Israelites sang the Great Hallel. This Hebrew word means "Praise!" just as Hallelujah declares: "Praise Yah [or YHWH]!" It consists of Psalm 136. Sometimes Ps 135:3-21 is added. Psalm 136 is properly a litany in which a leader or cantor sings the invocation or motivation and the congregation responds with: *kî le ʿôlam hasdô!* (Indeed the Lord's bounding love forever!)

The refrain deserves more attention. The introductory particle, *kî,* can be translated as "Indeed!" As explained earlier in this book, *kî* is almost equal to an exclamation mark, a symbol of excitement or wonder. Because anything of such importance usually induces repercussions, *kî* came to be translated as "for" or "because." In a litany of mighty momentum, the original sense of *kî* is preferable. The next word is central: YHWH's *hesed* (the original form) or *hasdô* with the masculine singular suffix "his." This word of long, rich tradition is generally reserved for a warm love and a loyalty dependent upon blood or a treaty. It is a special kind of love. Therefore, *hesed* is not the proper word for the love and concern, as genuine as it may be, bestowed on strangers. YHWH's loving bond is "forever!" It will survive every trial and pass through every barrier. Because it is as deeply rooted as blood, every action of God is ultimately to be attributed to this bond of love and life.[2] Thirty-six times Israel acclaims YHWH's bonding love gratefully and excitedly.

After acknowledging YHWH as "God of gods" and "Lord of lords," supreme over all world forces and all superhuman beings like spirits and angels, the litany begins with God creating the universe and covers Israel's history from their slavery in Egypt to their settlement in the land. Everything happens as influenced and directed by God's loving strength and loyalty.

Psalm 136 does not shy away from violence:

- "who struck Egypt through their firstborn" (v. 10);
- "overthrew Pharaoh and his army in the Red Sea" (v. 15);
- "who struck down great kings" (v. 17);
- "and killed famous kings" (v. 18);
- "Sihon, king of the Amorites" (v. 19);
- "and Og, king of Bashan" (v. 20).

All is summed up as God's remembrance of Israel in its low estate (see v. 23). Individual events, therefore, belong to a long drama, extending over centuries of time. No single act should be isolated. The long history of Israel, like the lifetime of any individual person, includes sin and sadness as well as victories and joy. Even sin and sadness, in God's loving care, mysteriously contribute to forming a compassionate, understanding people. As mentioned earlier in this book while discussing Exodus 32–34, God wants to appear before all people and be remembered principally as:

> The LORD, the LORD,
> a God merciful and gracious,
> slow to anger,
> and abounding in steadfast love [*hesed*] for the thousandth generation
> (Exod 34:6).

One of the most profound difficulties in the Bible is the presence of violence in the context of God's loving providence. The biblical writers do not flinch from including it under the rubric of YHWH's *hesed* or bonding

---

[2] On a few occasions the Bible reaches beyond the narrow sense of blood bond or treaty. In Isa 40:6; Pss 59:10-11; 143:12, it may be preferable to translate *hesed* as "strength." Yet even this rendition stresses the sturdy dependability of God's attachment to Israel.

love. Divine incidents of violence and a sense of loyalty and compassion exist side by side in the biblical text. Furthermore, when Psalm 136 was composed, no earlier than 350 B.C.E.,[3] Israel no longer possessed the military force to march against any foreign people. Such names as Sihon and Og, by this time, had become as legendary or symbolic as Attila the Hun—and, sooner or later, as Hitler or Nazi would be.

In any case, events are remembered not just because they happened but for their contribution to Israel's appreciation and praise of a compassionate God.

History at the Glorious Temple at Jerusalem

As Israel's hymn writing came into its own domain, what was seen in the previous chapter as characteristic of the Torah (the five Books of Moses) became central in the hymn. Israel's composers of sacred music became less dependent upon the Canaanite styles and motifs which centered mostly on creation and the struggle of the gods and goddesses to overcome chaos and to secure order, at least for the ensuing year. Israelite poets began to blend the wonders of God Creator with the wonders of God Savior. This latter perception was more distinctive to Israel, as the Jewish first commandment proclaimed: "I am the LORD your God, who brought you out of the land of Egypt, out of the house of slavery" (Exod 20:2). Another of Israel's creeds or classic statements of faith (Deut 26:5-11) reviews this social history more completely. The creed turns into a long ceremony in Joshua 24, with statements, questions and answers, repeated questions and challenges, solemn protestations and promises, and finally a ritual action to memorialize the solemn renewal of the covenant.

The tendency was to see Jerusalem and its Temple as the climax of God's action in Israel's history. Whatever happened up to David's conquest of this strategic city (2 Sam 5:6-12) and Solomon's dedication of the magnificent Temple (1 Kings 8) was celebrated at the Temple and relived in its ceremonies. Solomon enshrined the ark of the covenant in the Holy of Holies of the Temple, to symbolize continuity with the days of Moses and Israel's early years in the Promised Land. The way in which the sacred history of Israel came alive in the ceremonies of the Jerusalem Temple appears in the brilliant, if difficult, Psalm 68.

Psalm 68 is comparable to a medieval cathedral. So much history has marched up and down its aisles with kings and armies, with weddings and funerals, at anniversaries and times of mourning. So much of history is

[3] See Carroll Stuhlmueller, *Psalms 2 (Psalms 73–150),* Old Testament Message 22 (Wilmington, Del.: Michael Glazier, 1983) 186.

interred in its pavements and walls, famous people whose corpses have disintegrated and whose inscriptions are rubbed smooth by thousands of footsteps. So much of culture and changing, clashing customs strike the eye, as ritual changes require new arrangements of altar, chairs, pulpit, and lectern. With liturgical developments the images of new saints are added or else, because of reforms for simplification, the images are removed. Even strange, popular practices find a place, like the gargoyles on the stained glass windows that represent the artist's enemies as devils. Psalm 68 not only draws a map through Israel's history, leading up to the Jerusalem Temple, but the psalm carries along with it the saints and sinners, the high and low moments of that history.

The psalm opens with two songs, summoning Israel to march in procession—liturgically, yes, but also through the major stages of its history. The first verse is adapted from the marching song in Num 10:35, said to be sung whenever Israel broke camp in the wilderness and moved onward. Verses 7-10 center on Mount Sinai and the trek through the desert; verses 11-14 describe the early settlement in the Promised Land; finally, there is a climactic, central moment when Israel arrives at the new Sinai and holy mountain, Jerusalem, in verses 15-20. The victories of King David proudly ring out in verses 21-23.

Psalm 68 abounds as much with ritual acts as it does with Israelite history: verses 7-10 describe a ritual with water that recalls God showering down manna during the Israelites' wilderness journey: "Rain in abundance, O God, you showered abroad" (Ps 68:9). Likewise, it rained manna from heaven at the presence of God.[4] Verses 13 and 19 recount enemy booty and slaves brought to the Temple; verses 24-27 detail the Temple procession; verses 28-31 offer petition; verses 32-35 close with a solemn conclusion. The psalm may even reflect a transfer from a northern sanctuary at Mount Tabor. Verses 11-14 seem inspired by the Song of Deborah (cf. Ps 68:8 with Judg 5:4-5), which has a special association with Mount Tabor (Judg 4:6). Motifs from ancient Canaanite temples enter the early verses of Psalm 68; YHWH is like the Canaanite Baal, "who rides upon the clouds" (v. 4). Indeed, Psalm 68 invokes a litany of divine names or titles and so blends many separate spiritualities or approaches toward the deity. In Hebrew, such names include God or *'elohim;* Lord or *'adonai;* Almighty One or *shaddai;* YHWH; YHWH *'adonai;* and YHWH *'elohim.*

Finally, the glory and shame of Israelite history are repeated in the Christian use of Psalm 68. It is the classic psalm of ancient tradition for celebrating the feast of Pentecost when the wonders of Mount Sinai and the showering of gifts are experienced anew (Acts 2). The ritual has found

---

[4] Exod 16:4 uses similar language for the manna.

the psalm especially appropriate for the consecration of churches and altars. It was sung by Savanarola and his monks as they were led to a fiery martyrdom at the stake. The crusaders found it a favorite battle hymn.

Other processional hymns are less strident and militaristic, like Psalms 84; 95:1-7a; 100; and 132. Later, two other psalms, partly processional and partly penitential (Psalms 15 and 24), will be the focus of the discussion. Now, however, the focus is on the great trilogy of Jerusalem or Zion psalms, Psalms 46–48.

Jerusalem, Symbolic of God, a Mighty Fortress

Psalm 46 leads readers and listeners on an intriguing journey, not only from mythology to solid faith, but also from prophecy and its influence on liturgy, and then from liturgy and its later impact upon prophecy. This later interpretation of prophecy will leave its mark when the Hebrew text is translated into the ancient Greek Septuagint, the Greek Scriptures upon which the New Testament frequently depended. Perhaps the journey seems more complex and convoluted than intriguing, but such is always the way of human history, even history that is the carrier of God's hopes of messianic salvation.

Before Psalm 46 is analyzed, it is freshly translated. This new translation, carried out according to the principles of dynamic equivalence,[5] attempts to render not so much word for word, but sense for sense as it dynamically involves one's imagination and contemporary rhythmic style.

a

God, our strong refuge,
　　our bulwark against enemies,
　　God ever present.
So we do not fear a tumultuous earth,
　　mountains collapsing to the bottom of the sea.
Oceans rage and foam,
　　mountains heave convulsively. *Selah*
[The Lord of hosts is with us,
　　our fortress, Jacob's God.]

---

[5] A translation making use of dynamic equivalence focuses on the receptor language (such as English) rather than the original language (such as Hebrew). See Mary Collins, "An Introduction to the Translation," *Psalms for Morning and Evening Prayer*, ed. Gabe Huck (Chicago: Liturgy Training Publications, 1995) xxxi–xxxiii.

b

Ocean currents, now a quiet stream,
    flow joyfully through God's city,
        the sacred dwelling of the Most High.
With God in her midst, she shall never collapse,
    God, her bulwark at the break of day.
Nations rage, kingdoms foam;
    God thunders, the earth crumbles.
The Lord of hosts is with us,
    our fortress, Jacob's God. *Selah*

c

Come! Look! A vision across the earth,
    the Lord acts with stunning might.
Wars stop
    to the ends of the earth.
God breaks bows and splinters spears,
    strikes chariots with fire.
Wait! Be aware that I am God,
    I rise over the nations,
    I rise over the earth.
The Lord of hosts is with us,
    our fortress, Jacob's God. *Selah*

The three stanzas of Psalm 46 closely interlock with each other, especially the first and second, even if each proceeds with a strong step forward into a very different setting. The first stanza abounds with mythological images common in Canaanite and Ugaritic literature. A new created universe rises out of chaotic fury. Quaking mountains are plunging into a roaring and foaming sea. The world seems to totter at the brink of extinction. Certainly no human being can stand up against this plunge to *tohû wabohû,* the Hebrew word for tumultuous chaos (Gen 1:2). Jeremiah offers one of the most graphic descriptions of this world explosion:

> I looked at the earth, and lo, it was waste and void;
>   and to the heavens, and they had no light.
> I looked on the mountains, and lo, they were quaking,
>   and all the hills moved to and fro.
> I looked, and lo, there was no one at all,
>   and all the birds of the air had fled.
> I looked, and lo, the fruitful land was a desert,
>   and all its cities were laid in ruins
>   before the LORD, before his fierce anger (Jer 4:23-26).

Yet as the prophet of the Isaiah tradition declares, all remains in God's control:

> I am the LORD, and there is no other. . . .
> I form light and create darkness,
>> I make weal and create woe;
>> I the LORD do all these things (Isa 45:5, 7).

Second Isaiah summarizes, by the words "darkness" and "woe," the destruction of the nation of Israel and the exile of its inhabitants under the fierce anger of the Babylonians, as declared earlier in Isa 44:24-28, a situation of *tohû wabohû* about to be corrected.

The second stanza of Psalm 46 reverses the chaotic rush to extinction in the earlier lines. The first stage, however, had already assured hearers and readers that God was in firm control, in the opening words: "God is our refuge and strength, / a very present help in trouble" (Ps 46:1). This faith in God's reassuring presence is all the more secure, if the refrain from verses 7 and 11 is added to the end of the first stanza, as reflected in the NRSV: "The LORD of hosts is with us; / the God of Jacob is our refuge" (vv. 7, 11). The second stanza, however, does more. It picks up the images and even the vocabulary of the opening stanza, to redirect and pacify its fury.

The second stanza opens with the Hebrew word *nahar*, best left in its Canaanite or Ugaritic meaning of a mighty ocean current (cf. Ps 93:3) At once, however, this leftover from the chaos of the previous stanza is tamed, to be God's servant. It becomes a gentle rivulet, rejoicing the city of God. This time, in place of the mythologized waters in the first stanza, it is nations that are raging and kingdoms that are foaming. While the second stanza historicizes the myth of creation, the prevailing memory of the myth puts Israel on guard that no human force, no mighty army of even King David, can overcome the onslaught of foreign armies. Only God can do that. Before God, therefore, the earth melts. Rightly, the congregation sings once again the refrain: "The LORD of hosts is with us; / the God of Jacob is our refuge" (Ps 46:7).

The third and final stanza locates in the Jerusalem Temple the stunning and fearful chaos of the first stanza as well as the fiery end of the monstrous machinery of war. Twice, with strong imperative verbs, God summons Israel's worshipers into ecstatic silence: "Come! Behold the works of the Lord" (Ps 46:8) and "Be still, and know that I am God!" (Ps 46:10).

Perhaps at this point in the ceremonies the choir chants loud and clear other victory hymns like Psalms 33; 68; or 76. The priests or lectors may proclaim the accounts of Israel's early exploits from literature like that found in the book of Joshua. These inspired songs and traditions insist that the victory belongs to God. Rightly Psalm 46 concludes with the refrain: "The LORD of hosts is with us; / the God of Jacob is our refuge" (Ps 46:11).

Psalms like this, with their accompanying liturgical ceremonies, created Israel's sacred history, a history that is more a tradition of faith which perceives God's marvelous though hidden presence and is strongly invigorated by this insight. Faith such as this, in the language of Psalm 46, welcomes a messiah and beholds visions, visions which the liturgical ceremonies reenact and which endow the people with a divine strength and endurance to sustain hopes and survive colossal disasters. What follows is a brief sketch of salvation history as Psalm 46 and the prophecy of Isaiah interact on each other. The Latin proverb expresses this relationship well: *causae ad invicem sunt causae*— "causes are causes upon each other," or better, "causes impact each other."

A number of parallels exist between Psalm 46 and Isaiah: the roaring of the nations (Ps 46:6; Isa 8:7-8; 17:12; 29:8); God's appearance in power (Ps 46:9-11; Isa 17:13; 29:6; 30:30); the divine victory over the nations (Ps 46:10-11; Isa 10:33-34; 17:13-14); and trusting in God (Ps 46:6, 10-11; Isa 7:9; 22:11; 28:16). The ancient Canaanite imagery of the roaring seas combined with the unique and wonderful salvation by YHWH appears in both texts (Ps 46:4; Isa 17:12-14). It is possible that Psalm 46 and Isaiah drew upon a common image or a common source. But most likely there were a series of interactions between the two over a period of time.[6]

While First Isaiah centers mostly on the Davidic dynasty, Psalm 46 attends exclusively to the holy city Jerusalem, especially its Temple. When the dynasty collapsed, never to revive (except for the few years of Zerubbabel immediately after the exile; see Haggai 1–2; Zechariah 4), Psalm 46 may have influenced Second Isaiah to transfer the everlasting promise, once bestowed on the dynasty, to the city Jerusalem. In the language of Isa 7:14 (which sees the maiden wife or ʿ*almah* as the new queen of King Ahaz, whose child will continue the dynasty), Psalm 46 alludes to Jerusalem in its title through its reference to maidens in the plural form of ʿ*almah*. Psalm 48 addresses Jerusalem with a similar sounding word, ʿ*al-mûth*, which means "beyond death" or "for ever." For these reasons, and for others beyond the scope and space of this book to discuss, the Greek Septuagint translated ʿ*almah* in 7:14, not as "maiden" or young woman, but as "virgin" or *parthenos* in the Greek, in accord with Isa 62:1-5:

> For as a young man marries a young woman,
>> so shall your builder marry you,
> and as the bridegroom rejoices over the bride,
>> so shall your God rejoice over you (Isa 62:5; cf 66:7-16).

---

[6] See Carroll Stuhlmueller, "Psalm 46 and the Prophecy of Isaiah Evolving into a Prophetic, Messianic Role," *The Psalms and Other Studies on the Old Testament: Presented to Joseph I. Hunt*, ed. Jack C. Knight and Lawrence A. Sinclair (Nashotah, Wisc.: Nashotah House Seminary, 1990) 21–3.

The intertwining of Psalm 46 with the prophecy of Isaiah, like the compenetration of Israel's liturgy and "history," could lead hearers and readers in faith to look upon God as a stronghold of security and continuity, whose impact upon the world can transform seemingly small incidents into historical moments, justice, and compassion. This Old Testament tradition, moreover, insists that faith that engenders character and fidelity will successfully stand up against world forces, even those as mammoth as the chaotic fury in the first stanza of Psalm 46. Finally, the concatenation of Isa 7:14; 62:5; and Psalm 46 offers some theological support for dogma that developed in their own separate way in both the Eastern Church and the Roman Catholic Church: namely, the inviolable person of Mary in her Immaculate Conception and bodily Assumption into heaven at the end of her earthly life, as well as Pope Paul VI's invocation of Mary at Vatican II as Mother of the Catholic Church.[7]

Entrance and Reconciliation Services at the Temple

There are indications that Psalms 15 and 24[8] may have provided the ritual for a reconciliation service at one of the Temple gates. Ps 118:19 may refer to one such entrance way where Levites would be posted for this religious function:

> Open to me the gates of righteousness,
>> that I may enter through them
>> and give thanks to the LORD.

A longer scenario for the service is described in the book of Numbers:

> The LORD spoke to Moses, saying: Speak to the Israelites: When a man or woman wrongs another, breaking faith with the LORD, that person incurs guilt and shall confess the sin that has been committed. The person shall make full restitution for the wrong, adding one fifth to it, and giving it to the one who was wronged. If the injured party has no next of kin to whom restitution may be made for the wrong, the restitution for wrong shall go to the LORD for the priest, in addition to the ram of atonement with which atonement is made for the guilty party. Among all the sacred donations of the Israelites, every gift that they bring to the priest shall be his. The sacred donations of all are their own; whatever anyone gives to the priest shall be his (Num 5:5-10).

---

[7] Carroll Stuhlmueller, "Old Testament Settings for Mary in the Liturgy," *The Bible Today* 24 (May 1986) 159–66.

[8] For other similar texts that may either support a temple service of reconciliation or be influenced by one, see Isa 26:1-6; 33:14-16.

It is helpful to review the stages and purpose of the ritual in Num 5:5-10: (1) to defraud a man or woman is to break faith with the Lord (cf. Ps 51:4, "Against you, you alone, have I sinned, / and done what is evil in your sight"); (2) the culprit must confess publicly the wrong he or she has committed; (3) the culprit restores the ill-gotten goods plus 20 percent; (4) if the person who was defrauded is deceased and has no next of kin, the restitution is made to the priests; (5) an atonement ram is offered in sacrifice at the sanctuary, symbolic of full reconciliation with the community in God's presence. The atonement ram does not remove sin or substitute for the sorrow and penance to be performed by the guilty person. The guilt has been removed by the earlier stages, especially the public confession and the restoration plus 20 percent.

The Temple serves a double purpose, both of equal importance. It affords a final scrutiny as to whether the guilty person has indeed made restoration plus 20 percent. Second, it declares publicly that the once-guilty person has been restored fully to the community and to God. No one, henceforward, is to harbor any suspicion. Fellow Israelites are to be as forgiving as God is.

Psalm 15 elaborates upon the ceremony at the Temple gate. When the once-guilty person—or any devout person who wishes greater purity in God's eyes—arrives at the "gates of righteousness" (Ps 118:19), the priest or Levitical gatekeeper (1 Chr 9:17-27; 26:12-18) solemnly asks: "O LORD, who may abide in your tent? / Who may dwell on your holy hill?" (Ps 15:1). The following verses serve as an examination of conscience and as a public repudiation of these offenses. Like Num 5:5-10, none of the sins are ritual taboos or cultic misdemeanors. Like prophetic preaching in Amos, Isaiah, or Jeremiah, all the demands touch upon social justice. After the lay person renounces the evil deeds, the priest or gatekeeper declares: "Those who do these things shall never be moved" (Ps 15:5b). The person may now freely enter the Temple and innocently, without suspicion, take his or her place with the assembly, and participate fully in the ceremonies.

Psalm 24 represents a still more elaborate ritual at the Temple gate. This time the group is much larger, with a choir—possibly trained—and priests. The choir begins the ceremony by singing verses 1-2. These lines extol God the Creator who has overcome all hostile forces of chaos and disorder and founded what every devout Israelite expects at the Temple: a place of security and prosperity. The choir sings:

> The earth is the LORD's and all that is in it,
>   the world, and those who live in it;
> for he has founded it on the seas,
>   and established it on the rivers (Ps 24:1-2).

The Levitical gatekeepers then ask the formal question: "Who shall ascend the hill of the LORD? / And who shall stand in his holy place?" (Ps 24:3). As in Ps 15:2-5, a series of ethical demands are voiced:

> They will receive blessing from the LORD,
> > and vindication from the God of their salvation.
> Such is the company of those who seek him,
> > who seek the face of the God of Jacob (Ps 24:5-6).

The third section of Psalm 24 refers to a full ritual of returning the ark of the covenant to the most holy place (Exod 26:31-34; 1 Kgs 8:6-7). Still another processional hymn, for marching with the ark of the covenant, occurs in Psalm 132. This psalm may celebrate the yearly anniversary of David's installing the ark in a tent in Jerusalem after it had lodged in "the house of Obededom the Gittite," at Kiryath Yearim (2 Samuel 6).

Chapter Five

Celebrating the Lord as King and Creator

*O sing to the L*ORD *a new song;*
  *sing to the L*ORD*, all the earth.*
*Worship the L*ORD *in holy splendor;*
  tremble before him, all the earth;
*Say among the nations: "The L*ORD *is king!" (Ps 96:1, 9, 10).*

Israel's religion, like that of most religions of any time or place, blended its unique, strictly orthodox form with a popular, more syncretistic expression. While the former generally prevailed, especially when the latter degenerated into superstitious and even sensual ways, the popular form was nonetheless just that, more popular with the majority of the people. The people's religious needs seemed to be met more immediately and more practically by the popular form than by the more distant, regulated, and disciplined orthodox form.

Some examples, first from contemporary times and then from the ancient days of the psalms, will help to clarify the discussion. While Christians profess Jesus as Lord and Savior, some may feel more comfortable centering their prayer on Mary and the saints, particularly the saints known as patrons for the dying (St. Joseph), for lost objects (St. Anthony), or for hopeless situations (St. Jude). Other saints such as Rose of Lima, Martin de Porres, and Ann, the mother of Mary, often attract enthusiastic devotion. Feast days associated with the life cycle of birth, marriage, children, and death are always appealing. Among Christians, Christmas, Good Friday, Easter, and Pentecost are central celebrations.

Within Protestantism, popular piety took the form of private reading and interpretation of the Bible, emphasizing the important role of the lay priesthood. This situation has led to the proliferation of churches. The phenomenal success of charismatic churches, as distinct from the mainline Protestant denominations such as Lutheranism, Presbyterianism, and

Methodism, shows again where popular support gravitates, sometimes like an avalanche.

This discussion can be extended to the marked success of local, independent churches in Africa. These churches are contemporary examples of syncretism, blending many ancient African customs in ritual and lifestyle with the traditional rubrics and sacred vestments of Catholicism. They have even revived many features of Old Testament religion close to their own customs, such as circumcision and polygamy.

The intent here is neither to defend and applaud nor to condemn and deplore this strong support for popular forms of religion. It is simply to alert readers to the parallel situation within Christianity to better understand biblical religion.

Blending Creation and Redemption

Earlier in Chapter 3 it was noted that Israel's official charter or document of religion, the Torah (the five Books of Moses), stressed the redemptive acts of God which begin especially with Israel's deliverance from Egypt under Moses. As was stated at that time, Israel's first commandment was no commandment at all but a strong statement of faith in this Savior God: "I am the LORD your God, who brought you out of the land of Egypt, out of the house of slavery" (Exod 20:2). If one reaches back still further to the origins of Moses' vocation to bring Israel out of slavery, one hears these passionate words of a compassionate God addressed to Moses out of the burning bush: "I have observed the misery of my people who are in Egypt; I have heard their cry on account of their taskmasters. Indeed, I know their sufferings, and I have come down to deliver them from the Egyptians" (Exod 3:7-8a).

Israelite tradition associated three principal feasts with great moments in their redemption. In March or April the feast of Passover recalled Israel's deliverance from slavery, when, as the biblical text suggests, the LORD struck down the first-born of Egypt (Exod 12:12-13). This historical remembrance is mentioned several other times (Deut 16:1). Seven weeks later the feast of Weeks (the Christian word is Pentecost) commemorated the giving of the Law on Mount Sinai (Lev 23:15-22). The third major feast, the feast of Tabernacles in what is now the month of October, celebrated God's care of Israel in the wilderness, God's later tabernacling in their midst within the Temple, and finally the Temple as a sign of the messianic age (1 Kgs 8:2; Zech 14:16-19). The feast of Tabernacles seems to have gathered the richest set of memories in its long development. Still other feasts were instituted, such as New Year's Day (Lev 23:23-25) and the

Day of Atonement (Lev 23:26-32). The Day of Atonement or Yom Kippur, probably the holiest of all feasts, is sometimes called simply *Yoma,* "the Day."

Leviticus 16 describes the elaborate ritual of Yom Kippur, including the weird, yet most popular, ceremony of the scapegoat. The high priest "confesses over it all the sinful faults and transgressions of the Israelites" (Lev 16:21). Then several attendants take turns leading the most unfortunate animal "to an isolated region" in the desert toward Jericho, where it is hurled over a precipice to its death—"for Azazel" (Lev 16:8-10). This bizarre ritual can be nothing other than a bow to popular superstition that is found in the Torah.

That other Canaanite practices and beliefs came into Israel's ritual was already brought to our attention in studying Psalms 8; 19; and 29. Here one can see how Canaanite agricultural feasts and practices were absorbed within Israel's three main festivals of Passover, Weeks, and Tabernacles. In reading about these feasts in Deuteronomy 16 and especially in Leviticus 23, the historical remembrances, for the most part, have fallen by the way. Harvest rejoicing spreads songs and feasting throughout the festivals. It seems that a Creator God, not a Redeemer God, is at the center. Yet when one turns to another, somewhat detailed celebration of first fruits of the harvest in Deuteronomy 26, the person making an offering recites a creed of God's great redemptive acts. God continues as redeemer in providing food and drink. Israel's remembrance of a Savior God and the great deeds of this God in Israel's history persisted down the centuries as the controlling feature.

Nevertheless, Israel's religion continued to adapt itself to the nation's agricultural existence, to enhance its ritual with Canaanite customs (or possibly to degrade the ritual in the case of the goat for Azazel), and to surround Israel's faith with a deepening sense of its Redeemer God. This development of redemption in the direction of world creation, so vast and so universal, was God's hope for sharing Israel's redemption, a central theme in Isaiah 40–55. While it is beyond the scope of our study to explore creative redemption in Deutero-Isaiah,[1] we still take note of the fact that creation tends to bring a universal scope to what otherwise would be limited to the redemption of the single chosen people Israel. Israel's first commandment, cited earlier in this chapter, professes faith in "the LORD . . . who brought you out of the land of Egypt, that place of slavery" (Exod 20:2). As noted in Chapter 3, belief in a Redeemer God separates Israel from the non-elect, in this case the cast-off Egyptians.

---

[1] See Carroll Stuhlmueller, *Creative Redemption in Deutero-Isaiah* (Rome: Pontifical Biblical Institute, 1970).

YHWH-King within Israel's Sacred History

Already examined were Psalms 19; 29; and 95. Here one recalls how the psalmists blend creation-faith with the Torah's emphasis upon a Redeemer God in Israel's history. While Psalm 19A proclaims the wonders of God across the universe and especially acclaims the sun in the language due to a deity, Psalm 19B is a litany of praise for the beauties and life-giving power of the Law. It even singles out its sweetness, more delectable than honey. One is reminded of Ps 81:16, which compares the manna to "honey from the rock." Psalm 81 points to a sacred meal (like the Passover meal) at the conclusion of a Temple ceremony. The gift of the Law, over which Psalm 19B becomes ecstatic, originated with Moses at Mount Sinai. The final word in Psalm 19B turns to YHWH as "Redeemer." In stitching creation and redemption together, the Law gradually absorbs the universal qualities of creation, including its boundless beauty and innate generative power.

Psalm 19 does not explicitly introduce the title of king for YHWH. The roll of thunder over the roaring water, against the towering mountains, and upon the trembling desert climaxes in the enthronement of YHWH. A psalm whose opening lines explode with peals of thunder, called the voice of God, ends with YHWH's blessing the people with shalom. Yet, even here in the final line the Hebrew grammar balances the gift of peace with the twice repeated naming, in the emphatic opening word, of YHWH. It is the divine person of YHWH as savior and protector, not the Lord's enthronement, which centers Israel's piety and worship.

Psalm 95 delays even less than Psalm 29 on the royalty of YHWH. As motivation in the procession to the Temple, a specially trained choir sings out: "For the LORD is a great God, / and a great King above all gods" (Ps 95:3). The epithet of "great king over all gods" does not seem combative like Ps 81:10 or Psalm 91, nor demeaning as in Psalm 82 or Psalm 115. Rather, YHWH is surrounded by lesser deities (called angels), as in any number of biblical passages (1 Kgs 22:19-22; Pss 29:1; 58:1; Isa 40:1-8; Job 1:6, 12). This is an idea symbolized in the Temple, where YHWH was surrounded with cherubim or seraphim (Exod 25:22) who come alive in prophetic visions (Isa 6:1-4; Ezekiel 1). In Deut 4:19; 29:26; 32:8-9; and 33:2-3, these lesser gods take charge of other nations. Late Jewish tradition thinks of the archangel Michael as guardian of the synagogue—as Christian tradition does for the church, a duty shared with the legendary St. George, often portrayed in struggle with a demon.[2]

---

[2] See Carroll Stuhlmueller, *Psalms 2 (Psalms 73–150)* Old Testament Message 22 (Wilmington, Del.: Michael Glazier, 1983) 41–2.

These examples from across the Bible inform us that the enthronement of Yhwh was not the focus of a specific ceremony, much less the preoccupation of a feast day. Rather, it was part of a wide assortment of Canaanite religious practices and intuitions that Israel accepted as the props or "furniture" for its ritual. These words are too wooden to communicate properly the fearful, majestic world of the spirits that surrounded Yhwh. As mentioned several times, this Canaanite mythology helped to sustain a sense of awe and mystery, lest Israel's religion degenerate into rationalistic excursus over law, senseless fears associated with animism, helplessness before an impersonal superpower, or crude naïveté without majesty or dignity in its form of worship.

Yhwh, a Just King

Important features of Mosaic religion controlled or corrected superstitious excesses. One of the most important ways consisted in emphasizing Yhwh's impartial jealousy and ever-loving concern for the poor, the defenseless, and the disabled. "Justice" is a rich and many faceted word for this attribute of Yhwh. The many Hebrew expressions—like *tsedeq* or *yashar* or *ᶜemeth* or *mishpat*—defy adequate translation into the English language where "justice" has become such a legal, quid pro quo, balancing act—giving exactly, no more and no less, than what is due.

Before returning to those psalms that acclaim Yhwh King, a look at Exod 34:6-7 provides a backdrop for the discussion that follows. According to the Exodus text, Moses stood atop the mountain, holding the two tablets of the Law in his arms, and the Lord came down in a cloud,[3] stood there and proclaimed:

> The LORD, the LORD,
> a God merciful and gracious,
> slow to anger,
> and abounding in steadfast love and faithfulness,
> keeping steadfast love for the thousandth generation,
> forgiving iniquity and transgression and sin,
> yet by no means clearing the guilty,
> but visiting the iniquity of the parents
> upon the children
> and the children's children,
> to the third and the fourth generation (Exod 34:6-7).

---

[3] For cloud symbolism see Ps 104:3 and Dan 7:13.

"Steadfast love" and "faithfulness"[4] have become the trademark of the covenant, the criterion of authentic religion, the mark of distinguishing the one, true God from all others.

This characteristic shines through clearly and concludes a very early psalm—in fact one of the earliest to lift into prominence the acclamation of YHWH as King. Psalm 93:1-2 reads:

> The LORD is king, he is robed in majesty;
>> the LORD is robed, he is girded with strength.
> He has established the world; it shall never be moved;
>> your throne is established from of old;
>> you are from everlasting.

These verses are a liturgical call to worship, and establish the ritual's setting. Verses 3-4 describe the liturgical action:

> The floods have lifted up, O LORD,
>> the floods have lifted up their voice;
>> the floods lift up their roaring.
> More majestic than the thunders of mighty waters,
>> more majestic than the waves of the sea,
>> majestic on high is the LORD!

Verse 5 concludes the hymn:

> Your decrees are very sure;
>> holiness befits your house,
>> O LORD, forevermore.

This division or description recalls Psalm 19 where the opening line invites hearers and readers into the "liturgical setting" of the universe. Verses 3-5a allow them to witness the "liturgical action" within this cosmic sanctuary: day to day gurgling, a sound like water bubbling from rocky springs; night to night, experiencing the silent sound of its darkness; one end of the world shouting its message to the other end, yet without sound or words. No human statement nor any earthly expressions can possibly contain the awesome mystery of God.

Mystery such as this rises with the majestic grandeur of African clouds, preparing for the ensuing collapse of the heavens upon the earth in tropical downpour. The opening words, like a trumpet call piercing the distant silence, declare that YHWH—and none other—reigns as King.

---

[4] Steadfast love and faithfulness are seen as prominent characteristics of YHWH. See Pss 86:15; 103:8-18; 145:8; Joel 2:13; Jonah 4:2. These divine characteristics are especially apparent in God's covenant relationship with Israel. See Deut 7:9-12; 1 Kgs 8:23.

Normally, in the coronation of a new king, the verb comes first, then the name of the monarch (see Heb. of 2 Sam 15:10; 1 Kgs 1:11: "then reigns [the new king] Absalom/Adonijah)." Psalm 93 names YHWH immediately, with the clear assertion: "The LORD is king, he is robed in majesty; / the LORD is robed, he is girded with strength" (Ps 93:1).

Liturgical actions function as memorials. As such, they are not announcing the start of something new but the remembrance of what has always been the case. If there is anything new, the newness lies in its fresh and effective renewal within the worshiping community. That YHWH is not newly becoming king but personally has ruled from ages immemorial becomes the clear, repeated assertion of the short verse 2: "your throne is established from of old; / you are from everlasting." The final word in the introductory verses 1-2, effective in Hebrew grammar but somewhat awkward in English, unless in song, is the pronoun subject, "you."

Returning again to verse 1, one finds that the Hebrew words here also stress grammatically the complete or full action that is spoken: the Lord's reign as king, the Lord's adornment with splendor and might. The language, depicting the Lord clothed and girt with fearful brilliance and strength, prepares for battle. The same vocabulary occurs in Second Isaiah where the cosmic struggle leads to Israel's redemption from slavery in Egypt and exile in Babylon:

> Awake, awake, put on strength,
>   O arm of the LORD!
> Awake, as in days of old,
>   the generations of long ago!
> Was it not you who cut Rahab in pieces,
>   who pierced the dragon?
> Was it not you who dried up the sea,
>   the waters of the great deep;
> who made the depths of the sea a way
>   for the redeemed to cross over?
> So the ransomed of the LORD shall return,
>   and come to Zion with singing;
> everlasting joy shall be upon their heads;
>   they shall obtain joy and gladness,
>   and sorrow and sighing shall flee away (Isa 51:9-11).

The "liturgical setting" in Psalm 93 reaches across the universe where YHWH appears as king, clothed majestically and fearsomely. The "liturgical action" in verses 3-4 amounts to a full orchestration of Canaanite mythology. It too concludes with the solemn singing of the sacred name, here, "the LORD" and YHWH in Hebrew. The person of the Lord is more important than the Lord's kingship. The ceremony concludes with a double proclamation:

Your decrees are very sure;
>   holiness befits your house,
>   O Lord, forevermore (v. 5).

In this final verse the psalmist offers a word of confidence about God's Law and God's house, and reaffirms the basic meaning of the sacred Hebrew name for God, Yhwh: the one who is always there with you.[5]

Yhwh-King: A New Song

Psalms most fully and formally proclaiming Yhwh-King came late, like Psalms 96–99 and 149. Most of these psalms are entitled "a new song," possibly under the influence of Second Isaiah:

>   Sing to the Lord a new song,
>   his praise from the end of the earth!
>   Let the sea roar and all that fills it,
>   the coastlands and their inhabitants.
>   Let them give glory to the Lord,
>   and declare his praise in the coastlands (Isa 42:10, 12).

This hymn concludes a major section of the poetry of Second Isaiah (41:1–42:13). The longer poem begins by announcing Cyrus the Great as the champion and liberator of Israel (41:1-20). Cyrus is later to be acclaimed God's "anointed," or literally the Lord's "messiah" (45:1). Cyrus' conquest of the world provides a panoramic setting for Israel's salvation and return from exile. This is the "new thing," unheard of until now (41:21-29). Yet, mysteriously, God really achieves it through "my servant" Israel, silent and humble, the Lord's instrument for justice (42:1-4). Israel will become "a light for the nations" (42:6), something "new" that even now is springing to light (42:9). The "new song" in 42:10-12 celebrates this wonder of Israel's salvation that somehow becomes a light to the nations.

Psalms 96; 98; and 149 begin with Second Isaiah's "O sing to the Lord a new song!"(Ps 149 omits "O"). What is new is not exactly new in every way. Already in Psalms 8; 19A; and 29 the heavens and the earth provided

---

[5] The root of the Hebrew name Yhwh seems to be the verb *hyh* (or *hwh*), which means "to be" or "to be present." God's nature is intimately related to being, and divine activity is associated with presence. However, the particular form of the name Yhwh also indicates a causative meaning: God not only is but also causes to be. God is the origin of everything else. At the same time the form of the name shows action in progress rather than completion. Thus Yhwh is a God continually coming to be, a God constantly moving into the future (see Exod 3:14, where "I am who am" can also be translated "I will be who I will be"). See Irene Nowell, "Yahweh," *The Collegeville Pastoral Dictionary of Biblical Theology*, ed. Carroll Stuhlmueller (Collegeville: The Liturgical Press, 1996) 1111–2.

the liturgical setting or sanctuary for God's redemptive act, for the manifestation of the Lord's justice in fulfilling all promises. Yet the song is new. Israel is not expressing its religious beliefs with Canaanite language and motifs but with its own traditional style of worship and song. This style is often called "anthological." What is also new in these late psalms is the realization that God will not set up a world kingdom through military adventure and the armies of a King David. These psalms are different from Psalm 87, in which a series of international treaties and conquests enables people from Egypt and Babylon, Philistia, Tyre, and Ethiopia all to look to the holy mountain and the gates of Zion and to declare, "All my springs are in you" (Ps 87:7b). Another important new aspect of Psalms 96–99 and 149 shows up in a comparison with Ps 68:18, where captives are set free:

> You ascended the high mount,
>> leading captives in your train
>> and receiving gifts from people,
> even from those who rebel against the LORD God's abiding there.

This theme resounds in Second Isaiah where one hears:

> Here is my servant, whom I uphold,
>> my chosen, in whom my soul delights;
> I have put my spirit upon him;
>> he will bring forth justice to the nations.
> He will not cry or lift up his voice,
>> or make it heard in the street;
> a bruised reed he will not break,
>> and a dimly burning wick he will not quench;
>> he will faithfully bring forth justice.
> He will not grow faint or be crushed
>> until he has established justice on the earth;
>> and the coastlands wait for his teaching (Isa 42:1-4).

This new posture of a humble yet victorious Israel, athirst for justice (mentioned twice in this servant song), inspires Second Isaiah to "Sing to the LORD a new song" (Isa 42:10), an inspiration again for the authors of Psalms 96–99 and 149.

The new creation of Israel, shared with the ends of the world, is the work of God; Israel waits silently, humbly—except to sing the joyful songs of the liturgy. As just mentioned, justice characterizes the new song and the new kingdom of God. In Psalms 96; 97; 98; and 99, various verses ring out with strength:

> Say among the nations, "The LORD is king!
>> The world is firmly established; it shall never be moved.

He will judge the peoples with equity."
Let the heavens be glad, and let the earth rejoice;
 let the sea roar, and all that fills it;
 let the field exult, and everything in it.
Then shall all the trees of the forest sing for joy
 before the LORD; for he is coming,
 for he is coming to judge the earth.
He will judge the world with righteousness,
 and the peoples with his truth (Ps 96:10-13).

The LORD is king! Let the earth rejoice;
 let the many coastlands be glad!
Clouds and thick darkness are all around him;
 righteousness and justice are the foundation of his throne.
The heavens proclaim his righteousness;
 and all the peoples behold his glory.
All worshipers of images are put to shame,
 those who make their boast in worthless idols;
 all gods bow down before him.
Zion hears and is glad,
 and the towns of Judah rejoice,
 because of your judgments, O God.
The LORD loves those who hate evil;
 he guards the lives of his faithful;
 he rescues them from the hand of the wicked.
Light dawns for the righteous,
 and joy for the upright in heart.
Rejoice in the LORD, O you righteous,
 and give thanks to his holy name! (Ps 97:1-2, 6-8, 10-12).

The LORD has made known his victory;
 he has revealed his vindication in the sight of the nations.
He has remembered his steadfast love and faithfulness
 to the house of Israel.
All the ends of the earth have seen
 the victory of our God.
Let the floods clap their hands;
 let the hills sing together for joy
at the presence of the LORD, for he is coming
 to judge the earth.
He will judge the world with righteousness,
 and the peoples with equity (Ps 98:2-3, 8-9).

Mighty King, lover of justice,
 you have established equity;
you have executed justice
 and righteousness in Jacob (Ps 99:4).

This litany of justice matches one that can be drawn from the prophecy of Isaiah. One of the major themes, threading its way through all sixty-six chapters, is the keen sense of God's justice. As mentioned already, justice carries with it: first, the primary sense that God lives up to the divine promises and to the bonds of love expected by the renewal of the covenant in Exodus 34; second, that Israelites abide lovingly by the same lines of blood, one with all others; and third, communicated throughout the long book of Isaiah and by those psalms honoring YHWH-King, that these bonds of love and loyalty reach out to men and women everywhere.

> Say among the nations, "The LORD is King!
> The world is firmly established; it shall never be moved.
> He will judge the peoples with equity" (Ps 96:10).

Verses 6-9 of Psalm 149 leave in God's mighty hands and in God's sense of justice the fate of the people Israel, who have so often been, from the post-exilic age until modern times, the victims of massive injustice:

> Let the high praises of God be in their throats
>   and two-edged swords in their hands,
> to execute vengeance on the nations
>   and punishment on the peoples,
> to bind their kings with fetters
>   and their nobles with chains of iron,
> to execute on them the judgment decreed.
>   This is glory for all his faithful ones.
> Praise the LORD! (Ps 149:6-9).

Because these lines draw upon Second and Third Isaiah and resonate the spirit of Zechariah 9–14 and the prophecy of Obadiah, they anticipate the final judgment scene, the eschatological age, the complete victory of God over evil.

Meditative Style

One of the telltale signs of late composition for the YHWH-King psalms shows up in their heavy dependence upon earlier psalms and prophecy. In many ways these psalms offer an excellent model for modern sacred songs, since they are often a mosaic of biblical phrases.

Psalm 96		Biblical Source	
v. 1a:	O sing to the LORD a new song.	Isa 42:10a:	Sing to the LORD a new song.
v. 2b:	Tell of his salvation	Isa 52:7b:	who announces salvation

v. 4a:	greatly to be praised	Ps 48:2a:	beautiful in elevation
v. 4b:	above all gods	Ps 95:3:	above all gods
vv. 7-9a:		Ps 29:1-2:	

Ascribe to the LORD, O families of the peoples,	Ascribe to the LORD, O heavenly beings,
ascribe to the LORD glory and strength.	ascribe to the LORD glory and strength,
Ascribe to the LORD the glory due his name;	Ascribe to the LORD the glory of his name;
bring an offering, and come into his courts.	
Worship the LORD in holy splendor.	Worship the LORD in holy splendor.

v. 10b:	The world is firmly established; it shall never be moved.	Ps 93:1b:	[God] has established the world; it shall never be moved
v. 10c:	He will judge the peoples with equity.	Ps 98:9b:	and the peoples with equity.
v. 11a:	Let the heavens be glad, and let rejoice;	Ps 97:1:	Let the earth rejoice; let the many coastlands be glad!
v. 11b:	let the sea roar, and all that fills it;	Ps 98:7a:	Let the sea roar, and all that fills it;
v. 13:	before the LORD; for he is coming, for he is coming to judge the earth	Ps 98:9	at the presence of the LORD, for he is coming, to judge the earth.

He will judge the world with righteousness,	He will judge the world with righteousness,
and the peoples with his truth.	and all the peoples with equity.

This same style of biblical anthology appears in Psalm 97 (although in a more restricted way), this time with Second and Third Isaiah. One should not overlook, however, the free way in which the psalmist also drew upon Pss 18:7-16; 50:1-6; and 77:16-20. Here the focus is on the prophecy of Isaiah, certainly the principal "meditation" and "memory" book for the psalmist. The quotations are not verbatim but, especially in the Hebrew, close enough to track their sources.

Psalm 97	Isaiah
v. 1: Let the earth rejoice; let the many coastlands be glad!	Isa 42:10,12; 49:13; 51:5
v. 3: Fire . . . consumes [God's] adversaries	Isa 42:25
v. 6: All the peoples behold [God's] glory	Isa 40:5

v. 7:   All worshipers of images are put   Isa 42:17; 45:16
    to shame
v. 11: Light dawns for the righteous   Isa 58:10b; 60:1

This method of the Bible quoting the Bible, so familiar to contemporary readers, was new in biblical times. The first instance of quoting a biblical passage by name occurs when Mic 3:12 is cited by the elders of the land who defended the prophet Jeremiah against the death threats of the priests and temple prophets (Jer 26:18). Up until this time, inspired spokespersons were forming or, better, were creating the Bible new. Only close to the Exile and especially afterward did people begin to view Scripture as set and unchangeable and therefore as something to be quoted.

As was seen in Chapter 2 of this book, in quoting the Bible the people were not historical-critical scholars. They never felt obliged to abide exclusively by what the original author meant in his or her context. If individual verses were lifted out—and changed or corrected, as was seen when Ps 96:7-8 quotes Ps 29:1-2—the later authors thought of themselves as members of a living tradition, able to adapt for the benefit of a later assembly of worshipers.

The community of believers are commissioned not only to be thoroughly Bible people but also to be a thoroughly vibrant, dynamic, and sensitive part of their respective churches as they struggle, preach, instruct, and pray within the contemporary world. Communities and churches today are not neatly confined as was ancient Israel, a country of some six thousand square miles, whose interaction with other nations was generally limited to the Near East. Today, believing communities form "world churches," at home on all continents, where there are many living languages and distinctive cultures. If the YHWH-King psalms, depending upon the prophecy of Isaiah, stressed justice, the task is all the more pressing in today's world where millions of people are suffering severe forms of oppression. The task of adaptation—in quoting the Bible—is far more complex and demanding but equally as crucial as in Bible times, so that believers may repeat today:

> Worship the LORD in holy splendor;
>   tremble before him, all the earth.
> Say among the nations, "The LORD is king!
>   The world is firmly established; it shall never be moved.
>   He will judge the peoples with equity" (Ps 96:9-10).

Chapter Six

The Royal Dynasty of David

You are my son,
Today I have begotten you (Ps 2:7).

Your people offer themselves willingly
  on the day you lead your forces
  on the holy mountains.
From the womb of the morning,
  like dew, your youth will come to you (Ps 110:3).

These two opening psalms, especially the second, became very significant in the New Testament as well as among the Dead Sea Scrolls. In fact,
they are among the most quoted of the psalms in the New Testament. Yet
in the context of the New Testament, these two psalms take on a new sense,
one that is quite different from their original use and purpose. Readers and
listeners are baffled not only by the New Testament references to Jesus' resurrection but also by the whole question of ancient monarchy. In today's
world many countries and cultures, such as that of the United States, have
transferred the pomp and protocol of kings and queens, princes and
princesses into an entirely different form of expression. The psalms, originally composed with important celebrations for the monarchy of ancient
Israel in mind, present a challenge.

Yet one cannot, or at least should not, dodge this challenge. These
psalms are far too important, not only for the New Testament theology of
Jesus' resurrection and Pentecost but also for the Christian communities'
liturgical celebration of the resurrection on Saturday eves or Sundays and
major feasts, to be left aside. Introducing his commentary on the prophecy
of Isaiah, Jerome wrote "ignorance of Scripture means ignorance of
Christ!" A paraphrase of this statement would sound something like this:

"Ignorance of the royal Davidic psalms means a lack of understanding of Jesus' resurrection and his gift of the Holy Spirit."

The gifts of the Holy Spirit prepare believers for work in their respective communities. Paul wrote to the Corinthians:

> Now there are varieties of gifts, but the same Spirit; and there are varieties of services, but the same Lord; and there are varieties of activities, but it is the same God who activates all of them in everyone. To each is given the manifestation of the Spirit for the common good. To one is given through the Spirit the utterance of wisdom, and to another the utterance of knowledge according to the same Spirit, to another faith by the same Spirit, to another gifts of healing by the one Spirit, to another the working of miracles, to another prophecy, to another the discernment of spirits, to another various kinds of tongues, to another the interpretation of tongues. All of these are activated by one and the same Spirit, who allots to each one individually just as the Spirit chooses (1 Cor 12:4-13).

Each person has received unique gifts or charisms of the Holy Spirit. These special qualities are shared with others whom the Spirit may have endowed with wisdom in discourse, or the gift of healing or prophecy, or with the duties in another list of offices, those of apostles, pastors, and teachers (Eph 4:11). As Paul declares further in writing to the Ephesians:

> [All of these gifts are] to equip the saints for the work of ministry, for building up the body of Christ, until all of us come to the unity of the faith and of the knowledge of the Son of God, to maturity, to the measure of the full stature of Christ (Eph 4:12-13).

The royal Davidic psalms are reminders that whatever may be one's gift of influencing and guiding others—as parent or teacher, as neighbor and friend, as religious leader in a church community—one acts "for the work of ministry, for building up the body of Christ."

Hope: A Blessed, Purified Memory

Royalty seems not to have been the initial divine intention for Israel. Actually, a different kind of leadership seems to have begun with Moses. The great lawgiver, prophet and priest, leader and intercessor left Israel with a system of religious leaders—either Levites or prophets—as well as with judges for more immediate, civil cases. Only the Levites possessed a hereditary right. Yet as we see in Judges 17, Levites, although preferred, were not indispensable for religious services. The prophet Samuel was not a Levite yet offered sacrifice (1 Sam 7:16-17). One also learns from Deuteronomy 18:6-8 that not all Levites were functioning professionally or continually at a sanctuary. Mosaic legislation preferred less centralization in responding to needs and opportunities. This at least seems to describe the organization of life for the Israelite tribes in the first two centuries after Moses, as one reads in Judges, the book of Joshua, and the early chapters of First Samuel.

Moreover, nothing in the five Books of Moses, the basic charter of Israel, speaks against this interpretation—despite the fact that these books, like amendments to the U.S. Constitution, developed over the centuries with serious revisions at key moments of reform. The only clear reference to royalty in the Books of Moses, that in Deut 17:14-20, sounds much more like a warning against excesses committed by kings than an enthusiastic endorsement of monarchy. No doubt, it comes from one of the revisions referred to earlier, after Israel had suffered from evil or incompetent kings.

If royalty came as a second thought upon the traditions of Moses, then certainly it could have been thought about and abolished—as the text admits. Monarchy survived in Israel's consciousness as a bad memory. Yet this memory also contained, as will be seen later, extraordinary promises and exceptional hopes for something far better. Over time, memories of the monarchy became purified so that Israel did not lose what God inspired at the heart of prophecy. Out of this process emerged Israel's messianic hopes.

Israel composed psalms for its kings. These sacred songs followed the kings through three stages: the kings' exalted moments of eternal promises; their sad and tragic collapse; and finally, the people's hopes for a new messianic king. Each stage, but particularly the first and third, speaks directly to listeners and readers of the text. What follows is a quick review of them as the setting for appreciating the royal Davidic psalms and applying them to one's life, prayer, and work.

Origins, Development, and Collapse of Monarchy

Even though the Davidic monarchy was to exert profound theological consequences in the religion of Israel and eventually take center stage in messianic discussion, its origins were not theological at all. First introduced in the shadow of moral problems with personnel in the existing structure, monarchy soon took on the urgency of sheer political survival for Israel. The Philistines, who invaded the land of Canaan from the western sea at about the same time as Israel, from the east, crossed the river Jordan under Joshua, possessed the secret of iron and so enjoyed military superiority (1 Sam 13:19-22). They destroyed the sacred city of Shiloh and captured the ark of the covenant (1 Samuel 4–5). Even united under Saul, its first king, Israel ended up in total collapse and disarray (1 Samuel 31).

Saul was chosen leader of all the tribes after the elders had come to the old man Samuel and had complained to him about his sons, "they took bribes and perverted justice" (1 Sam 8:3). The elders came quickly to the point: "appoint for us, then, a king to govern us, like other nations" (1 Sam 8:5). Royalty thus began as a desperate necessity, copied from neighboring peoples. Even so, it remained too radical a change to be completely integrated immediately. Although anointed with oil like a king (1 Sam 10:1), Saul never carried the title of king, *melek* in Hebrew. Rather, he was called *nagid,* commander or leader.

After Saul's suicide and military debacle, the people turned to David, this time with the full title of king. Although David could not proceed with his plans to build a sumptuous temple—too much of a break from the desert and tent traditions of Mosaic days (2 Sam 7:4-7)—he received assurances of eternal possession of the throne:

> When your days are fulfilled and you lie down with your ancestors, I will raise up your offspring after you, who shall come forth from your body, and I will establish his kingdom. He shall build a house for my name, and I will establish the throne of his kingdom forever. I will be a father to him, and he shall be a son to me. When he commits iniquity, I will punish him with a rod such as mortals use, with blows inflicted by human beings. But I will not take my steadfast love from him, as I took it from Saul, whom I put away from before you. Your house and your kingdom shall be made sure forever before me; your throne shall be established forever. In accordance with all these words and with all this vision, Nathan spoke to David (2 Sam 7:12-17).

These everlasting assurances are repeated in Psalm 89, where they merge with the eternal promises of the Mosaic covenant:

> I will sing of your steadfast love, O LORD, forever;
>> with my mouth I will proclaim your faithfulness to all generations.
> I declare that your steadfast love is established forever;
>> your faithfulness is as firm as the heavens.
> You said, "I have made a covenant with my chosen one,
>> I have sworn to my servant David:
> 'I will establish your descendants forever,
>> and build your throne for all generations'" (vv. 1-4).

> He shall cry to me, "You are my Father,
>> my God, and the Rock of my salvation!"
> I will make him the firstborn,
>> the highest of the kings of the earth (vv. 26-27).

At the heart of this covenant between God and the Davidic dynasty are two oft repeated phrases: the agreement will last forever, conferring on David and his successors a unique divine sonship. What all Israel was,

God's special children, God's "first-born" (Exod 4:22; Hos 11:1), the Davidic king possessed *par excellence*. At the central moment of the coronation ritual, a prophet proclaimed divine sonship over the crown prince. One finds different formulas in the Bible—just as there are various Eucharistic prayers in the Roman Catholic Church for celebrating the essentially one and the same Mass. Already cited is the one for King David from 2 Sam 7:12-17. Another, composed by the prophet Isaiah most probably for Hezekiah's coronation, reads with grandeur and pomp even in English translation. The Hebrew is included because of its unparalleled cadence:

For a child has been born for us,	*kî-yeled yulad-lanû*
a son given to us;	*ben nittan-lanû*
authority rests upon his shoulders;	*wattehî hammisrah 'al-shikmô*
and he is named	*wiyyiqra' shemô*
Wonderful Counselor, Mighty God,	*pele' yô'es' el gibbôr*
Everlasting Father, Prince of Peace	*'abî'ad sar-shalôm.*
(Isa 9:5).	

Several other coronation formulas exist from the psalms, as already seen in Ps 89:26-27. Another is found in Ps 2:7: "I will tell of the decree of the LORD: / He said to me, 'You are my son; today I have begotten you.'" Two others come from two different readings of the same Hebrew text, specifically, the consonantal text. By inserting different sets of vowels within the consonants, one finds two different formulas for royal coronations. The standard Hebrew text favors one, the Greek Septuagint, the other:

Hebrew Text	Greek Version
Your people offer themselves	With you in dominion
freely in the day of your power*	in the day of your power
in holy splendor	in the splendor of your holy ones**
from the womb, from the dawn	from the womb before the morning star
yours the dew of your youth.	I have begotten you.
(* *with a slight change, the Hebrew can*	(** *"holy ones" refers to the divine*
read "in the day of your birth")	*assembly*)

In either case a wondrous birth is taking place, explicitly so in the Greek version, implicitly in the Hebrew use of imagery. Daylight appears miraculously, in a burst of splendor, in this land with very little dawn or twilight. Dew too has a miraculous appearance; the ground is moistened, but without a bit of rainfall! As God declares to Job: "Has the rain a father, / or who has begotten the drops of dew?" (Job 38:28; cf. Judg 6:37-40).

Yet the Davidic monarchy collapsed under the weight of Solomon's scandalous lasciviousness (1 Kings 11), Ahaz's apostasy (2 Kgs 16:1-4), Manasseh's subservience to foreign powers and their deities (2 Kgs 21:1-18),

Jehoiakim's luxurious lifestyle (Jer 22:13-23), and poor Zedekiah's indecisive and blundering politics (Jer 37:1–39:1). The dynasty went down in the flames that destroyed Jerusalem and its Temple.

As seen in the biblical text, God does not revoke promises, however, nor does God renege on the divine word of an eternal dynasty. Without any incumbent king, Israel continued to recite the royal Davidic psalms, only now they proclaimed converging hopes for a Davidic Messiah in the distant future. Some traditions continued with this loyalty to the Davidic tradition—like the two books of Chronicles and Zechariah 9–12. Still other traditions preferred to ignore the Davidic promises. Isaiah 55:3-5 returns to the people what had been an "everlasting covenant," and "sure love for David" (v. 3). One is now back again in the days before 1 Sam 8:5 when the people asked for a king like all the nations. In Isaiah 56–66 all hopes are centered in the city of Jerusalem. The apocalyptic visions in Daniel 7–12 recognize no mediators between God and the people; God immediately sets up the glorious, final state of Israel.

In collecting the psalms into five books, the editors saw to it that David was "democratized." He appears in the titles to the psalms not as king but as psalm writer and fellow human being. The largest number of psalms are under the patronage of his name. The psalms originally composed for royal rituals (coronation, marriage, anniversaries, special needs) are scattered throughout the five books. One of the most important, Psalm 110, as mentioned already, was almost lost. It was recovered, in tattered shape with textual difficulties, from a long-standing tradition and included in the last of the five books of Psalms.

With respect to the New Testament writings, Jesus avoided the title of king. The larger context, moreover, where the people attempted to make him king after a multiplication of loaves and fish, confuses messianic prophet with messianic king (John 6:14-15). Only after Jesus died, rose from the dead, and sent the Holy Spirit upon the apostles and early Christians did the disciples recognize Jesus as the messianic King. They began to see in Jesus' resurrection the fulfillment of Davidic hopes. The phrases "sit at my right hand" (from Ps 110:1) and "you are my son" (from Ps 2:7) suggest Jesus' resurrection and coronation as messianic king (Acts 2:34-36; 13:32-35). Only still later, in one of the final New Testament books, is the latter formula from Psalm 2 read in terms of Jesus' preexisting divinity from all eternity (Heb 1:5).

The New Testament fulfillment reaches far beyond the generic and vague hopes of late Judaism (such as those found in the two books of Chronicles) and even the expectations of the Dead Sea Scrolls. The New Testament is light years beyond the original sense of the royal Davidic psalms. Yet careful scrutiny recognizes a line of continuity. An attempt will be made to trace that continuity and its meaning into contemporary life and work. First, however, it is necessary to reconstruct the ceremony of coronation from the details in these psalms, and from other biblical passages in the two books of Kings, especially the description of the coronation of King Solomon (1 Kgs 1:32-48) and of King Joash (2 Kgs 11:12-20).

Long Live the King!

The research of Roland de Vaux, O.P., aids in laying the foundation needed to summarize the main events in the coronation ritual. Previously the important role of one's imagination for interpreting the psalms was stressed. In reviewing the following details, one is able to see that each part of the ceremony was accompanied with music, song, and dancing (see Pss 45:8b-9; 68:24-28; 150), with the active presence of priests and nobility, Israelite and foreign (Pss 68:17-20; 72:8-11; 87). The central events in the coronation ritual would have been:

- escorting the crown prince, within the Temple, to the royal throne, which in the Bible was called "the pillar," a place reserved for the king (2 Kgs 11:14; 23:3);

- smashing the seal of the deceased king, definitively closing his reign so that a new chapter or new tenure now begins with the new king;

- bestowing the royal insignia, a diadem or crown, a sword, a scepter (Pss 2:9; 45:4; 110:2). These would have included, at one point of the ceremony, the clothing with priestly vestments. The king was supremely in charge of all aspects of Israelite life and, on most important occasions, offered sacrifices (2 Sam 6:17-19; 1 Kgs 3:4; 8:54-66);

- the solemn proclamation and inscription declaring the divine birth of the king. This action is central and essential and constitutes the transition from crown prince to king (2 Kgs 11:12; see as well the many passages already quoted in the preceding section);

- proclaiming the royal name. Kings received a new name at this time. Recall the elegant titles or names in Isa 9:6b. See also 2 Sam 12:24-25; 2 Kgs 23:34; 24:17; Jer 22:11, 24, 28;

- anointing with oil and a prayer for the bestowal of the spirit of God (1 Sam 9:16; 10:10; 2 Sam 2:4; 5:31; 1 Kgs 1:39; 2 Kgs 9:3, 6);

- the acclamation by the people: "So and so is king." This phrase is very similar to what was noted in Chapter 5 in the enthronement psalms of Yhwh (Pss 96:10; 97:1), literally, "Solomon [or whatever be the name of the new king] reigns!" This shout of acceptance began with the blaring sound of a trumpet, transmitted from hilltop to hilltop by trumpeters (2 Sam 15:9; 1 Kgs 1:34, 39);

- the enthronement in the palace which, with other royal and administrative buildings, lay immediately south of the Temple (1 Kgs 1:46; 2 Kgs 11:19);

- the homage from high officials and foreign dignitaries (1 Kgs 1:47);
- feasting, dancing, and general rejoicing (1 Kgs 1:9, 19, 25, 40).

This background furnishes the best interpretation for Psalms 2 and 110. Almost each line of the psalms announces a new, separate ceremony in the prolonged celebration. No one seemed to be in a hurry. Some of the lines, too, about the humiliation of the enemy and the removal of rivals have a touch of rhetorical exaggeration—always permissible at such a time of grandiose hopes and elegant acclaim—but they also carried a note of stern realism. The decline and death of a king always stirred ambitious intrigue among the various royal sons or princes (2 Sam 15:1-12; 1 Kgs 1:1-27). It also stirred ideas of revolt and strategies for independence among conquered peoples, who were forced to give tribute and sumptuous gifts at the time of the coronation of a new king (Pss 2:1-3; 68:19; 110:1-2).

Psalms 2 and 110

The opening stanzas of Psalm 2 set up a contrast between rival or tributary nations (vv. 1-3) and the Lord YHWH (vv. 4-6). Proper liturgical style manifests itself in that, in each case, the nations or YHWH are first spoken about in the third person and then, in the final verse (vv. 3 and 6), in their own name.

Ps 2:1-3	Ps 2:4-6
Why do the nations conspire, and the peoples plot in vain?	He who sits in the heavens laughs; the LORD has them in derision.
The kings of the earth set themselves, and rulers take counsel together, against the LORD and his anointed, saying,	Then he will speak to them in his wrath, and terrify them in his fury, saying,
"Let us burst their bonds asunder, and cast their cords from us."	"I have set my king on Zion, my holy hill."

Liturgy often begins with symbolic stage props—whether these are musical instruments or calls for praise or lament—and with descriptive language about the person or event. Gradually, or sometimes abruptly, symbolism and narrative stop and one finds one's self in the immediate presence of God. An excellent example is the Eucharist. After songs and prayers that the assembly addresses to God, after biblical readings instructing the assembly about God's wondrous deeds, after the assembly offers themselves and their gifts of bread and wine, the ceremony comes to its central action. This too begins in the third person, recalling what Jesus said and did. The third Eucharistic Prayer in the Catholic Liturgy reads:

On the night he was betrayed, he took bread and gave you thanks and praise. He broke the bread, gave it to his disciples, and said, Take this, all of you, and eat it: this is my body which will be given up for you. When supper was ended, he took the cup. Again he gave you thanks and praise, gave the cup to his disciples, and said: Take this, all of you, and drink from it: This is the cup of my blood, the blood of the new and everlasting covenant. It will be shed for you and for all so that sins may be forgiven. Do this in memory of me.

Returning to Psalm 2, one can appreciate the opening stanzas as introductory hymns. The congregation is approaching the center of the Temple courtyard before the Holy Place. Here the crown prince takes his place "at the column" or royal dais. A temple prophet steps forward, for it seems to have been their privileged role of anointing kings (see the texts cited in the previous summary of the ceremony). The prophet produces a solemn edict and declares: "I will tell of the decree of the LORD" (v. 7a). Turning to the crown prince and addressing him in God's name, the prophet most solemnly intones the sacred formula: "He said to me, 'You are my son; / today I have begotten you'" (v. 7b). At this point the choice of this man as king belongs exclusively to the Lord. The decision no longer relies upon any political process. As already mentioned, at this, the heart of the ceremony, one notes that God speaks in the first person singular, in the divine name.

Most probably the assembly now formally retires to the royal administrative buildings south of the Temple courtyard. Here the ceremony continues, first in verse 8 with homage from representatives of vassal states and tributary nations. Each brings forward his formal credentials and, of course, his sumptuous gifts. Then in verse 9—perhaps on another day?— the priests enact two important rituals: bestowing the royal scepter and smashing the seal by which the deceased king had endorsed decrees and official documents. Finally, the priest or an elder statesman pronounces wise instructions to the new king. The counsels of Deut 17:14-20 may have originated on an occasion like this and were frequently put to use.

The final line in Psalm 2, "Happy are all who take refuge in him" (v. 11c), was added very late. It links up with the opening line of Ps 1:1:

> Happy are those
> > who do not follow the advice of the wicked,
> or take the path that sinners tread,
> > or sit in the seat of scoffers.

The instructions in Ps 2:10-11b also correspond to the wisdom motif in Psalm 1. The editor achieves an excellent *inclusio,* an envelope to include or enshrine what goes in between. This literary device comes from the late period when Psalms 1–2 were placed here as an introduction to at least the first book of the Psalter (Psalms 1–41) and possibly to a longer collection.

Our explanation of Psalm 110 will be shorter, relying as we can upon the previous scenario of the ritual for the enthronement of new kings. The ceremony this time begins in the Temple courtyard. After introductory hymns and announcements, one of the temple prophets calls for the start of an elaborate procession south to the royal palace: "The LORD says to my lord, / 'Sit at my right hand . . .'" (v 1a). "Right" is another designation for "south," as Israelites always took their directions facing the east.

Once all are assembled at the palace, the representatives of vassal states join with Israelite nobility, pledging obedience and assuring the new king of a victorious reign: "'. . . until I make your enemies your footstool' . . . / Rule in the midst of your foes" (vv. 1b, 2b). In the midst of this pledge of victory and fealty, the crown prince receives the insignia of his office: "The LORD sends out from Zion / your mighty scepter" (v. 2a).

As mentioned already, at the central point of the coronation the crown prince formally becomes king. Most likely the assembly is back again in the Temple courtyard. Here a prophet steps forward to speak directly in God's name and proclaims the king begotten of God (v. 3). The ritual of Psalm 110 provides for the priestly investiture of the new king. The formula endows the Israelite king with one of the ancient titles of the Jebusite kings who ruled Jerusalem before its conquest by David: "The LORD has sworn and will not change his mind, / 'You are a priest forever according to the order of Melchizedek'" (v. 4). Melchizedek, it will be remembered, was featured in the story of Abraham:

> And King Melchizedek of Salem brought out bread and wine; he was priest of God Most High. He blessed him and said,
> "Blessed be Abram by God Most High,
>   maker of heaven and earth;
> and blessed be God Most High,
>   who has delivered your enemies into your hand!" (Gen 14:18-20).

Salem has been traditionally explained as Jerusalem. The rights of the Davidic kings to priesthood reach back before Moses. The epistle to the Hebrews applies Ps 110:4 and Genesis 14:18-20 to Jesus' eternal priesthood.

Verses 5-6 in Psalm 110 reach out rhetorically and acclaim the military powers of the new king. The king by this time is seated at his throne, northeast of the Holy Place. Therefore, the text refers to the Lord as at the king's right hand. In the final act of the ritual, at least as it is described in Psalm 110, one reads of a ceremony in which the new king drinks sacred water from the spring Gihon which supplied all Jerusalem: "He will drink from the stream by the path; / therefore he will lift up his head" (v. 7). Either the priests carried the water from the stream in solemn procession to the Temple, or else the entire assembly proceeded to the stream. This stream included a shrine. In fact, it was here that Solomon was anointed king (1 Kgs 1:33-34). The ending of this elaborate and complex psalm seems at first anti-climactic, even trite. Once again one needs to imagine the scene of procession, the blessing of the water and the pouring of it into sacred vessels, the offering of it to the king and his partaking of it, and finally, the solemn conclusion of music, song, shouts, and clapping, signaled when the king "lifts up his head."

I This Day Beget You

Yet all this ceased. Even Psalm 110 was almost lost when the dynasty collapsed in flames with the holy city of Jerusalem. Psalm 89, which begins with God's promise to David, as firm and eternal as the Mosaic covenant (Ps 89:2-5), ends with tragedy and pathetic pleading:

> But now you have spurned and rejected him;
>> you are full of wrath against your anointed.
> You have renounced the covenant with your servant;
>> you have defiled his crown in the dust.
> How long, O LORD? Will you hide yourself forever?
>> How long will your wrath burn like fire? (vv. 38-39, 46).

"How long?" The Jewish people are still awaiting the Davidic messiah. Christian faith finds the answer in Jesus' resurrection from the dead and bestowal of the Holy Spirit upon the Church. Acts 2:32-36 quotes from Psalm 110, while at 13:32-34, Acts cites Psalm 2. Each time the fulfillment came thus: "This Jesus God raised up, and of that all of us are witnesses. Being therefore exalted at the right hand of God, and having received from the Father the promise of the Holy Spirit, he has poured out this that you both see and hear" (Acts 2:32-33). For Christians, this Spirit-pledge of the bodily resurrection is already dwelling in us and transforming our earthly existence:

> For you did not receive a spirit of slavery to fall back into fear, but you have received a spirit of adoption. When we cry, "Abba! Father!" it is that very Spirit bearing witness with our spirit that we are children of God, and joint heirs with Christ—if, in fact, we suffer with him so that we may also be glorified with him (Rom 8:15-17).

The Spirit is active, influencing one's thoughts and directing our decisions:

> Likewise the Spirit helps us in our weakness; for we do not know how to pray as we ought, but that very Spirit intercedes with sighs too deep for words. And God, who searches the heart, knows what is the mind of the

Spirit, because the Spirit intercedes for the saints according to the will of God (Rom 8:26-27).

This phenomenon of being begotten by the Spirit and living by the Spirit is expressed in Ps 2:7b and, in light of the New Testament, can also be understood in relation to Jesus: "You are my son; / today I have begotten you."

Each Day Continuously Begotten by God

The Bible deliberately and repeatedly compares the divine and human process of begetting children. Here attention is once again drawn to the similarity and difference, each markedly significant, to set the stage for personal application that can span from mundane daily needs to mystical moments of intuition and prayer.

Conception is a most secret moment. Not only is intercourse between spouses wrapped in intimate secrecy, but the joining of ovum and semen takes place within the dark chambers of the new mother, unknown and uncertain to her and her spouse until many days later. Psalm 139 reflects on this dark, glorious mystery:

> For it was you who formed my inward parts;
>   you knit me together in my mother's womb.
> I praise you, for I am fearfully and wonderfully made.
>   Wonderful are your works;
> that I know very well.
>   My frame was not hidden from you,
> when I was being made in secret,
>   intricately woven in the depths of the earth (Ps 139:13-15).

God's creative presence is directing the process, as the opening lines of the preceding quotation declared.

So immediate and so directive is this presence that biblical writers, beginning with Jeremiah, recognize the source and major direction of their whole life, certainly of their vocation and major life work, as decided by God at this moment. The lines from Jeremiah are very familiar:

> Before I formed you in the womb I knew you,
>   and before you were born I consecrated you;
> I appointed you a prophet to the nations (Jer 1:5).

As one will see later, other biblical writers pick up this insight of Jeremiah in order to understand, at least in a small way, the profound mystery of their life vocation, especially in its dark, difficult moments. Perhaps the secrecy which surrounds conception prompted this application.

The first application comes from the strong similarity and total difference between human parents begetting a child and God's way of begetting us. In each case, as mentioned already, the action occurs in secrecy, even if the effects become quite evident at later periods of time. Very seldom does the Holy Spirit descend with the awesome signs of the first Pentecost (Acts 2:1-13). In fact, later in the same New Testament book, Peter is surprised that Gentiles—pagan Romans—have already begun to search for Jesus and for salvation in his name. This sign of the Holy Spirit's initial action in their hearts induces Peter to admit unashamedly: "I truly understand that God shows no partiality" (Acts 10:34).

The key words occur at the start and end of Peter's confession. "I begin" means that I have much more to learn of the Spirit's action; "no partiality" removes all human barriers to the coming of the Holy Spirit. Peter's surprise turns into amazement: "While Peter was still speaking, the Holy Spirit fell upon all who heard the word" (Acts 10:44). Peter then received the first Gentiles into the Church, bypassing the requirement—up until that moment—of being first incorporated into Judaism.

The gift of the Spirit and the Spirit's begetting of new life in Jesus crept up on Peter and the early Church and took them first by surprise, then by storm. The surprise element is one point of comparison with the begetting of new life. One is humanly prepared and humanly cooperating, yet the new life is mysterious.

Each time a person arrives at important decisions, in fact each time one acts under the influence of the Holy Spirit, God is actively begetting further new life in that person. Here is where the comparison with human generation stops. In begetting a child, the father's part is restricted to that act of intercourse that led to fertilization of the ovum. The mother's part extends for nine months. The analogy with the spiritual life may extend the parent's part for some years further. Yet, once the child arrives at full maturity, it is independent of its parents and on its own. On the contrary, a person is never independent of the Spirit of God. One is led day by day by the Spirit, affirmed once again by Paul's words to the Romans:

> For all who are led by the Spirit of God are children of God. For you did not receive a spirit of slavery to fall back into fear, but you have received a spirit of adoption. When we cry, "Abba! Father!" it is that very Spirit bearing witness with our spirit that we are children of God, and if children, then heirs, heirs of God and joint heirs with Christ—if, in fact, we suffer with him so that we may also be glorified with him (Rom 8:14-17).

This life, begotten in a person continuously by the Holy Spirit, manifests itself, as Paul wrote to the Galatians, in the fruits of the Spirit. These are:

"love, joy, peace, patience, kindness, generosity, faithfulness, gentleness, and self-control" (Gal 5:22-23).

Hearers and readers of the psalms have come a long way from Psalms 2 and 110 and the begetting of the new king as "son of God." Such is this mystery that, "in former generations . . . was not made known to human-kind, as it has now been revealed to his holy apostles and prophets by the Spirit" (Eph 3:5). Once prophecy reached its fulfillment in Jesus Christ, everyone became "royal" children of God through the Spirit.

Crucified and Led by the Spirit

In the passage quoted from Gal 5:22-25, Paul writes that "those who belong to Christ Jesus have crucified the flesh with its passions and desires" (v. 24). Earlier in this same epistle, Paul expanded upon this insight: "I have been crucified with Christ; and it is no longer I who live, but it is Christ who lives in me. And the life I now live in the flesh I live by faith in the Son of God, who loved me and gave himself for me" (Gal 2:19b-20). This insight of Paul also brings to mind the series of Old Testament passages in which God consecrates a person from their mother's womb with their unique call and vocation. In almost every case, this vocation involves exceptional trials—or, in the language of Paul, becoming "crucified with Christ" (Gal 2:19b).

As already noted, at the source of the Old Testament tradition is the great prophet Jeremiah whose vocation is announced in the beginning of the book of Jeremiah:

> Before I formed you in the womb I knew you,
>> and before you were born I consecrated you;
>> I appointed you a prophet to the nations (Jer 1:5).

YHWH's words as delivered by Jeremiah form an *inclusio* with Jer 20:15-18. In Jeremiah's prophecy, 20:14-18 concludes the last of his five so-called "confessions" or "laments" (12:1-4; 15:10-18; 17:14-18; 18:19-23; and 20:7-18). Each of these poems constitutes a most poignant prayer of a person under severe tension and persecution. Jeremiah seems close to despair, lost in darkness, hanging on by the skin of his teeth. And yet, according to the biblical texts that describe his moanings, there is within him a glimmer of hope, a word of confidence.

The first confession begins: "You will be in the right, O LORD, / when I lay charges against you" (Jer 12:1). The final lines of the confession are couched in imagery:

> How long will the land mourn,
>> and the grass of every field wither?

For the wickedness of those who live in it
    the animals and the birds are swept away,
    and because the people said, "He is blind to our ways" (Jer 12:4).

In sum, things must get worse before they get better. Until now Jeremiah has been contending with fellow human beings; now God offers the prophet a challenge. Until now Jeremiah has been inhabiting a land of peace, whatever may have been his conflicts; now he plunges into the jungle of the Jordan River, at that time a habitat of lions. Jeremiah's confessions/laments conclude with the prophet's decision to remain faithful to God and God's ways no matter what difficulties may ensue.

In the fifth confession/lament Jeremiah returns to the moment of his first vocation, actually to the moment of his conception, and expresses his frustration:

Cursed be the day
    on which I was born!
The day when my mother bore me,
    let it not be blessed!
Cursed be the man
    who brought the news to my father, saying,
"A child is born to you, a son,"
    making him very glad.
Let that man be like the cities
    that the LORD overthrew without pity;
let him hear a cry in the morning
    and an alarm at noon,
because he did not kill me in the womb;
    so my mother would have been my grave,
    and her womb forever great.
Why did I come forth from the womb
    to see toil and sorrow,
    and spend my days in shame? (Jer 20:14-18).

Within this confession, other lines allow readers and listeners a visit to the deepest heart of this marvelous person:

O LORD of hosts, you test the righteous,
    you see the heart and the mind;
let me see your retribution upon them,
    for to you I have committed my cause

Sing to the LORD;
    praise the LORD!

For he has delivered the life of the needy
    from the hands of evildoers (Jer 20:12-13).

Jeremiah thinks of God testing the just, not destroying them but purifying and strengthening them by means of the obstacles that must be dealt with, as the Hebrew implies. Hidden within the swirling storm—yet most assuredly present—is a valley of peace, joy, and praise. Mountain climbers know this experience, so do God's faithful people.

Jeremiah's hope in the thick of his frustration, his glimpse of light while enveloped in darkness, his experience of peace during the storm and of praise beneath the cacophony of raucous noise—all these show up again in his theme of conception and birth, of new life in the Spirit, which accompanies the passage. In the second song of the Suffering Servant within the prophecy of Isaiah, one reads:

> Listen to me, O coastlands,
>> pay attention, you peoples from far away!
> The LORD called me before I was born,
>> while I was in my mother's womb he named me.
> He made my mouth like a sharp sword,
>> in the shadow of his hand he hid me;
> he made me a polished arrow,
>> in his quiver he hid me away.
> And he said to me, "You are my servant,
>> Israel, in whom I will be glorified."
> But I said, "I have labored in vain,
>> I have spent my strength for nothing and vanity;
> yet surely my cause is with the LORD,
>> and my reward with my God" (Isa 49:1-4).

Another echo of Jeremiah is found in Psalm 139:

> O LORD, you have searched me and known me.
> Even the darkness is not dark to you;
>> the night is as bright as the day,
>> for darkness is as light to you.
> For it was you who formed my inward parts;
>> you knit me together in my mother's womb.
> I praise you, for I am fearfully and wonderfully made.
>> Wonderful are your works;
> that I know very well.
>> My frame was not hidden from you,
> when I was being made in secret,
>> intricately woven in the depths of the earth.
> Your eyes beheld my unformed substance.
> In your book were written
>> all the days that were formed for me,
>> when none of them as yet existed.

Do I not hate those who hate you, O LORD?
And do I not loathe those who rise up against you?
Search me, O God, and know my heart;
test me and know my thoughts (Ps 139:1, 12-16, 21, 23-24).

Still other examples are found in Ps 22:10-11; Job 1:21; 3:3-7. In the New Testament the figure of Paul comes to mind. While involved in a severe controversy (Can Gentiles be immediately accepted within the disciples of Jesus, without compliance with the Mosaic Law?), with strong suspicions cast upon his call to be an apostle and evangelizer (see Galatians 2), Paul establishes his case firmly in the mystery of God's call, in the language of the first chapter of Jeremiah and of the Suffering Servant Songs (see Isaiah 49): "But when God, who had set me apart before I was born and called me through his grace, was pleased to reveal his Son to me, so that I might proclaim him among the Gentiles, I did not confer with any human being" (Gal 1:15-16).

A Blend of Traditions

Once again application of the royal Davidic psalms has wandered far from their initial purpose, a ritual for the coronation of kings at Jerusalem before the Babylonian destruction of the city in 587 B.C.E. and the effective removal of the Davidic family from ruling Israel. A notable development has led hearers and readers from the fulfillment of these passages, first in Jesus' resurrection from the dead, and later to his "coronation" at the right hand of God (the language or image from Psalm 110), and then to his exercise of royal power by sending the Holy Spirit into the first group of disciples (Acts 2). The Holy Spirit shared with the disciples what Jesus was seen to be, this time in the language of Psalm 2: begotten of God and therefore a Son of God (see Acts 13:32-34).

Paul drew out additional implications of this expression of faith, such as Jesus begotten by the Spirit as a child of God. Paul looked more closely at Jesus' crucifixion and saw it as a decisive factor leading up to this life in the Spirit. Here Paul found guidance, not only in his own experience of Jesus' cross and rejection (2 Cor 4:5-11; 10:10-11; 12:7-10; Gal 4:13-15), but also from the prophets Jeremiah, Second Isaiah, and possibly Psalms 22 and 139. Thus Paul formulated "his own" gospel (cf. Gal 2:5, 7), centered on the message of the cross, the absurdity of the preaching of the gospel, and Christ the power of God and the wisdom of God (1 Cor 1:21-24). In order to be at peace with such intense suffering and severe conflict, Paul declared that such was God's intention and call from his mother's womb. Yet a lifetime of faith also impacts the mystery imparted from the first moment of life, for God calls all people from life, through death, by the Spirit to new life that is no more than the fulfillment of the first gift of life.

Chapter Seven

Community Laments

Rouse yourself! Why do you sleep, O Lord?
Awake, do not cast us off forever!
Why do you hide your face?
Why do you forget our affliction and oppression?
For we sink down to the dust;
our bodies cling to the ground.
Rise up, come to our help.
Redeem us for the sake of your steadfast love (Ps 44:23-26).

In more ways than one, a new chapter in the study of the psalms commences. Sorrow and suffering, it is true, have already entered the discussion yet, in general, they are a later development. With the royal Davidic psalms, victory and joy dominated Psalms 2; 45; 72; and 110. Only in the application of Acts 2 and 13 to the death and resurrection of Jesus and, to a greater extent, in Paul's more elaborate theology, did suffering and even death move to the center of discussion.

In the hymns praising God for the glories of nature or of Israel's history, sorrow and death appear only as a distant echo experienced by Israel's enemies, now overcome in Israel's journey to liberation and new life. Or else as seen in Psalms 8 or 29, the forces of chaos across the universe rolled back in the wonder of God's care for Israel. These chaotic monsters still hover on the distant horizon. Should Israel sin, they can roar with destructive fury. The wonder of creation is always on the brink of collapse—but, according to the biblical text, God will not permit such tragedy, provided Israel remains faithful. Psalm 82 tells how, under divine power, these "gods" and "children of these deities" can collapse, even die like human beings. Psalm 91, therefore, directs Israel to find its refuge in a faithful God, Israel's "shield" and "buckler" (v. 4) against "the terror of the night" (v. 5), against "the pestilence that stalks in darkness, / or the destruction that wastes at noonday" (v. 6). YHWH commands angels to "guard you in all your ways" (v. 11)—these are all references from Psalm 91. Israel is assured, as in Psalm 46, "the LORD of hosts is with us; the God of Jacob is our refuge" (v. 7) against the raging and foaming ocean waters, convulsing as mountains ascend into them.

This roar of cosmic chaos and the fearful tramp of mammoth international armies remain at a distance, serving only to orchestrate the wonder of YHWH's concern for the chosen people and the lavish proportions of YHWH's gifts to Israel. Such, at least, is the joyful panoramic setting of the hymns of praise.

The psalms of lament are of a completely different type. The awkwardness of these psalms' compatibility with Israel's religion in its origin and in its basic development shows up in the question or exclamation found in many of their introductions or at key transitions, and addressed either to God:

> My God, my God, why have you forsaken me? (Ps 22:1).
> Rouse yourself! Why do you sleep, O LORD? (Ps 44:23).
> How long, O LORD? Will you be angry forever? (Ps 79:5).

or to wicked persons:

> Why do you boast, O mighty one,
>   of mischief done against the godly?
>   All day long you are plotting destruction.
> Your tongue is like a sharp razor,
>   you worker of treachery (Ps 52:1-2).

> Transgression speaks to the wicked
>   deep in their hearts;
> there is no fear of God
>   before their eyes.
> For they flatter themselves in their own eyes
>   that their iniquity cannot be found out and hated (Ps 36:1-2).

> Do you indeed decree what is right, you gods?
>   Do you judge people fairly?
> No, in your hearts you devise wrongs,
>   your hands deal out violence on earth (Ps 58:1-2).

The questioning and exclamations sadly reflect the shock of disbelief. It cannot be true, yet it is. One needs to look more carefully at why Israel found such difficulty in associating sorrow and evil with the worship of God. Christian devotion to Jesus Crucified intensifies the seriousness of the question for Christian believers.

YHWH, the Living God

Two titles or epithets for God in Israel's early religious traditions set the direction for the long development of Old Testament theology, especially as this theology directed the composition of the psalms. The scene now turns again to Mount Sinai and the Lord's revelation there to Moses:

> "The LORD, the LORD,
> a God merciful and gracious,
> slow to anger,
> and abounding in steadfast love and faithfulness" (Exod 34:6).

"Abounding in steadfast love and faithfulness"—this phrase summarizes God's attitude toward Israel and invites listeners and readers into the mysterious heart of God. "Steadfast love" and "faithfulness"—in Hebrew *hesed we'emeth*—offer God's eternal pledge of fidelity to a bond as intimate and cohesive as the blood and/or relationships that unite members of a family. "Steadfast love" or *hesed* is the key word or, to use a better image, the thread that binds Israel's entire history in Psalm 136, the "Great Hallel" or "Praise" psalm, sung every Sabbath. God's "bonding love" with Israel becomes the key to opening up the mystery of creation; it is the thread woven through every moment of Israel's life. The psalm turns even the slaying of hostile kings into God's *hesed;* God will not stand by idly when the divinely beloved people are mistreated. In another important incident, that of God's appearance to Moses in the burning bush, God declares:

> Then the LORD said, "I have observed the misery of my people who are in Egypt; I have heard their cry on account of their taskmasters. Indeed, I know their sufferings, and I have come down to deliver them from the Egyptians, and to bring them up out of that land to a good and broad land, a land flowing with milk and honey, to the country of the Canaanites, the Hittites, the Amorites, the Perizzites, the Hivites, and the Jebusites" (Exod 3:7-8).

With this background, two troubling questions surface: How can Israel's affliction become a standard part of the people's liturgy? Is not suffering more a preamble, not an important or central feature of Israel's worship?

Another perhaps more pressing reason for excluding sin, sorrow, and lament from the liturgy lies in Israel's appreciation of YHWH as a "living God." The title occurs often enough (see Deut 5:26; Josh 3:10; 1 Sam 17:26, 36; 2 Kgs 19:4, 16; Ps 84:3; Isa 37:4, 17; Jer 10:10; Dan 6:20, 26; Hos 1:10). In order to perceive some of its scope for ancient Israel, one needs only to recall Israel's strong, official monotheism: "Hear, O Israel: The LORD is our God, the LORD alone" (Deut 6:4). Such monotheism did not tolerate other gods equal to YHWH. One of the serious threats to Israel's belief in one God came from the fascination of neighboring people—especially the Egyptians—with the abode of the dead, the underworld inhabited by spirits and gods. That Israelites could be drawn to worship or at least fear these deities and, at times, seek ways of communicating with them has already entered this discussion. Saul consulted the witch of Endor in order to receive information from the ghost of Samuel. The witch declares when Samuel appears: "I see a divine being coming up out of the ground" (1 Sam 28:13). Psalm 91 also takes seriously the gods of pestilence and terror who stalk the night. At this point in the study, however, the focus is on Israel's more official, orthodox position which worshiped only one God, YHWH, who was always living, compassionate, and faithful.

Unlike the Canaanites, Israel did not worship any god like their Muth or Moth (the Hebrew word means "death"). With their multiple gods for this world and for the underworld of the dead, the Canaanites provided a reasonable way of dealing with mystery, especially the mystery of problems, plagues, and sickness in this life, as well as the mystery of the dead in Sheol. In some paradoxical way, polytheism responded "rationally" to the mysteries of life—just as modern civilization explains its erstwhile mysteries in its rational way by science.

The country with the most elaborate system of life after death was Egypt. Its pyramids, luxurious tombs, and mummies testify to the Egyptian belief in the afterlife. Israel's teachers reacted strongly against the multiple gods, magic passwords, and the caste system of the Egyptian afterlife. Only priests or nobility could afford it or master its secrets. Egyptian and Canaanite deities found a place in Israel's popular expression of religion, either as separate gods or as associated with YHWH (1 Sam 16:14; 2 Sam 24:1, 12-13; 2 Kgs 1:2). The law book of Deuteronomy, otherwise mild and compassionate, severely reprimanded: "No one shall be found among you who makes a son or a daughter pass through fire, or who practices divination, or is a soothsayer, or an augur, or a sorcerer, or one who casts spells, or who consults ghosts or spirits, or who seeks oracles from the dead" (Deut 18:10-11). One sees that what was religious for some Israelites was magic for others.

This very negative reaction against contacting the dead or seeking to control sickness through the spirits led to a position that such areas were outside the presence and concern of YHWH. The sick and the dead, therefore, were unclean. Laws restricted priests and especially the high priests from touching them, or even from being present—for the high priest even in the case of his parents (Lev 21:1-15). Levites and priests who were in any way physically handicapped or whose physical appearance did not measure up to norms set by the majority were not allowed to function publicly in the Temple or to approach the altar or the veil of the Holy Place. As

Leviticus explains: "But he shall not come near the curtain or approach the altar, because he has a blemish, that he may not profane my sanctuaries; for I am the LORD; I sanctify them" (Lev 21:23).

A New Prophetic Direction

Prophecy appears to turn Israel's religion in a new direction. Yet, very often, apparent novelty was actually either recognizing a genuine value in an aspect of popular religion or reviving what had previously been lost in Israel's own tradition. Prophets like Elijah and Elisha never feared any uncleanness from touching the dead and bringing them back to life again (1 Kgs 17:17-24; 2 Kgs 4:31-37). The prophet Elijah rose to the otherworld in a whirlwind (2 Kgs 2:1-18) to indicate that real saintly persons inhabited it. In the prophetic book 1–2 Samuel, the ghost of the dead Samuel is put in contact with Saul (1 Samuel 28).

The books of the major prophets did not outrightly and totally condemn diviners and soothsayers, only their motive. Isaiah groups together

> warrior and soldier,
>> judge and prophet,
>>> diviner and elder . . .
> counselor and skillful magician and expert enchanterer (Isa 3:2).

Earlier in the passage, the prophet comments that

> For now the Sovereign, the LORD of hosts,
>> is taking away from Jerusalem and from Judah
> support and staff—
>> all support of bread,
>> and all support of water . . . (Isa 3:1).

Micah condemns seers and diviners, along with priests and prophets, not because of their religious activity but on account of their greed, lying, and bribery (see Mic 3:5-12).

Rather than consider blind or deaf people, or those who were dumb or lame, to be unclean and outside the presence of God, Isaiah proclaims their presence as the nucleus of the messianic age. They are symbols of the redeemed, as God reaches out first to them and calls them to see and hear, to speak and leap in a new, marvelous way (Isa 35:5-6).

Perhaps the most significant shift in the development of the psalms consisted in:

- the condemnation of what Israel considered most clean and sacred, like the Temple, its priests, and the royalty (Jeremiah 7; 26);

• the divine sentence of destruction, death, and evil in a foreign, unclean land (Amos 7:17; Isa 8:5-8; 29:1-16);

• the purification and transformation of Israel by these "unclean" punishments (Isa 10:5-27; Jeremiah 30–31).

In fact, a key word in Jeremiah, appearing nineteen times and transmitted to many psalms, is that which speaks of disciplinary suffering. The Hebrew word is *yasar.* For instance:

Your wickedness will punish you,
    and your apostasies will convict you.
Know and see that it is evil and bitter
    for you to forsake the LORD your God;
    the fear of me is not in you,
    says the Lord GOD of hosts (Jer 2:19).

In vain I have struck down your children;
    they accepted no correction.
Your own sword devoured your prophets
    like a ravening lion (Jer 2:30).

Indeed I heard Ephraim pleading:
    "You disciplined me, and I took the discipline;
    I was like a calf untrained.
Bring me back, let me come back,
    For you are the LORD my God" (Jer 31:18).

The impossible, blasphemous prophecy came true—impossible and blasphemous to the priests and temple prophets who called for Jeremiah's death (Jer 26:8, 11). Indeed, the prophet of the Babylonian exile argued extensively the case of such prophecies as Jeremiah's, and so also the certainty of the new prophecy that Israel will return from exile. The reference here is to the many poems on "new things" and the "former things" in the poems of Second Isaiah: Isa 41:21-29; 42:9; 43:9-12, 18-19; 44:6-8; 46:8-10; 48:6-8. The new prophecy will even reach out to the nations (Isa 40:1-5) and the instrument will be the "Suffering Servant," most probably the prophet himself in his own rejection. His innocent suffering will become a center of wonder and, in the reflection that it stirs, a source of salvation for the people Israel and for the nations. This is especially evident in Isa 49:3-6:

And he said to me, "You are my servant,
    Israel, in whom I will be glorified."
But I said, "I have labored in vain,
    I have spent my strength for nothing and vanity;
yet surely my cause is with the LORD,
    and my reward with my God."

> And now the LORD says,
>> who formed me in the womb to be his servant,
> to bring Jacob back to him,
>> and that Israel might be gathered to him,
> for I am honored in the sight of the LORD,
>> and my God has become my strength—
> he says,
> "It is too light a thing that you should be my servant
>> to raise up the tribes of Jacob
>> and to restore the survivors of Israel;
> I will give you as a light to the nations,
>> that my salvation may reach to the end of the earth."

This innocent suffering becomes identified with the suffering of all the people. The servant's innocence and silent submission to such unjust suffering are catalysts that help to transform the suffering caused by sin into a suffering that becomes a source of liberation and life for others. Israel and the nations say in their astonishment over the silent, Suffering Servant:

> Surely he has borne our infirmities
>> and carried our diseases;
> yet we accounted him stricken,
>> struck down by God, and afflicted.
> But he was wounded for our transgressions,
>> crushed for our iniquities;
> upon him was the punishment that made us whole,
>> and by his bruises we are healed (Isa 53:4-5).

In the first line of this quotation, Second Isaiah picks up Jeremiah's key word, *yasar,* now as the noun *mûsar,* to declare that, through the innocent servant plunged into the heart of a suffering but guilty people, suffering becomes wondrously transformative, changing them first into a suffering, innocent people, and then into a people who are healed.

From this prophetic background, the psalm will formally introduce into temple worship what previously had been forbidden or at least avoided. Yet, as stated earlier, this change for the new was not entirely new. Rather, it revived what had existed in the people's popular piety or in some spontaneous acts of mourning before the ark in earlier times (Josh 7:6-7; Judg 20:23, 26; 1 Sam 7:6). These latter demonstrations did not become normative in the Torah (the five Books of Moses). Prophecy reaches to the earliest times and to the prayer and worship of the common person, in order to bring sorrow and suffering, military defeat and destruction, sickness, and eventually death into temple worship.

Attention is now given to communal lament, those written in the plural and generally preoccupied with community sin and tragedy. The following section focuses on individual laments, in the first or second person singular, more personal conflicts, and trauma, like sickness and death.

Psalm 44

A careful reading of Psalm 44 uncovers the paradox of, on the one hand, firm attachment to tradition and the orthodox interpretation of it and, on the other, of honest confrontation with this same tradition. The psalmist seems to cry out in desperation: by unconditional loyalty, I have suffered its limitations. The psalmist is not declaring at all that orthodoxy is now unorthodox and false; rather, its traditional expression is not adequate to the new situation. In the previous chapter, this insufficiency of earlier interpretation became evident. In the case of the Davidic dynasty and the poems composed for the ritual of coronation (Psalms 2 and 110), the early expectation collapsed. Yet Israel never gave up on the promises to David. Rather, they invited God to fulfill them in new, marvelous ways. Those ways became still more stupendous than ever anticipated when, with evolving insight, the psalms were to speak of Jesus' death, resurrection, and bestowal of the Holy Spirit upon the first disciples.

Psalm 44, like the book of Job up to its final conclusion in chapters 38–42, locates listeners and readers very close to the tragedy. Because the psalm laments a military defeat yet says nothing about the destruction of the Temple (unlike Psalms 74 and 79 or the book of Lamentations), its composition seems to be toward the end of Jeremiah's career, most likely after the Babylonians took the city of Jerusalem the first time in 597 B.C.E.

The psalmist remained within two seemingly diverse traditions. The one precipitated his crisis of faith while the other pointed in the direction of its solution. This attachment to tradition shows the importance of memories, a significant factor in the series of psalms, of which Psalm 44 is a part, attributed according to the title or introductory verse to the "sons of Korah" or, better, according to a guild of psalm writers within the Levitical family of Korah (1 Chr 9:22; 2 Chr 20:19). The first of the Korah psalms in the Psalter is Psalms 42–43, a psalm of nostalgic memory:

> These things I remember,
>> as I pour out my soul:
> how I went with the throng,
>> and led them in procession to the house of God,
> with glad shouts and songs of thanksgiving,
>> a multitude keeping festival (Ps 42:4).

Memory, in Psalms 42–43, leads to sorrow over what is lost:

> My tears have been my food
> > day and night,
> while people say to me continually,
> > "Where is your God?" (Ps 42:3).

The same memory provides the language to express one's sorrow in liturgical ways (while longing for the liturgy) and, because of God's presence in the Temple, the psalmist composes the refrain:

> Why are you cast down, O my soul,
> > and why are you disquieted within me?
> Hope in God; for I shall again praise him,
> > my help and my God (Pss 42:5-6, 11; 43:5).

The major recollection in Psalm 44, occupying the entire first stanza, verses 2-9, comes from Israel's military tradition. As in the book of Joshua, God promised the land to Israel and pledged to fight with Israel's armies. YHWH even calls it "my land" (Jer 16:18). In a style that moves from strong trust to humble dependence and community confidence and praise, Ps 44:1-8 is a classic hymn of praise:

> We have heard with our ears, O God,
> > our ancestors have told us,
> what deeds you performed in their days,
> > in the days of old:
> you with your own hand drove out the nations,
> > but them you planted;
> you afflicted the peoples,
> > but them you set free;
> for not by their own sword did they win the land,
> > nor did their own arm give them victory;
> but your right hand, and your arm,
> > and the light of your countenance,
> for you delighted in them.
>
> You are my King and my God;
> > you command victories for Jacob.
> Through you we push down our foes;
> > through your name we tread down our assailants.
> For not in my bow do I trust,
> > nor can my sword save me.
> But you have saved us from our foes,
> > and have put to confusion those who hate us.
> In God we have boasted continually,
> > and we will give thanks to your name forever (Ps 44:1-8).

The beauty of these lines shines out in the movement from the community voice to the solo part of an individual in verses 4 and 8. Another movement is subtler to detect in reading the psalm, but must have been quite evident in viewing the bodily direction of hands and arms of the singers. The third person plural refers to the nations as well as to the Israelites:

> you with your own hand drove out the nations,
>> but them you planted;
> you afflicted the peoples,
>> but them you set free (v. 2).

The memory of the psalmist included more than temple traditions and ceremonies; it treasured as well the tradition of the prophets, especially Jeremiah. The psalmist's arguing for his innocence in verses 17-22 recalls the pleas of Jeremiah (Jer 15:10-18; 17:16; 18:19-20). The phrase "sheep for slaughter" in verse 12 echoes Jeremiah 11:10; 12:3. To be a "laughing stock," literally wagging or shaking one's head, aligns Psalm 44 with a number of other laments (Pss 22:7; 64:8; Job 16:4). These references are later, yet they help to associate the author of Psalm 44 with a tradition of lamentation in Israel. Prophetic tradition, while challenging the excessive formalism and limitations of the Temple, also served to sustain Israel through the ordeal of Jerusalem's destruction and the Babylonian exile of the people. It functioned in the same paradoxical way in Psalm 44.

The limits of orthodoxy show up in a comparison of the second stanza, a lament (vv. 9-16), with the opening hymn (vv. 1-8). The second stanza actually repeats phrases, only to reverse them. This daring feature is most evident in verses 7, 10, and 11:

> But you have saved us from our foes,
>> and have put to confusion those who hate us (v. 7).
> You made us turn back from the foe,
>> and our enemies have gotten spoil (v. 10).
> You have made us like sheep for slaughter,
>> and have scattered us among the nations (v. 11).

The language of dramatic reversal borders on blasphemy in verse 23: "Rouse yourself! Why do you sleep, O Lord?" One can compare this desperate cry with two other biblical passages. In 1 Kgs 18:27, Elijah taunts the priests of the god Baal: "At noon Elijah mocked them, saying, 'Cry aloud! Surely he is a god; either he is meditating, or he has wandered away, or he is on a journey, or perhaps he is asleep and must be awakened.'" Elijah's God, by contrast, is never caught in such human moments of tiredness. In fact, Ps 121:4 states it bluntly: "He who keeps Israel / will neither slumber nor sleep."

The question style of Psalm 44, in verses 24-25, links the psalmist not only again with Jeremiah (cf. Jer 12:1; 15:18) but also with the prophet Habakkuk, who twice questioned God. In fact, this interrogation of the deity gets the prophecy underway and brings it to one of its major conclusions. God attempts an answer to the first question—unsatisfactorily for Habakkuk—but God closes the conversation at the second question. The first question:

> Why do you make me see wrongdoing
> > and look at trouble?
> Destruction and violence are before me;
> > strife and contention arise (Hab 1:3).

Habakkuk is complaining about the situation in Jerusalem in which

> . . . the law becomes slack
> > and justice never prevails.
> The wicked surround the righteous—
> > therefore judgment comes forth perverted (Hab 1:4).

God decides to punish such wickedness at Jerusalem with foreign invasion. First answer:

> For I am rousing the Chaldeans,
> > that fierce and impetuous nation,
> who march through the breadth of the earth
> > to seize dwellings not their own.
> At kings they scoff,
> > and of rulers they make sport.
> They laugh at every fortress,
> > and heap up earth to take it (Hab 1:6, 10).

Such a solution, in Habakkuk's eyes, seems far worse than the problems—therefore (second question):

> Why do you look on the treacherous,
> > and are silent when the wicked swallow
> those more righteous than they? (Hab 1:13b).

After all, protests Habakkuk, there are limits to wickedness and the Babylonians, not the inhabitants of Jerusalem, exceed those boundaries. Habakkuk bravely declares:

> I will stand at my watchpost,
> > and station myself on the rampart;
> I will keep watch to see what he will say to me,
> > and what he will answer concerning my complaint (Hab 2:1).

[second answer] Look at the proud!
    Their spirit is not right in them,
but the righteous live by their faith (Hab 2:4).

As in the case of the confessions/laments of Jeremiah, God's second answer is no answer at all, at least to the second question. It reaffirms the need for faith and trust. One is reminded of the questions of Abraham: "Suppose there are fifty righteous within the city; will you then sweep away the place and not forgive it for the fifty righteous who are in it?" (Gen 18:24). Having received the answer he desired, Abraham reduces the number to forty-five, forty, thirty, twenty, and then ten. God agrees to ten but, at that point, the narrator of the story has God exercising the divine prerogative of closing the conversation: "And the LORD went his way, when he had finished speaking to Abraham; and Abraham returned to his place" (Gen 18:33; see also Gen 18:16-33).

Again, from this example in Israel's earliest history, prophecy reaches back to the first contact with God and the initial intuitions so that what seems new with Habakkuk, Jeremiah, and Psalm 44, namely, the questioning of God and the response of faith, has an ancient precedent that was lost in the formalization of religion in ritual and doctrinal statements. Temple liturgy and theology are essential not only for daily living but also for the questions which challenge both temple liturgy and theology. There would be no interrogation if faith was doubtful and theology was "maybe" or "maybe not." When faith fails, the solution is simple: this was a "maybe not" day and a divine exception to truth and fidelity. God too can be "asleep or on a day off." But YHWH does not sleep and remains forever compassionate and faithful, according to the key passage in Exod 34:6-7, quoted at the beginning of this chapter and throughout this book.

To be noted is still another important observation about the question-style, inherited by the psalmist from prophecy. The question put to God by the prophet or psalmist, by the very fact that it is a part of the Bible, becomes the inspired word of God. Put simply, a person's question is God's answer. God affirms a person's questioning as a divinely approved way to an answer. At times, even Jesus answers a question, either with another question (see Matt 21:16; 22:45) or with a baffling statement, no better than a question. What is humanly good, even if divinely inspired, can be improved upon or at least adapted further to meet pastoral needs. Luke frequently does this. For instance, in Matthew the Gospel writer depicts Jesus offering a specific teaching: "If you then, who are evil, know how to give good gifts to your children, how much more will your Father in heaven give good things to those who ask him!" (Matt 7:11). In Luke, however, the Gospel writer brings the final statement in closer accord with one of his favorite themes, that of the presence of the Holy Spirit: "If you then, who are evil, know how to give good gifts to your children, how much more will the heavenly Father give the Holy Spirit to those who ask him!" (Luke 11:13). To be noted is that in the NRSV these words of Jesus in Matthew conclude with an exclamation mark. The grammatical form, however, is a question. Is Jesus, we wonder, answering again with a further question?

Psalm 44 never attempts to answer its question, "Why do you sleep, O Lord?" (v. 23). In the second to last line, listeners and readers are reminded again of a refrain in the other psalm of Korah, Psalms 42–43. The psalmist declares: "For we sink down to the dust; / our bodies cling to the ground" (Ps 44:25). The refrain of the other psalm reads: "Why are you cast down, O my soul?" (Ps 42:5). The two Hebrew words are almost but not quite identical. Psalms 42–43 use a form of *shakhah* (the final letter a heavy gutteral "h"), and Psalm 44 a variety of *shakakh* (the final letter, a lighter guttural "h"). In each case, one is prostrate upon the earth and lost in its dust or dirt: in Psalm 44, "sink down" in adoration; in Psalms 42–43, "cast down" in dejection. In both cases, however, the physical posture is identical and, as we already remarked, the sound of the two Hebrew words is almost indistinguishable.

Two further reflections follow upon this close parallel of sound and posture. First, both psalms lead us into a silence that blends into adoration and ecstasy. Questions project our mind and heart beyond statements and words into the wondrous and overwhelming presence of God. As mentioned in the first chapter of this book, the emphasis upon *"Word"*—in the "Word of God"—has rightly shifted to *"God."* Second, lost in the dirt or dust of the earth, the psalmist, and now all God's people, can be formed anew, just as Genesis speaks of the initial formation of humanity: "then the LORD God formed man from the dust of the ground, and breathed into his nostrils the breath of life; and the man became a living being" (Gen 2:7). Silently lost in adoration within the dust before God is preparation for the ultimate answer to all questions: one's becoming a new creature in Christ Jesus. Buried in Christ, one will rise to new life in Christ (Rom 6:4), to become a new person in God, re-created by the Holy Spirit, according to the New Testament interpretation of the royal Davidic psalms (Psalms 2 and 110) in the preceding chapter. Enlivened by the Holy Spirit, then, God's people who lie prostrate on the earth will rise to follow the way of the psalmist in prayer and adoration. Paul's words resonate in our minds and hearts:

> Likewise the Spirit helps us in our weakness; for we do not know how to pray as we ought, but that very Spirit intercedes with sighs too deep for words. And God, who searches the heart, knows what is the mind of the

Spirit, because the Spirit intercedes for the saints according to the will of God (Rom 8:26-27).

If one returns to the first reflection in the preceding paragraph—the transition from "*Word* of God" to "word of *God*," one finds that Psalm 44 ends in a way similar to another observation in Psalm 1. The Scriptures, it was suggested, uncover Israel's continually developing perception of their God. In "word of *God*"—here one is working with the new emphasis—God steps forward much less as Creator and much more as Redeemer, much less as prophet and much more as compassionate savior. The psalmist concludes Psalm 44 with the prayer: "Rise up, come to our help. / Redeem us for the sake of your steadfaast love" (v. 26).

"Steadfast love," the translation of the Hebrew *hesed*, insists upon the common blood shared in a family and, consequently, of the family obligation expected of each member. God has freely entered one's family. The image is that of blood; the reality is still more intimate and intense. God is life of one's life, in whom a person lives and moves and has his or her being (Acts 17:28). The psalm returns to an essential point: YHWH is a living God. The Torah pushed this concept to the extreme so that anything that spoke of suffering, sickness, and death was outside the boundary of God's presence and therefore "unclean." Psalm 44, however, and its appeal to the Lord's *hesed*, give the sense of God as a living God, its true and deep meaning—life shared in one blood. Strangely enough, Psalm 44 led to this extraordinary insight into the reality of a living God. Verse 23 of psalm 44 dared to question God: "Why do you sleep, O Lord?" The challenge invites one to enter the mystical ecstasy of the living God.

Psalm 12 and the Purification of God's Word

Another communal lament, Psalm 12, invites one to participate in Israel's prayer in an equally mysterious although perhaps less violent way than was expressed by the opening stanzas of Psalm 44. In Psalm 44 the trial to faith erupts when the Israelites address God directly and tell of their pain because of what God has done or allowed to happen when Israel was plundered at will by foreigners and scattered among the nations:

> You have made us like sheep for slaughter,
>   and have scattered us among the nations.
> You have sold your people for a trifle,
>   demanding no high price for them.
> You have made us the taunt of our neighbors,
>   the derision and scorn of those around us (Ps 44:11-13).

In Psalm 12 faith is challenged by other Israelites. This sentiment is also echoed in the book of Jeremiah:

> For even your kinsfolk and your own family,
>> even they have dealt treacherously with you;
>> they are in full cry after you;
> do not believe them,
>> though they speak friendly words to you (Jer 12:6).

This betrayal by his own relatives precipitated the most touching and certainly the deepest soul-searching of all Jeremiah's writings. The verse just quoted is part of Jeremiah's first confession. The serious trial endured by prophet and psalmist, as well as the recorded response of questioning and complaint, seems new in comparison to the earlier hymns of praise or to the strong statements of the Torah. Yet, once again, the style is not totally new. Abraham, childless and seemingly forced to leave his possessions and promises to the hired steward (Gen 15:2), complained to God. Hagar, one of Abraham's wives, wept at being driven out into the desert with her son (Gen 21:14-19). According to the book of Exodus, even God was about to give up on the people Israel, until Moses pleaded for them (Exod 32:7-14). Yet Moses himself could not obey God and strike a rock for water without first complaining against this rebel people and in anger (or was it in doubt?) striking the rock twice (Num 21:7-13). For this transgression God refused Moses the necessary permission to enter the Promised Land, despite Moses' repeated entreaties (Deut 1:37). In fact, God seems fed up with Moses' repeated prayer: "But the LORD was angry with me on your account and would not heed me. The LORD said to me, 'Enough from you! Never speak to me of this matter again!'" (Deut 3:26). Betrayed by his own people's transgressions and momentarily having doubted, Moses still continued to entreat God for them. "For I was afraid that the anger that the LORD bore against you was so fierce that he would destroy you. But the LORD listened to me that time also" (Deut 9:19). Later, in the same chapter of Deuteronomy, one sees him further declaring:

> Throughout the forty days and forty nights that I lay prostrate before the LORD when the LORD intended to destroy you, I prayed to the LORD and said, "Lord GOD, do not destroy the people who are your very own possession, whom you redeemed in your greatness, whom you brought out of Egypt with a mighty hand" (Deut 9:25).

The psalms, therefore, remember Moses almost more as an intercessor with God than as a lawgiver:

> Moses and Aaron were among his priests,
>> Samuel also was among those who called on his name.
>> They cried to the LORD, and he answered them (Ps 99:6).

This selfless defense of the people and the willingness to suffer with them and even within their transgression prevented Moses, sadly enough, from entering the Promised Land. This attitude of faith and prayer in the midst of betrayal and stubborn sinfulness led to Moses' deepening relationship with God who, according to the biblical text, declared him "very humble, more so than anyone else on the face of the earth," with whom alone the Lord speaks "face to face" (Num 12:3, 8). The Torah itself ends with verses of praise for Moses:

> Never since has there arisen a prophet in Israel like Moses, whom the LORD knew face to face. He was unequaled for all the signs and wonders that the LORD sent him to perform in the land of Egypt, against Pharaoh and all his servants and his entire land, and for all the mighty deeds and all the terrifying displays of power that Moses performed in the sight of all Israel (Deut 34:10-12).

Such is the final memory of Moses in the Torah—indeed its final words. The biblical writers wanted Moses remembered forever as a prophet, not as a person who fulfilled in himself the prediction of entering the Promised Land but as a faithful intercessor, as a man who persevered with the people regardless of obstacles and struggles. Psalm 12 allows listeners and readers to return midstream—or better, mid-desert—as Moses and Jeremiah struggled with their temptations against faith in God because of betrayal from within. Psalm 12, in fact, not only leads back mid-desert but also stops there. In a true sense, it brings listeners and readers nowhere.

In order to give some context to the last sentence of getting nowhere, lest it stand condemned by Psalm 12's own disdain for clever people who use their cleverness to speak deceptively "with flattering lips and a double heart" (v. 2), one has only to observe that the opening affront repeats itself, even more shamelessly, in the final verse: "Help, O LORD, for there is no longer anyone who is godly; / the faithful have disappeared from humankind" (v. 1) [literally, from the children of humanity—Hebrew, *benê ʾadam*]; "On every side the wicked prowl, / as vileness is exalted among humankind" (v. 8) [Hebrew, *benê ʾadam*]. By glancing further at the overall literary structure of Psalm 12, another very important detail comes to the fore. It is not the psalmist alone who is mid-desert—the desert here being the deceit and smooth talk of one's relatives—but God too is at the center, literally at the center of the literary shape of the psalm.

Psalm 12, upon careful reading, divides its lines with careful balance, even though the opening call, "Help, O LORD," seems to depart from the plan:

      v. 1a: call for help: "Help, O LORD"
a   v. 2: lament

b   v. 3: prayer or petition
c   v. 4: evil people speak
d   v. 5: God speaks a word of salvation
c'   v. 6: good people reflect on God's word
b'   v. 7: another prayer
a'   v. 8: final lament

Here is an elaborate form of "chiasm," one of the rhetorical techniques already discussed above in Chapter 3. In this example, the downward stroke (a-b-c) is repeated in the upward stroke, only in reverse order (c'-b'-a'), while at the center is a simple line, unique in itself, to unite both strokes (d).

No amount of smooth and arrogant talk will drive God away. Torah would protect God from this profanation within the Holy of Holies (Exod 25:17-22; 26:31-34; 1 Kgs 8:10-13); prophecy and the psalms of lament plunged God into the rough and tumble of earthly life. It would seem that God would be enough of a realist to admit how burdensome is the deceit and boasting within the community of Israel:

> "Because the poor are despoiled,
>   because the needy groan,
>   I will now rise up," says the LORD;
>   "I will place them in the safety for which they long" (Ps 12:5).

Strangely, yet realistically enough, it almost seems as if sin is a precondition for God to manifest the mystery of God's merciful self.

If one scans the chiastic structure of Psalm 12, then one notices that the opening call for help seems outside the otherwise rigid literary shape of the psalm. This, however, is not so on a second reading. God, in declaring, "I will place them in safety" (v. 5), is repeating the very idea of the call for help, "Help, O LORD." Verse 6 allows the entire congregation to meditate on God's word, as the choir sings:

> The promises of the LORD are promises that are pure,
>   silver refined in a furnace on the ground,
>   purified seven times.

In this verse, the psalmist speaks candidly: divine promises are "pure," in the Hebrew sense of *taher*. They can be relied upon and embraced by one's heart. They are, accordingly, the exact opposite of what one hears from the "flattering lips" and "a double heart" in verse 2. To embrace God's words is to embrace life in its purity and fullness. In verse 7 one hears: "You, O LORD, will protect us; / you will guard us from this generation forever." These words express a sense of confidence in God in spite of continued struggles and challenges.

God's word needs to find a resting place in people's hearts. As in the prophecy of Isaiah, times come when self-reliance no longer suffices. In Isaiah 7, the prophet advises the king in a couplet first positive, then negative: "Take heed, be quiet, do not fear, and do not let your heart be faint" (Isa 7:4). The king seems to have only three choices, one of which he had already decided against: to join the coalition against Assyria and pitch his kingdom into the international chess game Assyria had always won. Another choice is to march his army against the Syro-Ephraimite league that was moving south against Jerusalem. His third choice is to appeal to Assyria for help. The second alternative was inviting sure defeat, for his army was greatly outnumbered. The final way meant the loss of independence, annual tribute to the Assyrians, and the encouragement of a strong Assyrian influence in politics and, worse of all, in religion. The prophet offers a fourth possibility: do nothing but wait upon God trustfully. Isaiah expands upon this, his recommended choice, especially in the light of the king's rejection of it:

> For thus said the Lord GOD, the Holy One of Israel:
> In returning and rest you shall be saved;
> > in quietness and in trust shall be your strength.
> But you refused and said,
> "No! We will flee upon horses"—
> > therefore you shall flee!
> and, "We will ride upon swift steeds"—
> > therefore your pursuers shall be swift!
> A thousand shall flee at the threat of one,
> > at the threat of five you shall flee,
> until you are left
> > like a flagstaff on the top of a mountain,
> > like a signal on a hill.
> Therefore the LORD waits to be gracious to you;
> > therefore he will rise up to show mercy to you.
> For the LORD is a God of justice;
> > blessed are all those who wait for him (Isa 30:15-18).

Without faith in God's goodness and God's ability to empower people, one's own strength and hope remain fleeting virtues.

Isaiah, in another written passage closely connected with the former passage in Isaiah 7, uses the image of water—the silent, slow-moving yet life-giving waters of Shiloah, the name given to those that bubbled out of the spring of Gihon that supplied the city of Jerusalem. Rejecting God as the source of life was compared to the foolish disaster of repudiating the spring water ready at hand for Jerusalem and of turning to distant, muddy, angry torrents. Isaiah's words speak for themselves:

Because this people has refused the waters of Shiloah that flow gently, and melt in fear before Rezin and the son of Remaliah; therefore, the Lord is bringing up against it the mighty flood waters of the River, the king of Assyria and all his glory; it will rise above all its channels and overflow all its banks; it will sweep on into Judah as a flood, and, pouring over, it will reach up to the neck; and its outspread wings will fill the breadth of your land, O Immanuel.

> Band together, you peoples, and be dismayed;
>> listen, all you far countries;
> gird yourselves and be dismayed;
>> gird yourselves and be dismayed!
> Take counsel together, but it shall be brought to naught;
>> speak a word, but it will not stand,
>> for God is with us (Isa 8:6-10).

Even so, as the final stanza announces, even in Israel's rejection of God, God still abides by an eternal covenant with this people and will still redeem Israel, albeit through further sorrow.

Returning to Psalm 12, one notes that the psalm is not dealing with a private concern of an individual. Already the psalm's context of smooth lips and double hearts, as well as its literary form of separate sections of lament, prayer, words of the wicked, words of good people, and the Lord's own words—all this presumes community interaction. Different choirs probably sang the separate sections; the priest or temple prophet pronounced the divine oracle in verse 5. The psalmist cannot trust any personal response to the wider community, and deems that it is best to place one's trust in God. This prayer positioning of one's self refines a person sevenfold. The word is active within God's people; it is a two-edged sword cutting to the marrow (Heb 4:12). This attitude of trust is a central theme in the second letter to Timothy:

> The saying is sure:
>> If we have died with him, we will also live with him;
>> if we endure, we will also reign with him;
>> if we deny him, he will also deny us;
>> if we are faithless, he remains faithful—
>> for he cannot deny himself (2 Tim 2:11-12).

Thus, when the winds blow fiercely or the ocean currents drive steadily onward, just to stay the course and remain in position uses up all of one's energy supply, but it often leads to a positive outcome. Trust can help one overcome all sorts of obstacles, and it can allow for deeper, more open interaction with one's God and with all of life.

Chapter Eight

Individual Laments

My God, my God, why have you forsaken me?
   Why are you so far from helping me, from the words of
      my groaning?
O my God, I cry by day, but you do not answer;
   and by night, but find no rest (Ps 22:1-2).

The largest number of psalms fit into the category of individual laments. The division between communal and individual laments is somewhat arbitrary. No psalm is in the Psalter unless intended for the community of Israel. Thus the individual, possibly as a cantor in a religious service, speaks for all Israel in their sorrow or desperation. This cultic function shows up rather clearly in the first three chapters of the book of Lamentations (the last two lamentations come from the voice of the community's "we" or "us"). As the third chapter begins:

> I am one who has seen affliction
>   under the rod of God's wrath;
> he has driven and brought me
>   into darkness without any light (Lam 3:1-2).

Some of the lines, spoken by an individual mourner, echo in the memory of Christian piety, as the following one, often addressed to Mary at the foot of Jesus' cross:

> Is it nothing to you, all you who pass by?
>   Look and see
> if there is any sorrow like my sorrow,
>   which was brought upon me,
> which the LORD inflicted
>   on the day of his fierce anger (Lam 1:12).

These laments in the first-person singular originated in the devastated ruins of Jerusalem. The Babylonians had razed the city to the ground a month after its capture (2 Kgs 25:8-10). In the later part of the book of Jeremiah one hears about groups of Jews, "the poor people who owned nothing" (Jer 39:10), left behind after the majority of the people, especially the nobility and skilled workers, had been deported. These came to the ruined Temple for worship: "eighty men arrived from Shechem and Shiloh and Samaria, with their beards shaved and their clothes torn, and their bodies gashed, bringing grain offerings and incense to present at the temple of the LORD" (Jer 41:5). Still later, after the first of the exiles began returning to Jerusalem, permitted by an edict of Cyrus the Great (2 Chr 36:22-23; Ezra 1:1-4), the people began to inquire about days of mourning and fasting (Zech 7:1-4). These days at first did not need to be legislated. Israel spontaneously commemorated such tragic days as the capture of Jerusalem and its burning a month later (2 Kgs 25:3-4, 8-9). Only gradually was public or official recognition given these days.[1]

Individuals may have composed the psalms not only to express and sustain their personal sorrow in God's presence, but also to share their sorrow with other Israelites on days of mourning. By this time, the prophet Jeremiah emerged with the recognition denied during his lifetime (Jer 25:11; 2 Chr 36:21; Zech 1:3-6; 7:8-14). Jeremian influence shows up in many psalms of individual lament.

These psalms, like the prophecy of Jeremiah, manifest such intense poignancy, personal involvement, and intimate emotional details, as well as signs of physical illness and shame, that they may have originally been composed to satisfy the needs of individual piety. Yet this individual was, at the same time, a person fully dedicated to community and involved in community life—and, in this case, community loss and death. The psalmist would, therefore, easily slip into public days of mourning; others, perhaps less gifted, would gratefully accept and use the psalm for their prayer.

Picking up the momentum, which was already occurring in ancient Israel, by which individual laments became public property adapted to community liturgy, this chapter focuses on individual laments, specifically Psalms 22; 42; and 43, to examine their role in the life and work of believing communities.

Psalm 22 and the Eucharist

Connections can be made between Psalm 22 and the life of Jesus. Specifically, the cross exhibits to the world the sacred humanity of Jesus,

---

[1] The rituals of Yom Kippur, the Day of Atonement, most likely developed or expanded after Judah's experience of exile.

not only in the body nailed naked to a cross, twisted in death agony, but also in another touching detail, so delicate in the paradox of a setting racked with the violent convulsion of crucifixion. Jesus recites the opening words of Psalm 22, not according to the sacred Hebrew text, ʾ*eli* ʾ*eli lamâ* ʿ*azabtanî*, but rather in the vernacular Aramaic, the form of popular prayer: ʾ*eloi* ʾ*eloi lema sabachtani* (Mark 15:34; Matt 27:46). These words, especially in the Aramaic, draw one into the human life of Jesus who prays peacefully at home in Nazareth and sweats in night vigils the agony of his mission. He often experienced being rebuffed and ridiculed (see Matt 26:36-44; Mark 3:20-30; 14:32-42; Luke 4:28-29; 6:12; 11:14-23; 22:39-46; John 6:41-52, 60-66; 8:48). Simultaneously one can become lost in another intimate moment, the bonding of Jesus the man with God. A glimpse of Jesus' experience comes from the inclusion of Psalm 22 where two songs of thanksgiving form community prayer, drawing the poor and afflicted of the world into worship and a sacred meal.

This latter fact, one among many others, alerts listeners and readers to the need of reviewing the overall structure of Psalm 22; this study provides the literary basis for theological conclusions. The opening section of the psalm (vv. 1-28) includes most parts of an individual lament—with one notable exception. Nowhere is the enemy identified or cursed. Psalm 22 gleams with innocent peace, whatever may be the horrendous pain. The other notable features of a lament show up:

I

vv. 1-2:	Call for help
vv. 3-5:	Confession of faith
vv. 6-8:	Lament
vv. 9-11:	Prayer of confidence
vv. 12-18:	Lament
vv. 19-21:	Prayer for help
vv. 22-28:	Prayer of thanksgiving

II

vv. 29-31: Second, later prayer of thanksgiving

This structure of a lament is traditional in that these features are usually present; and, although the sequence may vary, all laments conclude with thanksgiving. The value of tradition is exemplified in the lament. It offers a structure for what is the most unstructured, disorderly experience—sickness and violence. Already a sick or persecuted person perceives, however dimly, a plan and purpose. God wastes no moment of human existence. In fact, when someone is unjustly reduced to shame and helplessness, as in the case of the psalmist, God is empowering that person with dignity and extending the invitation to share in the salvation of others.

A structure that leads beyond abandonment to thanksgiving offers consolation, but the stark contrast intensifies each emotion. No literary structure ever masks the stark, naked realism in the psalm: the shame suffered by an innocent person and the callous shamelessness of those inflicting it.

Other literary features intensify the agony of the psalmist but also allow listeners and readers to understand the seemingly abrupt transition from agony to thanksgiving at the end of verse 22. The exceptionally close bonding of the psalmist with God as expressed in the opening words of the psalm is striking: "My God, My God."

v. 1:	My God, my God	v. 5:	To you they cried
v. 2:	O my God!	v. 6:	But I am a worm
v. 3:	Yet you!	v. 9:	Yet it was you
v. 4:	In you our ancestors trusted	v. 10:	On you I was cast

In the face of such intimacy, where mysterious darkness unites most distant aspects of life, one is also reminded of Psalm 139, to be studied later in this chapter:

> If I say, "Surely the darkness shall cover me,
>   and the light around me become night,"
> even the darkness is not dark to you;
>   the night is as bright as the day,
>   for darkness is as light to you (Ps 139:11-12).

Returning to Psalm 22, one hears:

> My God, my God, why have you forsaken me?
>   Why are you so far from helping me, from the words of my groaning?
> O my God, I cry by day, but you do not answer;
>   and by night, but find no rest (vv. 1-2).
> But you, O Lord, do not be far away!
>   O my help, come quickly to my aid!
> Deliver my soul from the sword,
>   my life from the power of the dog!
>   Save me from the mouth of the lion!
> From the horns of the wild oxen
>   you have rescued me (vv. 19-20).

The silent aloofness of God ends. The psalmist feels in the depths of craving loneliness a divine touch, ever so personal at such a secret place of one's life. God's presence is life sustaining.

Divine intimacy envelops the psalmist in still another way, again while immersed in agony and the dark distance of God. The key word "far" occurs three times, in verses 1, 11, and 19. The psalmist appears to be meditating on the Suffering Servant songs of Second Isaiah and on the prophecy of Jeremiah. The clue to this background of the psalmist's spirituality shows up in verses 9-10:

> Yet it was you who took me from the womb;
>> you kept me safe on my mother's breast.
> On you I was cast from my birth,
>> and since my mother bore me you have been my God.

It was the prophet Jeremiah who introduced into the Bible the theme of vocation from the mother's womb, as seen in the study of Psalms 2 and 110 in Chapter 6 and in God's begetting new life in humankind. The text of Jer 1:5 features the prophet quoting God and telling how God called and appointed him to a mission before he was even born:

> Before I formed you in the womb I knew you,
> and before you were born I consecrated you;
> I appointed you a prophet to the nations (Jer 1:5).

Jeremiah came to the conclusion that God must have called him from the beginning, because nothing in his life seemed to make sense and lead up to what he felt ought to be done. In frustration he wrote:

> Why did I come forth from the womb
>> to see toil and sorrow,
>> and spend my days in shame? (Jer 20:18).

Associating life's frustration with a divine vocation from the first moment of conception, Jeremiah influenced later Old Testament writers, notably Second Isaiah, in composing the Suffering Servant songs (Isa 49:1-7, see especially v. 1), Psalm 22, and Psalm 139 (especially vv. 13-15). Paul applied this insight to his own difficult mission and to humanity's rebirth in God by participating in the death and resurrection of Jesus. This point was explored earlier in Chapter 6 of this study. One is now in a position to review the outline and sequence of Psalm 22 and to recognize in it the major sections of the eucharistic ceremony.

Verses 2-21, with a strong sense of God's presence, expressions of faith, reading and reflection in Jeremiah and Second Isaiah, and prayers, contain the ingredients for the Liturgy of the Word at the Catholic Mass. This part of the Eucharist contains the confession of sin and forgiveness, prayers, reading of Scripture, sermon or homily, and the creed or expression of faith.

Between verse 21 and the prayer of thanksgiving beginning with verse 22, a ceremony called the priestly oracle may have occurred, similar to what was already seen in Psalm 12 where the text features God stepping in, through a priest or temple prophet, to respond to the sad case and entreaty of the psalmist:

> "Because the poor are despoiled, because the needy groan,
>> I will now rise up," says the LORD;
> "I will place them in the safety for which they long" (Ps 12:5).

Similar words of salvation punctuate the poetry of Second Isaiah, one of Psalm 22's main prophetic influences (see Isa 41:8-20; 43:1-7, 16-21; 44:1-5).

Verse 26 continues with a song of thanksgiving that includes a sacred meal:

> The poor shall eat and be satisfied;
>> those who seek him shall praise the LORD.
>> May your hearts live forever!

To this section of Psalm 22 corresponds the Roman Catholic liturgical Eucharistic Prayer, the central moment of consecration, and the body and blood of Jesus, present in one's midst under the form of bread and wine.

Verses 28-32 constitute a second prayer of thanksgiving, apparently added later for it breaks the metric pattern of the earlier song of thanksgiving. Another element pointing to later composition is the psalm's acceptance of life after death, which in Israel always included bodily resurrection. Although this doctrine of future life was always circulating on the fringes of Israel's thinking, due to strong Egyptian and Canaanite influence (see the introduction to Chapter 7 above), the temple prophets and priests resisted it as a foreign, unorthodox intrusion. The popular origin of the earlier sections of Psalm 22 made it possible for other new sections to be attached from the popular piety of the people. In this final section there occur the petitions for the living and the deceased:

vv. 27-28:   the ends of the earth and all the families of nations: foreigners and non-Israelites;

v. 29:   all those sleeping[2] in the earth and those going down into the dust of the earth: the sick and the dying, possibly the deceased;

v. 31:   the unborn, typical of all defenseless people.

---

[2] Hebrew here seems to be corrupt. Literally it means "all the fat ones of the earth have eaten and have bowed down." A slight change in the Hebrew letters, justified by the parallel in the second half of the verse, gives a different meaning: "all who sleep in the earth will bow low before him [God]."

These verses invite all such groups, like the oppressed in verse 26, to eat and be satisfied. The sacred meal is open to all, as long as they remember and return to the Lord (v. 27). Here one is reminded of the petitions for the living and the deceased, generally after the words of institution or consecration, in the liturgical Eucharistic Prayer.

It is possible that Jesus frequently turned to Psalm 22 for inspiration and guidance, and what follows is a proposal of a type of movement that shows up in his ministry:

- The psalmist truly knows, from the experience of persecution, rejection, and imprisonment, the lot of the poor and oppressed, so often called in the Bible by the Hebrew word ʿanawîm.
- The psalmist invites these ʿanawîm to join in the prayer of thanksgiving for a table service (v. 26).
- It was on the insistence of this group, their number multiplied by the Exile and the poverty of the post-exilic world, that Psalm 22 found its way into the songbook of the second temple, rebuilt after the return from exile.
- This community, as represented by Third Isaiah (Isaiah 56–66), aligned itself more readily with "the families of all nations" (Ps 22:27) than with the Jerusalem priest. The position of the latter tended to harden and to reject foreigners, as in the prophecy of Joel.

A similar four-step stage appears in the ministry of Jesus and in the mission of the early Church:

- Jesus himself seems attracted to "outsiders," to tax collectors and prostitutes, to foreigners within and outside of the land.[3] One wonders if this is why Jesus chose Capernaum as his home base (Matt 4:13; Mark 2:1), a city where caravans passed going north and south, where a post for collecting taxes was placed (Mark 2:14). Jesus seemed torn between his primary mission to "the lost sheep of the house of Israel" (Matt 10:6; 15:24) and an inner compulsion to admire the faith and attitude of those Jesus considered outside the law and of foreigners, certainly far outside the law. As Jesus began to suffer ridicule, opposition, intrigue and, finally, open persecution, he was certainly in the condition of the psalmist. Quite naturally, Jesus turned to Psalm 22 when dying a crucified criminal.
- There is a close link in the Gospels between Jesus' death and the institution of the Eucharist. Mark's and Matthew's accounts recognize this link, and it is also noted in the Gospel of Luke and the writings of Paul. In Luke 22:19-20, one hears and reads:

---

[3] See Donald Senior and Carroll Stuhlmueller, *The Biblical Foundations for Mission* (Maryknoll, N.Y.: Orbis Books, 1983) 147–55.

Then he took a loaf of bread, and when he had given thanks, he broke it and gave it to them, saying, "This is my body, which is given for you. Do this in remembrance of me." And he did the same with the cup after supper, saying, "This cup that is poured out for you is the new covenant in my blood" (Luke 22:19-20).

The eucharistic body and blood of Jesus are linked with the cross, and the cross is linked by Jesus with Psalm 22. The psalm, in its turn, influenced the development of the Eucharist.

• Paul's outreach to Gentiles opened the sacred meal to non-Jews. Yet, even before Paul campaigned for this openness, Peter had already received the first Gentiles into the company of the disciples, baptizing them without any requirements of the Mosaic Law (Acts 10:1–11:18). The instincts of Jesus to reach beyond boundaries and even to break down barriers, very difficult to accept at first, were gradually coming alive and active among his disciples. Through the persuasive presence of the Holy Spirit, new birth and new life in Jesus were drawing Christians through the mystery of Jesus' death and resurrection (see again Chapter 7).

• The controversy within post-exilic Judaism between the larger outreach of Isaiah 56–66 and the more rigid requirements of Joel were repeated in the early Church. This time, openness to the nations prevailed. Prophets like Jeremiah as well as Second and Third Isaiah, psalms like Psalm 22 and Psalm 139 all exerted their subtle yet effective influence on Jesus, through Jesus on the Eucharist, and through the Eucharist on the Church.

With respect to the Catholic tradition, the decisions of Pope John XXIII and Paul VI to give precedence to the documents on liturgy and revelation enabled the Second Vatican Council to take its first firm steps toward being a council of the Church's world mission. The liturgy, especially the Eucharist, continues to be a barometer of openness on the part of the Church to the poor, the oppressed, the neglected, and the ostracized.

Psalms 42–43: A Sense of Loss

These two psalms—actually a single composition but divided for reasons unknown—begin a new section in more ways than one.[4] In the Bible they inaugurate the second book of psalms (Psalms 42–72). The move from Psalm 41 to Psalm 42 can be as simple as turning a page of the Bible or, if both psalms are printed on the same page, as allowing one's eyes to slip down another line. It was not so simple in biblical times.

---

[4] Psalms 42–83 are sometimes referred to as the "Elohist Psalter." In these psalms, it seems that an effort was made to substitute the Hebrew word *Elohim* (God) for the divine name YHWH. In the rest of the Psalter the name YHWH is used.

A serious liturgical reform seemed to be underway at that time. While Book One of the Psalter (Psalms 1–41) predominantly laments for the individual, Book Two reflects a new interest in liturgy. One encounters three major Jerusalem or temple psalms (Psalms 46–48); a strong attempt to remove abuses (Psalms 50–51); the triumphant liturgy of Psalm 68; the gem composed for liturgical "remembrance," as the title of Psalm 70 informs us; and, finally, a psalm for the royal liturgy (Psalm 72), closing off the collection of Book Two with the patronage of King David. Here, a hypothetical suggestion is offered: Book Two was put together under the impetus of a renewal of liturgy as seen in 1 and 2 Chronicles, therefore around 500 B.C.E.

Psalms 42–43 begin the first collection of Korah psalms (Psalms 42–49); the second is found in Book Three (Psalms 84–85, 87–88). Each collection begins with memories and loss. The Korah guild of psalm writers, very attached to liturgy and especially to good music at the Temple (2 Chr 20:19), seems to have been demoted to lesser roles, like being in charge of preparing the cakes or loaves of bread used in the ritual (1 Chr 9:31), as well as the assigned task of guarding the threshold of the tent. This latter position may have allowed them to function in ceremonies of justice at the temple gate (see the earlier study of Psalms 15 and 24). Yet gatekeeper and baker were not as prominent or central as leaders of song. The Korah guild's reduction also seems to be reflected in the mysterious episode in Numbers 16–17. Loss of important functions, even exclusion or at least severe limitation, are reflected in Psalms 42–43 and 84:

> My tears have been my food
> > day and night,
> while people say to me continually,
> > "Where is your God?"
> These things I remember
> > as I pour out my soul:
> how I went with the throng,
> > and led them in procession to the house of God,
> with glad shouts and songs of thanksgiving,
> > a multitude keeping festival (Ps 42:3-4).

> My soul longs, indeed it faints
> > for the courts of the Lord;
> my heart and my flesh sing for joy
> > to the living God (Ps 84:2).

Memories here bring sorrow and tears, but memories do much more. Psalms 42–43 allow for the possibility of new understandings.

The Way of Memories

The three stanzas of Psalms 42–43 lead listeners and readers through depression, struggle, and hope. The refrain, sung at the end of each stanza, contains three parts that summarize the attitude of each.

Why are you cast down, O my soul,	first stanza
and why are you disquieted within me?	second stanza
Hope in God; for I shall again praise him,	third stanza
my help and my God.	

It is helpful to look more closely at each stanza. One can detect the stages of dealing with memories, especially sorrowful ones.

Memories in the first stanza do not allow the Korah guild to forget their exclusion and distance from the temple liturgy. Rather than get on with life in a different profession, or even abandon God altogether, the psalmist thirsts for God like a female doe thirsts for water in dry, barren terrain. The empty caverns of memory reverberate with the taunting question, "Where is your God?" not once but "continually." The sound tortures the psalmist, as it must compete with "glad shouts and songs of thanksgiving" of former times. The new loneliness turns all the more into isolation as memory rebounds with the temple multitude at festival time. The memories are depressing. The psalmist wants it to be different and pathetically asks in the refrain, "Why are you cast down, O my soul?" The question is the opposite: How can you not be downcast? Or, one can be still more practical: smother the memories, distract one's self, and forget the past. God, however, continues to pursue the psalmist with memories.

The second stanza, accordingly, moves from depression to struggle and confrontation. The dry wilderness and burning thirst of the first stanza turn into a cascade of mountain streams, tumultuously roaring over the precipice and thundering over the psalmist:

> Deep calls to deep
>   at the thunder of your cataracts;
> all your waves and your billows
>   have gone over me (Ps 42:7).

"Deep" translates the Hebrew *tehôm,* a word that evokes mighty ocean currents and sea monsters not only in Babylonian myths but also in biblical poetry (Gen 1:2; Isa 51:9-10; Jonah 2:5). The liturgist's remembrance of myths and poetry provide the Korah guild with language for struggle and confrontation. Memories also evoke, in the very next verse, God's temple songs in the day and prayers during the night vigils. The contrast is more disturbing than consoling. In Psalm 43, the psalmist challenges God:

For you are the God in whom I take refuge;
> why have you cast me off?
Why must I walk about mournfully
> because of the oppression of the enemy?
O send out your light and your truth;
> let them lead me;
let them bring me to your holy hill
> and to your dwelling (vv. 2-3).

In verse 5 of Psalm 43, God becomes "my help." In a new spirit, more fervent and at peace in God, the psalmist declares:

Why are you cast down, O my soul,
> and why are you disquieted within me?
Hope in God; for I shall again praise him,
> my help and my God (v. 5).

Memories carry listeners and readers through necessary stages. In fact, memories actually evoke feelings of depression and anger, humanly or emotionally important. Otherwise, as will be discussed in a moment, worse problems erupt. Before proceeding onward, it is necessary to look once again at the literary structure of Psalms 42–43, to admire the skillful ways by which the poet persists, first in giving us time and space for each emotional response, and then in moving the audience onward. In rereading this poem, the following movement seems to evolve:

42:1-4	42:5-11	43:1-4
past is recalled	present sorrows	future hopes
timid and afraid	strong	triumphant
yearning for God	deserted by God	awaiting God's presence
water, life-giving	water, destructive	light after the storm
desert terrain	mountains	sanctuary

Liturgical Language of Memories

As often happens in the Bible, the mystery of God's redemptive presence finds its appropriate expression in paradox. Positive liturgical memories provide the language for loss and deprivation. This paradox can be expressed theologically: the explanation about God is sometimes *via negativa*. Perhaps God can best be described by saying what God is not—especially by comparison with human life and attitudes. God is not finite, not limited, not changing and, therefore, infinite, unlimited, unchanging. As the psalmist is led by memories from the early days of leadership and full-throated singing in temple praise, to the present privation of all that was precious, the psalmist has no other language but that of the liturgy. So dedicated was he to what he had lost. Among the many possible liturgical phrases or allusions is included:

v. 1	the deer and my soul long	This verb occurs only one other time in the Hebrew Bible, in the highly liturgical book of Joel 1:20. It carries the nuance of "crying out" or "strong inclination."
v. 2	behold[5] the face of God	As in Deut 31:11, this is a technical phrase, taken over from the Canaanites for going up to the Temple.
v. 2	a thirst for God, the living God	In many biblical passages God was the source of living water which springs from the altar (Ps 46:4; Ezek 47:1-12; Sir 24:23-27).
v. 3	my tears have become my food	In place of a sacred meal, as in Ps 22:26, the psalmist is left only with his own tears. What a humble admission for public persons like Levites.
v. 4	I remember	Sacrifices of remembrance were among the most important in the ritual (Lev 2:2; see Isa 66:3; Exod 12:1-28; Deut 16:1-12).
v. 4	I pour out my soul	In the ritual, water or other liquids were poured out (1 Sam 7:6; Isa 57:6); here the psalmist explicitly recalls temple ceremonies.
v. 5	Why are you cast down?	The Hebrew word for cast *(sh-h-h)* is almost identical with the word for worship *(sh-h-h)*, except that the final "h" is less guttural in sound.
v. 5	disquieted within me	The Hebrew word for "disquieted" is from the same root as multitude who are keeping a festival in verse 4.

---

[5] Hebrew originally had only consonants. When vowels were added later, the word came to be understood as "I will appear" rather than "I will see/behold." These vowels may reflect the theological notion that no human being can see God and live (Exod 33:20).

These examples are ample enough to illustrate the pervasive liturgical coloring of a psalm that bemoans its absence from the liturgy.

As a result, one is able to see how important are structure and memory, dedication and discipline. These points have been discussed already in relation to hymns of praise. In the latter case careful schooling in the structure of praise allowed the poet great spontaneity. They were trustworthy. Structure and memory enabled the psalmist to evaluate and appreciate whatever was noble and helpful in Israel's liturgy. By missing it, the liturgy became all the more valuable.

Lost from sight and living in memory, liturgical ceremonies turn out to be much more than ritual actions and sacred words. They are a way of assuaging one's thirst for God; they answer the question, "Where is your God?" (v. 10). Finally, the refrain summarizes the third stanza, one's hope in God. God—nothing less—is the source and center of one's gladness and joy (see Ps 43:4).

By keeping alive the best of the past as a way toward God, memories sustain us over tumultuous times. They can support one's hope in God who answers the prayer:

> O send out your light and your truth;
>> let them lead me;
> let them bring me to your holy hill
>> and to your dwelling (Ps 43:3).

Even at the end of Psalm 43, when the psalmist anticipates praising God ("and I will praise you with the harp, / O God, my God" [v. 4b]), the refrain still begins with, "Why are you cast down, O my soul" (v. 5). The memories are still of sadness, even while declaring how happy and peaceful one may be. Sometimes stages of depression and anger are necessary in order to proceed to hope and joy.

Psalms 42–43 and Memories for Baptism

Psalms 42–43 belong to the Christian community's most ancient baptismal ceremony. In the revised Easter Vigil service of the Roman Catholic Church, these two psalms are sung after the blessing of the baptismal water while in procession to the baptismal font or place of immersion. An early image found in the place of baptism consisted of deer or hinds, standing within wavy lines that indicated water and holding a serpent in their mouth. This symbol is inscribed on the lintel over the entrance to the baptistry at Ostia Antica, the ancient seaport or "door" ("*osta*") for Rome. Here St. Monica, mother of St. Augustine, passed to the Lord. This representation comes from a blend of Psalms 42–43 with Genesis 2–3. Water has a prominent place in the first paradise and in these two psalms. Psalms 42–43 contribute the image of the deer, Genesis 3 that of the serpent.

In these psalms one finds in poetical language the major ingredients of Paul's theology of baptism:

> Do you not know that all of us who have been baptized into Christ Jesus were baptized into his death? Therefore we have been buried with him by baptism into death, so that, just as Christ was raised from the dead by the glory of the Father, so we too might walk in newness of life.
>
> For if we have been united with him in a death like his, we will certainly be united with him in a resurrection like his. We know that our old self was crucified with him so that the body of sin might be destroyed, and we might no longer be enslaved to sin. For whoever has died is freed from sin. But if we have died with Christ, we believe that we will also live with him. We know that Christ, being raised from the dead, will never die again; death no longer has dominion over him. The death he died, he died to sin, once for all; but the life he lives, he lives to God. So you also must consider yourselves dead to sin and alive to God in Christ Jesus (Rom 6:3-11).

The final memory, that of Jesus' resurrection, ushers in new life with peace and joy.

In the tripartite division of Psalms 42–43, there is something very normal, completely in tune with human nature. The loss of something precious can leave one first stunned and depressed, then angry and upset, and finally adjusted and peaceful. The psalmist and Paul respect but also transform what is natural and very human. Faith for the psalmist involves a personal, faithful, and just God, so that there is a strong guarantee that the new life of baptism will continue to overcome all difficulties and lead believers again and again to peace within the community of the Church.

Paul also writes from the Church's tradition, that is to say, from Church memory. Memory, however, is much more than human recall. Jesus remembers, or is eternally present, for he "is the same yesterday, today, and forever" (Heb 13:8). The human community remembers in faith, because Jesus first remembers in them and with them. Faith always grants the initial movement to the spirit of Jesus. Because this spirit resides primarily in the community, where the Spirit first descended at Pentecost, the initiative of Jesus' remembering comes at first within the body of Christ, the Church. It is in this sense that one can interpret the axiom of Roman Catholic theology, that the sacraments impart grace *ex opere operato,* from the work done within the living Church by the Holy Spirit.

Memory, in the case of baptism, involves Jesus' actively "memorializing" or "reliving" or "continuing" to die and rise. This memory lies behind many biblical statements:

For through the law I died to the law, so that I might live to God. I have been crucified with Christ; and it is no longer I who live, but it is Christ who lives in me. And the life I now live in the flesh I live by faith in the Son of God, who loved me and gave himself for me (Gal 2:19-20).

. . . since on their own they are crucifying again the Son of God and are holding him up to contempt (Heb 6:6).

Or one could return to the simple statement of Jesus: "Then he said to them all, 'If any want to become my followers, let them deny themselves and take up their cross daily and follow me'" (Luke 9:23). Finally, Psalms 42–43 lead our appreciation of baptism through important stages of human existence, sanctified by Jesus' remembrance within Church sacraments.

In sum, Psalms 22, 42, and 43 reflect the life, times, and beliefs of the ancient Israelite community. These psalms, as well as others, continue to bear fruit in the lives and religious practices of the Christian community today.

Chapter Nine

Psalms for Sickness and Dying

Your wrath has swept over me;
  your dread assaults destroy me (Ps 88:16).

But it is for you, O LORD, that I wait;
  it is you, O LORD my God, who will answer.
For I pray, "Only do not let them rejoice over me,
  those who boast against me when my foot slips."
For I am ready to fall,
  and my pain is ever with me.
I confess my iniquity;
  I am sorry for my sin.
Do not forsake me, O LORD;
  O my God, do not be far from me . . . (Ps 38:15-18, 21).

An unusually large number of psalms express the poignant plight of
the sick and dying (Psalms 16; 22; 30; 31; 38; 39; 41; 69; 88; 91; 103). This
fact is surprising because the rest of the Old Testament seldom voices the
desperate and painful situation of people physically ill, disabled, or in serious danger of death. Indeed, the Torah (the five Books of Moses) limits itself either to disbarring such people, especially if they are Levites or priests,
from public worship (Leviticus 15; 21; Numbers 12) or to rituals for readmitting them to normal life in society and in worship (Leviticus 14).

Torah Versus Prophecy

As mentioned at the beginning of Chapter 7, not only were health
care and attitudes toward the sick a low priority in Israel's official religious
practice, but also Israel's laws seemed to react very negatively against any
health care norms and customs practiced by the Egyptians and Canaanites.

Because the latter's practices were interlaced with the worship of gods and goddesses (2 Kgs 1:1-2), many genuinely helpful cures contained a liberal dose of strange, superstitious practices unacceptable to the Israelites. And, lest one also be too harsh on the Egyptians and Canaanites and, much later, the Greeks, ancient documents and other evidence like signs of surgery on mummies testify to advanced knowledge far superior to what Israelites knew about the human body, healthy or sick.

What, then, do the biblical texts themselves reveal about Israelite health care and attitudes toward sickness? Primarily their vocabulary is limited to externals, principally to skin diseases that are simplistically lumped together under the designation of leprosy.[1] Indeed, the Israelite rules for the return of a seriously sick person, that is "a leper," to public life, itself mixed salutary cleansing of the body and respectable temple sacrifice with other strange activity:

> The LORD spoke to Moses, saying: This shall be the ritual for the leprous person at the time of his cleansing:
>
> He shall be brought to the priest; the priest shall go out of the camp, and the priest shall make an examination. If the disease is healed in the leprous person, the priest shall command that two living clean birds and cedarwood and crimson yarn and hyssop be brought for the one who is to be cleansed. The priest shall command that one of the birds be slaughtered over fresh water in an earthen vessel. He shall take the living bird with the cedarwood and the crimson yarn and the hyssop, and dip them and the living bird in the blood of the bird that was slaughtered over the fresh water. He shall sprinkle it seven times upon the one who is to be cleansed of the leprous disease; then he shall pronounce him clean, and he shall let the living bird go into the open field. The one who is to be cleansed shall wash his clothes, and shave off all his hair, and bathe himself in water, and he shall be clean. After that he shall come into the camp, but shall live outside his tent seven days. On the seventh day he shall shave all his hair: of head, beard, eyebrows; he shall shave all his hair. Then he shall wash his clothes, and bathe his body in water, and he shall be clean.
>
> On the eighth day he shall take two male lambs without blemish, and one ewe lamb in its first year without blemish, and a grain offering of three-tenths of an ephah of choice flour mixed with oil, and one log of oil. . . .

---

[1] The Hebrew word *saraʿat* is usually translated "leprosy," although scholars today deny that it is identical with what one knows as Hanson's Disease. Biblical "leprosy" probably included psoriasis, eczema, seborrhea, and ringworm. It could even affect clothing and buildings. Skin, clothes, and walls all mark boundaries that were important to the ancient Hebrews. Disorders in such boundaries were seen as threats to the social order, and so uncontrollable skin eruptions were viewed as unclean. See D. Benjamin, "Leprosy," *The Collegeville Pastoral Dictionary of Biblical Theology*, ed. Carroll Stuhlmueller (Collegeville: The Liturgical Press) 549–51.

The priest shall take some of the blood of the guilt offering and put it on the lobe of the right ear of the one to be cleansed, and on the thumb of the right hand, and on the big toe of the right foot. The priest shall take some of the log of oil and pour it into the palm of his own left hand, and dip his right finger in the oil that is in his left hand and sprinkle some oil with his finger seven times before the LORD. Some of the oil that remains in his hand the priest shall put on the lobe of the right ear of the one to be cleansed, and on the thumb of the right hand, and on the big toe of the right foot, on top of the blood of the guilt offering. The rest of the oil that is in the priest's hand he shall put on the head of the one to be cleansed. Then the priest shall make atonement on his behalf before the LORD (Lev 14:1-10, 14-18).

Only in prophecy and psalms—and therefore in popular expressions of religion—does the Bible become humane and practical toward the sick, touching upon the physical reality of sickness. For example, while addressing the moral and religious sickness of Israel, the prophet Isaiah alludes to several remedies of ancient health care, albeit only as regarding the surface of the human body:

> The whole head is sick,
>   and the whole heart faint.
> From the sole of the foot even to the head,
>   there is no soundness in it,
> but bruises and sores
>   and bleeding wounds;
> they have not been drained, or bound up,
>   or softened with oil (Isa 1:5b-6).

A similar analogy, moving from physical external illness to spiritual, interior transformation, occurs in the fourth song of the Suffering Servant. The text compares the servant to one who is repulsive:

> He had no form or majesty that we should look at him,
>   nothing in his appearance that we should desire him.
> He was despised and rejected by others;
>   a man of suffering and acquainted with infirmity;
> and as one from whom others hide their faces
>   he was despised, and we held him of no account.
> Surely he has borne our infirmities
>   and carried our diseases;
> yet we accounted him stricken,
>   struck down by God, and afflicted.
> But he was wounded for our transgressions,
>   crushed for our iniquities;
> upon him was the punishment that made us whole,
>   and by his bruises we are healed (Isa 53:2b-5).

In this latter passage, one notes particularly that all the verbs for becoming sick primarily denote a blow or strike, as in upon the surface of the body.

Typical of his intensely personal and sensitive style, the prophet Jeremiah, alone in the entire Old Testament outside of Sir 38:1-15, speaks honorably of the physician:

> Is there no balm in Gilead?
>> Is there no physician there?
> Why then has the health of my poor people
>> not been restored?
> O that my head were a spring of water,
>> and my eyes a fountain of tears,
> so that I might weep day and night
>> for the slain of my poor people! (Jer 8:22–9:1).

Other revealing or even more striking passages occur in the books of the "former prophets," to use their Jewish name, that is, the books of Joshua, Judges, 1–2 Samuel, and 1–2 Kings. Here, in several cases, the situation is different from readmitting lepers, now healed, into full community life. However, one continues to see a communal and regulated separation of perceived uncleanness. For the lepers, most of the strange practices are before and therefore outside the formal liturgical ritual; the same separation appears during the ceremony for Yom Kippur or Day of Atonement in the case of the goat for Azazel who carries all the sinful faults and transgressions of the Israelites on its head (see Lev 16:6-10, 20-28).[2] In the former prophets, mourning as well appears as a communal act, either in the sacred place of the meeting tent or presided over by an official leader, as when Israel suffered military defeat:

> Then Joshua tore his clothes, and fell to the ground on his face before the ark of the LORD until the evening, he and the elders of Israel; and they put dust on their heads. Joshua said, "Ah, Lord GOD! Why have you brought this people across the Jordan at all, to hand us over to the Amorites so as to destroy us? Would that we had been content to settle beyond the Jordan! (Josh 7:6-7).

One observes similar passages in Judges 20:23, 26 and 1 Samuel 7:6.

As to "latter prophecy," that is, the three Major Prophets (Isaiah, Jeremiah, and Ezekiel) and the Twelve Minor Prophets (Hosea to Malachi), passages sympathetic and positive toward health care have already been quoted. Still, these references were indirect; they alluded to sickness and healing as metaphors for God's attitude toward Israel. Looking further, one

---

[2] It is important to note that in Lev 16:20, where the famous ritual of "sacrificing" the goat to Azazel begins, the text declares: "When he [the high priest] has finished atoning for the holy place and the tent of meeting and the altar, he shall present the live goat."

sees the prophets Elijah and Elisha directly ignore the laws of uncleanness that kept the sick person from entering the sanctuary or Temple and which (along with the still more contaminating presence of a corpse) rendered anyone unclean who touched them (cf. Hag 2:10-14) or was even in the same house with them (Lev 21:1-15, especially v. 11). The two aforementioned, itinerant prophets deliberately intervened, not just to touch but to carry and embrace a corpse. Such an act of "uncleanness," separating the prophet legally from God's presence in the sanctuary, leads the widowed mother of the young man to exclaim: "Now I know that you are a man of God" (1 Kgs 17:24), a technical term for a revered prophet in earliest Israel (1 Sam 9:6-11). In fact, such a "man of God" acted as priest for community worship and sacrifice (1 Sam 9:12-13) where ritual was closer to popular forms of devotion.

One cannot help but notice how Jesus of Nazareth aligned himself with this prophetic side of Israel's religion, sometimes deliberately as during his "inaugural " sermon in the synagogue at Nazareth (Luke 4:16-30), at other times subconsciously or spontaneously as at Naim, where Jesus touched the litter bearing a corpse and gave the resuscitated young man back to his widowed mother. In the latter case the people recognized what had happened: "Fear seized all of them; and they glorified God, saying, 'A great prophet has risen among us!' and 'God has looked favorably on his people!'" (Luke 7:16).

The psalms for the sick and dying offer a privileged invitation into the heart of this world of prophecy, a heart of agony and compassion with many forms of human reaction. To be considered first and foremost are the stages of a person's emotions in sickness and dying. Here one can benefit from the research and publications of Elisabeth Kübler Ross and later writers who have drawn valuable insights from the experience of pastoral care in hospitals. The psalms also allow listeners and readers to delay over the loneliness of death, the Old Testament view (or rejection) of life after death (at least of personal, conscious survival), and its subsequent evolution through later Wisdom psalms, especially through one of the jewels of all laments, Psalm 139.

Stages of Sickness

Physical Torments

Israel's knowledge of sickness and its vocabulary for expressing it were restricted to external, observable phenomena. The Hebrew language, for instance, had no word for such internal organs as small and large intestines, spleen, prostate gland, ovaries, nervous system, veins, and arteries.

The Israelites recognized that conception resulted from intercourse, but they never knew the stages of pregnancy within the mother. The diagnosis of sickness, therefore, went no further than what appeared on the surface of the human body or what was felt by sick persons in different parts of their body.

At times the reference is generic: "But I am lowly and in pain"[3] (Ps 69:29). Other passages, equally generic, refer more to an emotional or mental condition:

> Be gracious to me, O LORD, for I am languishing;
> O LORD, heal me, for my bones are shaking with terror.
> My soul also is struck with terror,
> while you, O LORD—how long? (Ps 6:2-3).

Such a generic description shifts attention away from a sick stomach or pain in one's arm, finger, or whatever, to a sick person. Whatever be Israel's benighted, almost nonexistent health care system, at least what little there was was directed to a holistic response, to the person.

Still other psalms, while primarily concerned with what is externally observable, become more specific: "my eye wastes away from grief, / my soul and body also" (Ps 31:9). Or, even more extensively:

> in the night also my heart instructs me . . .
> . . . my heart is glad, and my soul rejoices;
> my body also rests secure (Ps 16:7, 9).

Psalm 38 reports most completely of bodily pain:

> There is no soundness in my flesh
> because of your indignation;
> there is no health in my bones
> because of my sin.
> My wounds grow foul and fester
> because of my foolishness;
> For my loins are filled with burning,
> and there is no soundness in my flesh.
> My heart throbs, my strength fails me;
> as for the light of my eyes—it also has gone from me.
> But I am like the deaf, I do not hear;
> like the mute, who cannot speak (Ps 38:3, 5, 7, 10, 13).

The lament in Psalm 6 is quite descriptive:

---

[3] The Hebrew word *ʿanî* is a generic term and means "poor," "wretched," or "afflicted." It is related to *ʿanawîm*, "the poor." The word *koʾeb*, "weak," has to do with pain felt in the human body.

> I am weary with my moaning;
>> every night I flood my bed with tears;
> I drench my couch with my weeping (Ps 6:6).

It also relates with vividness the pain of the psalmist. The psalmist prays with these words scattered through the poem:

> O LORD, do not rebuke me . . .
>> . . . your hand has come down on me.
> . . . my iniquities have gone over my head
> But it is for you, O LORD, that I wait;
>> it is you, O LORD my God, who will answer.
> I confess my iniquity.
> Those who are my foes without cause are mighty.
> Do not forsake me, O LORD (Ps 38:1, 2, 4, 15, 18, 19, 21).

These lines show how suffering leads the psalmist into God's presence. Psalm 19 continues the theme of reliance upon God in the midst of struggles:

> But who can detect their errors?
>> Clear me from hidden faults.
> Keep back your servant also from the insolent;
>> do not let them have dominion over me.
> Then I shall be blameless,
>> and innocent of great transgression (Ps 19:12-13).

Paradoxically, suffering also brings a sick person into the community—and from here come relief and hope. In the past it was from within the community that, according to the biblical text, God declared:

> Then the LORD said, "I have observed the misery of my people who are in Egypt; I have heard their cry on account of their taskmasters. Indeed, I know their sufferings, and I have come down to deliver them from the Egyptians, and to bring them up out of that land to a good and broad land, a land flowing with milk and honey, to the country of the Canaanites, the Hittites, the Amorites, the Perizzites, the Hivites, and the Jebusites" (Exod 3:7-8).

With confidence Psalm 38 concludes:

> Do not forsake me, O LORD;
>> O my God, do not be far from me;
> make haste to help me,
>> O Lord, my salvation (Ps 38:21-22).

The phrase "make haste to help me" became a standard introduction for community prayer.

In sum, Israel's tradition gave the sick, abandoned person a way to express suffering and grief. There was a subtle, subconscious realization that

God and other Israelites were aware of their pain. Standard forms of expression acknowledged that such human situations can and do exist.

Shame

One of the most demeaning and dangerous reactions to which a sick person can succumb is shame. Shame can be wholesome in some circumstances, for it can help a person avoid sin (see Jer 3:3; 6:15). Psalms of supplication, especially those which lurch forward from sickness, manifest a different kind of shame, however. Communal laments accuse God:

> Yet you have rejected us and abased us,
>> and have not gone out with our armies.
> You have made us a byword among the nations,
>> a laughingstock among the peoples (Ps 44:9, 14).

Psalm 22, the classic lament of the individual, contrasts God's promise never to abandon faithful people to shame (Ps 22:6; see Ps 44:9) with the present, sad reality: "But I am a worm, and not human; / scorned by others, and despised by the people" (Ps 22:6).

In the ancient Israelite culture, suffering and sickness were thought to be the results of sin. Therefore, shame often came bitterly to a sick person's attention through the way former friends shunned the person and acted as though they never knew the sick one. If they visited the sick, it was only to speak more forcefully against the sick one afterward:

> And when they come to see me, they utter empty words,
>> while their hearts gather mischief;
>> when they go out, they tell it abroad.
> All who hate me whisper together about me;
>> they imagine the worst for me.
> They think that a deadly thing has fastened on me,
>> that I will not rise again from where I lie.
> Even my bosom friend in whom I trusted,
>> who ate of my bread, has lifted the heel against me.
> But you, O Lord, be gracious to me,
>> and raise me up, that I may repay them (Ps 41:6-10).

Almost pathetically the psalmist prays that God does not fall into the category of these false, fair-weather friends. The sick person's faith in God is too sturdy, even during physical weakness, to give up on God:

> You know the insults I receive,
>> and my shame and dishonor;
>> my foes are all known to you.
> Insults have broken my heart,
>> so that I am in despair.

> I looked for pity, but there was none;
>> and for comforters, but I found none.
> They gave me poison for food,
>> and for my thirst they gave me vinegar to drink (Ps 69:19-21).

God's fidelity, by contrast, intensifies the betrayal of erstwhile friends who think the worst of the sick person and do not want any such shame to spread to themselves and their families. The Gospels apply the final verse to the ignominious death scene of Jesus on the cross (Matt 27:34). One can be strengthened to know that Jesus willingly shared human experiences that included shame and desolation.

Yet shame is always a dangerous moment. Whether for the young or for the sick, shame can induce a person to throw off all precaution and healthy inhibitions. Why try to be good and decent, the tempter whispers tauntingly, if people are already thinking the worst, beyond what I deserve? One wonders why, if everybody acts that way, I who seek goodness am stricken. Shame can turn into the serious temptation to erupt with anger—possibly a response in the curses of Ps 69:23-29. Rightfully so, then, one psalmist prayed for help:

> But I trust in you, O LORD;
>> I say, "You are my God."
> My times are in your hand;
>> deliver me from the hand of my enemies and persecutors.
> Let your face shine upon your servant;
>> save me in your steadfast love.
> Do not let me be put to shame, O LORD,
>> for I call on you;
> let the wicked be put to shame;
>> let them go dumbfounded to Sheol.
> Let the lying lips be stilled
>> that speak insolently against the righteous
>> with pride and contempt.
> O how abundant is your goodness
>> that you have laid up for those who fear you,
> and accomplished for those who take refuge in you,
>> in the sight of everyone!
> In the shelter of your presence you hide them
>> from human plots;
> you hold them safe under your shelter
>> from contentious tongues (Ps 31:14-20).

The bitter line "let the lying lips be stilled" may offend the norms for humility and self-control, but too much is at stake—decency and self-respect—for the psalmist to take anything but a stern posture of self-defense.[4]

Depression

The honest confession of weakness and dependency by sick persons in the psalms is something of an amazement. Already one has had a glimpse of the sense of isolation from former close friends, even of betrayal by them, in Psalm 69. The same fearful, distrustful attitude toward the sick person occurs in Psalm 38:

> My friends and companions stand aloof from my affliction,
>   and my neighbors stand far off.
> Those who seek my life lay their snares;
>   those who seek to hurt me speak of ruin,
>   and meditate treachery all day long (Ps 38:11-12).

Friends are now fearful, even hostile observers, keeping their distance, lest they be contaminated by disease and shame. They want no part in a situation of what must be—so they conclude—sinful and guilty. The sick person soon collapses into depression. The psalmist deplores what seems dark and hopeless:

> I am counted among those who go down to the Pit;
>   I am like those who have no help,
> You have put me in the depths of the Pit,
>   in the regions dark and deep.
> Your wrath lies heavy upon me,
>   and you overwhelm me with all your waves.
> You have caused friend and neighbor to shun me;
>   my companions are in darkness (Ps 88:4, 6-7, 18).

Repeatedly this psalmist cries out to God, trying to break the silent depression:

> O LORD, God of my salvation,
>   when, at night, I cry out in your presence . . .
> For my soul is full of troubles,
>   and my life draws near to Sheol.
> But I, O LORD, cry out to you;
>   in the morning my prayer comes before you.
> O LORD, why do you cast me off?
>   Why do you hide your face from me? (Ps 88:1, 3, 13-14).

---

[4] This sternness, however, should be viewed in balance with other psalms, especially Psalm 22, which avoid any bitterness toward friends who betray the sick and defenseless person and heap shame upon them.

And yet another psalmist expresses this depression in a way to allow Jesus the words for pouring out his own abandonment: "My God, my God, why have you forsaken me?" (Ps 22:1)

As was seen in the discussion of Psalms 42–43, prayer—or better, the desire for God—becomes the only relief, the only means to overcome depression: "O LORD, all my longing is known to you; / my sighing is not hidden from you" (Ps 38:9). Again as in the case of Psalms 42–43, an inner peace comes from the subtle reminder that the psalmist is really, after all, not alone. Making use of the language and form of community prayer keeps the psalmist within the sanctuary. Even though darkness pervades and no one is visible in the sanctuary, nonetheless, the long tradition expresses itself in the prayer of Solomon at the dedication of the Temple: "The LORD has said that he would dwell in thick darkness" (1 Kgs 8:12). Darkness must continue until daybreak. Ps 30:5b says it plainly: "Weeping may linger for the night, / but joy comes with the morning." The hours of night cannot be short-circuited or hurried. Such is the human psyche in dealing with sickness and dying.

Anger, Terror, and Guilt

Other emotions always interrupt the lonely heart of the sick or dying person, especially terror, anger, and guilt. Fear erupts from the dark hours of introspection. In the following verses, one hears the plea for mercy from the sick person:

> Be gracious to me, O LORD, for I am languishing;
> > O LORD, heal me, for my bones are shaking with terror.
> My soul also is struck with terror,
> > while you, O LORD—how long? (Ps 6:2-3).

Usually, no normal, healthy person, stricken with serious sickness, easily gives up. Yet here is a condition over which he or she has little or no control.

Because life is God's gift, sickness and dying must also be under God's determination. The psalmist fears, then, that God must be angry and so prays: "O LORD, do not rebuke me in your anger, / or discipline me in your wrath" (Ps 6:1). This opening line is repeated at the beginning of Psalm 38, another psalm from a sick and dying person. Lives, convulsing with panic and distress, reach us from Psalm 88:

> O LORD, why do you cast me off?
> > Why do you hide your face from me?
> Wretched and close to death from my youth up,
> > I suffer your terrors; I am desperate.

> Your wrath has swept over me;
> > your dread assaults destroy me.
> They surround me like a flood all day long;
> > from all sides they close in on me (Ps 88:14-17).

The despairing psalmist can but conclude: "my companions are in darkness" (Ps 88:18). It is a relief that darkness numbs the sick person into another stretch of depression.

Anger and terror are so strong and pervasive that they seem to embroil not only the psalmist and God but also the enemies, real or imagined. Psalm 6, where the sick person is wearied with sighing, also finds the same person mustering enough strength to shout against the lowering clouds: "All my enemies shall be ashamed and struck with terror; / they shall turn back, and in a moment be put to shame" (Ps 6:10). Thus ends Psalm 6. This psalmist will not surrender as easily to darkness as did the author of Psalm 88, whose words were quoted in the previous paragraph.

Emotions quickly change like storm clouds across the life of the angry, terrorized person. The psalmist turns upon his or her own person: "I confess my iniquity; / I am sorry for my sin" (Ps 38:18). This response seems very close to what modern psychology calls "bargaining." Perhaps God will still change the divine mind. Long ago God was determined to consume Israel yet relented at the prayer of Moses (Exod 32:11-14). God also allowed Abraham to bargain down the conditions for not destroying the evil cities of Sodom and Gomorrah—from fifty just persons within their walls to only ten just persons (Gen 18:16-33).

There seems to be a chain reaction: sin to sickness, guilt to grief. Yet, just as quickly the psalmist turns from personal guilt to lash out again at the enemy. In the very next two verses one hears the complaint to God against hostile or unfriendly people:

> Those who are my foes without cause are mighty,
> > and many are those who hate me wrongfully.
> Those who render me evil for good
> > are my adversaries because I follow after good (Ps 38:19-20).

It seems hopeless, and the psalmist turns again to God, with the closing plea: "Do not forsake me, O LORD; / . . . make haste to help me" (Ps 38:21-22).

It is instructive to compare the final lines of these three psalms of sick and dying persons:

Psalm 6	anger at the enemy
Psalm 38	prayer to God
Psalm 88	dark depression

Perhaps many sick persons end one night or other with one of these emotions. Before there can be peace, either for the critically sick or dying person, one must touch upon the forbidding subject of death.

Death and Afterlife

Although the psalms of lament and supplication follow a prophetical pattern—rather than the example of priests and temple thought—and bring into God's presence such "unclean" topics or conditions as sickness and dying, they nonetheless generally revert to a very traditional position when dealing with the passage from death to afterlife. The most extensive description occurs in Psalm 88:

> I am counted among those who go down to the Pit;
>> I am like those who have no help,
> like those forsaken among the dead,
>> like the slain that lie in the grave,
> like those whom you remember no more,
>> for they are cut off from your hand.
> You have put me in the depths of the Pit,
>> in the regions dark and deep.
> Do you work wonders for the dead?
>> Do the shades rise up to praise you?
> Is your steadfast love declared in the grave,
>> or your faithfulness in Abaddon?
> Are your wonders known in the darkness,
>> or your saving help in the land of forgetfulness? (vv. 4-6, 10-12).

This preoccupation with the silent, dark loneliness of death and afterlife explains the dismal conclusion to Psalm 88: "my companions are in darkness" (v. 18). To the questions in the latter part of the long quotation from Psalm 88, the answer is always assumed to be "No!" "Will you work wonders for the dead?" "Of course not!" "Do they declare your kindness in the grave?" "Of course not!" These lines of Psalm 88 become a dismal litany to which the psalmist is replying:

> like those forsaken among the dead,
>> like the slain that lie in the grave,
> like those whom you remember no more . . . .

For those who have died, life has become as silent and dark as the tomb that enfolds their corpse. In death God cannot be present to work wonders. The "steadfast love" and "faithfulness" promised to Moses on Mount Sinai for all Israel (Exod 34:6-7) do not reach into the afterlife—according to verses 11-12.

While the passage of Psalm 88 may be the longest and gloomiest, it is by no means a solitary exception in the Psalter. Similar lines, even identical phrases, occur in Pss 6:5; 16:10; 30:9; as well as in Isa 38:18. Officially Israel rejected the complex mythology of the Egyptians that peopled the afterlife with gods and goddesses and that prepared a person for life after death by an elaborate system of passwords to get by barriers. In the tomb, workmen provided the deceased person with all the amenities of life on earth. Normally only priests and noble persons of considerable wealth and prestige could afford all this. The pharaoh seems to have spent his entire reign preparing his tomb. Even the burial itself occupied considerable time to process the corpse so that it would last forever as a mummy.

Israel rejected this mythology and this caste system, but the chosen people put nothing in its place. Up until very late in their history, the Israelites could not look forward to peace and other rewards in a future life. At best it was a bleak, almost unconscious, non-personal survival—if survival it was—simply a corpse in the ground. A breakthrough comes only with Isa 25:7-8 and Dan 12:1-3. These passages from the third and second centuries before Christ provide happiness only to the just; wicked people are left to rot in the grave. Not until a century later, with the Pharisees and the Dead Sea Scrolls, did hell as an eternal place for the damned enter the theology of Israel. This development appeared more in popular or "lay" circles (the Pharisees) and with a rebel group of priests at Qumram. The official Sadducean priesthood at the Jerusalem Temple continued to reject the resurrection of the body, angels and demons, heaven and hell. Consequently, as mentioned in a previous chapter, people and even prophets went their own way, like Saul who requested the witch of Endor to bring back the ghost of Samuel (1 Sam 28:4-25), or King Jeroboam II who sent his wife to the prophet Ahijah at Shiloh (1 Kgs 14:1-18), or King Ahaziah who dispatched messengers to the temple of Baalzebub (2 Kgs 1:1-2), each to inquire about sickness and to ward off death.

A breakthrough appears in the Psalter, first with the Wisdom psalms, which are discussed in a later chapter, especially in Psalms 1 and 49, and with the very late Psalm 139. For a number of reasons Psalm 139 can be dated quite late in the post-exilic period, perhaps around 200 B.C.E. but maybe even later. One finds, for example, an unusual number of words or expressions that belong to the Aramaic language spoken commonly by the people in later times but different from classical Hebrew. One notices also the influence of the book of Job, especially in some unusual terms.

Psalm 139 reflects not only a time well into the post-exilic age but also a situation of persecution and darkness. The psalmist prays that God "would kill the wicked" and that the "bloodthirsty would depart from me"

(Ps 139:19). The psalm courageously ends with the prayerful and earnest desire: "See if there is any wicked way in me, / and lead me in the way everlasting" (Ps 139:24). This background of sorrow and betrayal adds a sense of desperation to the lines earlier in the psalm:

> Where can I go from your spirit?
> > Or where can I flee from your presence?
> If I ascend to heaven, you are there;
> > if I make my bed in Sheol, you are there.
> If I take the wings of the morning
> > and settle at the farthest limits of the sea
> even there your hand shall lead me,
> > and your right hand shall hold me fast.
> If I say, "Surely the darkness shall cover me,
> > and the light around me become night,"
> even the darkness is not dark to you;
> > the night is as bright as the day,
> > for darkness is as light to you (Ps 139:7-12).

Darkness pervades everywhere, all through the night, into one's mind and heart, into one's personal relationships and neighborhood.

For the psalmist to declare "if I make my bed in Sheol" is an open declaration that YHWH is also present in the abode of the dead. If YHWH abides there, then the spirits of deceased people are alive and at peace, they praise and thank God. How different from other, earlier statements about Sheol or the nether world:

> For in death there is no remembrance of you;
> > in Sheol who can give you praise? (Ps 6:5).
> What profit is there in my death,
> > if I go down to the Pit?
> Will the dust praise you?
> > Will it tell of your faithfulness? (Ps 30:9).

Psalm 139 therefore represents a break from the rigid, orthodox position in the direction of popular or prophetic religious beliefs. This new appreciation of life after death moves the psalmist in the opposite direction to life before birth. Darkness surrounds each of these two periods of time.

> For it was you who formed my inward parts;
> > you knit me together in my mother's womb.
> I praise you, for I am fearfully and wonderfully made.
> > Wonderful are your works;
> that I know very well.
> > My frame was not hidden from you,

> when I was being made in secret,
> > intricately woven in the depths of the earth (Ps 139:13-15).

This confidence in God's tender care for the embryo "in my mother's womb" links this psalm with Jer 1:5; Isa 49:1; Ps 22:9-10; Job 10:8-12. All of these passages speak of desperate suffering and of a final, peaceful settlement in God's presence.

At Peace with God

This new section has already been anticipated in the discussion of Psalm 139. The psalms do not abandon the sick and the dying. One finds moments of confident prayer even in Psalm 38 that, according to the biblical text, begins with punishment by an angry God and concludes with the urgent entreaty: "Do not forsake me, O LORD; / . . . make haste to help me." The psalmist turns to this same God to affirm: "But it is for you, O LORD, that I wait; / it is you, O LORD my God, who will answer" (Ps 38:15). Such a prayer is possible for the psalmist and for contemporary readers too, for one reads in another psalm:

> I will exult and rejoice in your steadfast love,
> > because you have seen my affliction;
> > you have taken heed of my adversities . . . (Ps 31:7).

If God sees, the psalmist can pray again with confidence:

> But I trust in you, O LORD;
> > I say, "You are my God."
> My times are in your hand;
> > deliver me from the hand of my enemies and persecutors.
> Let your face shine upon your servant;
> > save me in your steadfast love.
> Do not let me be put to shame, O LORD,
> > for I call on you;
> let the wicked be put to shame;
> > let them go dumbfounded to Sheol.
> Let the lying lips be stilled
> > that speak insolently against the righteous
> with pride and contempt (Ps 31:14-18).

This trust leads to moments when God seems already to have reached out with healing touch and brought the sick person back from the edge of the grave. In fact, all of Psalm 41 turns into a thanksgiving prayer after illness:

> The LORD sustains them on their sickbed;
> > in their illness you heal all their infirmities.

> By this I know that you are pleased with me;
>> because my enemy has not triumphed over me (Ps 41:3, 11).

This psalmist had been desperately ill, as has been made known from other verses:

> All who hate me whisper together about me;
>> they imagine the worst for me.
> They think that a deadly thing has fastened on me,
>> that I will not rise again from where I lie (Ps 41:7-8).

A still more exuberant voice of gratitude rings out in another psalm:

> Sing praises to the LORD, O you his faithful ones,
>> and give thanks to his holy name.
> You have turned my mourning into dancing;
>> you have taken off my sackcloth
>> and clothed me with joy,
> so that my soul may praise you and not be silent.
>> O LORD my God, I will give thanks to you forever (Ps 30:4, 11-12).

This psalmist too has come back to health from critical danger of death: "O LORD, you brought up my soul from Sheol, / restored me to life from among those gone down to the Pit" (Ps 30:3).

Finally, it is helpful to note the sequence of psalms that move from book three (Psalms 73–89) into book four (Psalms 90–106) of the Psalter. Personal sickness (Psalm 88) and national catastrophe (Psalm 89) evolve first into an expression of human frailty (Psalm 90) and then God's protection against "pestilence that roams in darkness" and "the devastating plague at noon." No sorrow or sickness, not even demons and evil spirits, are any match for God. Nor does God come alone but accompanied, as divine majesty deserves, with angels and good spirits. These "guard you in all your ways / . . . so that you will not dash your foot against a stone" (Ps 91:11-12).

Excursus: The Tension between the Sciences and Moral Teaching

It is curious and significant that, while there have been great advances in the conversation between science and religion, there continues to be, at times, a tension. As already mentioned in this chapter, Israel so completely and so adamantly rejected Egyptian and Canaanite mythology that anything associated with it was immediately rejected. This is especially the case with health care and a belief in the afterlife. Just as the pharaohs of Egypt spent most of their reign planning their burial and building their tombs, likewise a great deal of Egyptian religion revolved around health and sickness, death and immortality. Because of the long-standing practice of embalming the dead—which included not only the treatment of the skin against corruption but also the removal of internal organs—Egyptian priest-embalmers arrived at an advanced knowledge of the human body. Since they also embalmed animals and birds, their information reached into a wide range of life on earth. Those engaged in studying the mummies know that the priests or their medical assistants practiced surgery, even on the brain or skull to remove pressure.

While the Canaanites were less advanced in health care—if one judges from ancient documentation—nonetheless their various deities for sickness and death indicate a serious concern about sickness, death, and afterlife. Not until the spread of Greek culture with Alexander the Great did anything matching the earlier Egyptian medical knowledge and health care come to the fore. Significantly enough, one of the few Old Testament books strongly influenced by Greek culture, namely Sirach or Ecclesiasticus, alone offers a positive appraisal of medical doctors. The passage, somewhat long, deserves a place here in this discussion:

> Honor physicians for their services,
>> for the Lord created them;
> for their gift of healing comes from the Most High,
>> and they are rewarded by the king.
> The skill of physicians makes them distinguished,
>> and in the presence of the great they are admired.
> The Lord created medicines out of the earth,
>> and the sensible will not despise them.
> Was not water made sweet with a tree
>> in order that its power might be known?
> And he gave skill to human beings
>> that he might be glorified in his marvelous works.
> By them the physician heals and takes away pain;
>> the pharmacist makes a mixture from them.
> God's works will never be finished;
>> and from him health spreads over all the earth.
> My child, when you are ill, do not delay,
>> but pray to the Lord, and he will heal you.
> Give up your faults and direct your hands rightly,
>> and cleanse your heart from all sin.
> Offer a sweet-smelling sacrifice, and a memorial portion of choice flour,
>> and pour oil on your offering, as much as you can afford.
> Then give the physician his place, for the Lord created him;
>> do not let him leave you, for you need him.
> There may come a time when recovery lies in the hands of physicians,
>> for they too pray to the Lord

> that he grant them success in diagnosis
> and in healing, for the sake of preserving life.
> He who sins against his Maker,
> will be defiant toward the physician (Sir 38:1-15).

Jeremiah also writes favorably of medical doctors in a single verse:

> Is there no balm in Gilead?
> Is there no physician there?
> Why then has the health of my poor people
> not been restored? (Jer 8:22).

Otherwise, doctors are relegated to the ranks of a "soothsayer, or an augur, or a sorcerer, or one who casts spells, or who consults ghosts or spirits, or who seeks oracles from the dead" (Deut 18:10-11). An instance of such activity, condemned in the Bible, is the action of kings Jeroboam II and Ahaziah (1 Kgs 14:1-18; 2 Kgs 1:1-8). Another instance of curious confusion and of negative appraisal of medical doctors occurs in the Hebrew words "to heal" or "to be a doctor" *(rapha²)* and "to be a shade" or "to be a ghost" *(raphah)*. The difference in pronunciation and in forming the plural for doctors and ghosts is so slight that the ancient translator into the Greek Septuagint and even the Hebrew scribe mixed up the two words. In Ps 88:11, the normal translation is "Do the shades rise up to praise you?" even if the Hebrew reads "the doctors." The same misspelling of the Hebrew occurs in Isa 26:14: "The dead do not live; / shades do not rise." This overlap between "doctor" and "shade" is probably due to the Israelite prejudice that medicine was involved in witchcraft and necromancy.

One can observe how the Torah legislates for uncleanness and for declaration of cleanness (Leviticus 13–15), but offers no help for bringing an unclean sick person to the clean, noncontagious state of good health.

The New Testament as well regards medical doctors with suspicion for their avarice and useless treatments. Luke, by long tradition a medical doctor himself, deletes a severely critical remark of Mark's Gospel. It is interesting to compare two passages:

Mark 5:26	Luke 8:43
She had endured much under many physicians; and had spent all that she had . . .	Now there was a woman who had been suffering from hemorrhages for twelve years; and though she had spent all she had on physicians, no one could cure her.

Yet the Gospels particularly emphasize not only Jesus' role as a healer but also the fact that healing constituted an essential part of his ministry (Matt 4:23) and the ministry given to his disciples (Matt 10:1). This part of the disciples' commission remains in the early epistles of Paul (1 Cor 12:9) but disappears in the later epistle to the Ephesians (Eph 4:11). Jesus even entered what seems to have been a health spa, associated with the Greek patron of healing, Aesculapius (John 5:1-15).

The New Testament, however, never separated bodily cures from miraculous action, so health care of itself remains outside the Christian Scriptures. For many centuries, reaching into the age of Michelangelo (1475–1564 C.E.), autopsies were forbidden. Knowledge of the human organism did not equal that of the priest-embalmers in ancient Egypt. Only later, at the time of the humanist revolution, did religious orders emerge for caring physically for the sick. Since then the Church has been in the foreground of health care. It was much earlier that Judaism turned very favorably to approving the practice of medicine.[5] Jews have an excellent reputation for medical expertise and health care.

Yet severe tension still exists between moral theologians and scientists when it comes to experiments for medical purposes, especially in the area of sexuality. While traditional Christian beliefs on sexuality and natural law strongly support the dignity of the human person against physical exploitation, science often objects that these beliefs are still too dependent upon earlier traditions when all scientific investigation and experimentation with the human body were forbidden, even to the point of forbidding autopsies. This excursus is not intended to argue any side or to settle the controversies, only to place the tension within a biblical setting. In the past, for example, reliance on biblical tradition has sometimes led to embarrassment for the Catholic Church, such as the famous Galileo case and the sun's revolution around the earth. Like the Christian tradition and community, the Bible is conspicuous for its defense of the whole person. One saw that such was the case in praying for a cure—not for a person's injured arm or sick stomach, but for the person who was suffering the injury or sickness. However, the Bible's narrow and overly rigid rejection of the perceived excesses of Egyptian health care, especially its mythology, offers a continuous warning to religion not to reject a worldview wholesale but rather to distinguish religious misdirection from genuine scientific advances.

---

[5] Jewish physicians were instrumental in passing on Greek medical practices to the Arabs during the Middle Ages. See "Medicine," *Encyclopedia Judaica* (Jerusalem: Macmillan, 1971) XI:1186–7.

Chapter Ten

Cursing and Reconciliation

Pour out your indignation upon them,
*	and let your burning anger overtake them.*
Add guilt to their guilt;
*	may they have no acquittal from you (Ps 69:24, 27).*

Have mercy on me, O God,
*	according to your steadfast love;*
according to your abundant mercy
*	blot out my transgressions.*
Wash me thoroughly from my iniquity,
*	and cleanse me from my sin (Ps 51:1-2).*

Biblical religion, especially in the psalms, often expresses itself in paradox. The self-righteous hatred in Psalm 69 is hardly reconcilable with the penitent entreaty for mercy in Psalm 51. This phenomenon of seeming contradiction continues into the New Testament. On different occasions Jesus, heralded in John 14:6 as "the way, and the truth, and the life," seems to contradict himself: "Do you think that I have come to bring peace to the earth? No, I tell you, but rather division!" (Luke 12:51), and "Peace I leave with you; my peace I give to you. I do not give to you as the world gives. Do not let your hearts be troubled, and do not let them be afraid" (John 14:27). An opening in the fast-moving clouds appears in the words of another biblical writer, the wise and provocative Ecclesiastes:

> For everything there is a season, and a time for every matter under heaven:
> a time to be born, and a time to die;
> a time to plant, and a time to pluck up what is planted; . . .
> a time to love, and a time to hate;
> a time for war, and a time for peace (Eccl 3:1-2, 8).

This explanation sounds similar to the stages of serious sickness and dying: a stage of depression and a stage of anger, a stage of denial and a stage of acceptance and peace with God. Yet, almost everyone still feels uneasy. One certainly cannot stretch the litany of Ecclesiastes to include "a time to sin, and a time to be virtuous"—unless one were to add at once, "to be virtuous and repent." Even this venerable old man must have felt the same frustration with his explanation. He begins his book declaring: "Vanity of vanities. . . . All is vanity" (Eccl 1:2); "the eye is not satisfied with seeing, / or the ear filled with hearing" (1:8b). Ecclesiastes' final words lead us closer to a satisfactory conclusion:

> Of anything beyond these, my child, beware. Of making many books there is no end, and much study is a weariness of the flesh.
> The end of the matter; all has been heard. Fear God, and keep his commandments; for that is the whole duty of everyone. For God will bring every deed into judgment, including every secret thing, whether good or evil (Eccl 12:12-14).

These verses conjure up thoughts about the conclusion to a section of another Wisdom book, whose name is very similar to Ecclesiastes. In the NAB it is called "Sirach," but in many Bibles we find the name "Ecclesiasticus" (NRSV). It was called this because—after psalms—it was the book most quoted and used in the liturgy of the early Church. ("Ecclesiastes" probably means "one who convokes an assembly.") In Sirach one reads:

> We could say more but could never say enough;
>   let the final word be: "He is the all."
> Where can we find the strength to praise him?
>   For he is greater than all his works.
> Who has seen him and can describe him?
>   Or who can extol him as he is?
> Many things greater than these lie hidden,
>   for I have seen but few of his works.
> For the Lord has made all things,
>   and to the godly he has given wisdom (Sir 43:27-28, 31-33).

One prays for the wisdom to delve into the mystery of cursing and reconciliation, violence and penitence, within the single inspired collection of the Bible.

Cursing

The curse of the enemy—the invocation of God's anger and severe punishment upon another—occurs too frequently in the psalms to be ignored: Pss 10:15; 31:17-18; 40:14-15; 55:15; 58:6-11; 59:11-13; 68:22-23;

69:22-28; 83:9-18; 109:6-20; 137:8; 139:19-24; 140:9-11. Perhaps the most dreadful and therefore best known comes at the end of Psalm 137: "Happy shall they be who take your little ones / and dash them against the rock!" (Ps 137:9). No amount of explanation can remove the bitterness and the scandal of such a black imprecation. It is not only the violent hatred of such a verse—once would have been more than enough—but also the frequency of such curses.

The question, "Why these curses in the Bible?" can be approached from the base of Psalm 69. This psalm not only includes one of the longest curses in the Psalter but it is also, as we shall see, one of the most quoted in the New Testament. Even some of the cursing lines (vv. 23-29) are included in the list:

- v. 4 in John 15:25: It is cited by Jesus in his Last Supper discourse, where he also prayed for peace (John 14:27);
- v. 9a in John 2:17: Here Jesus manifests anger at people who traffic in the Temple and profane the house of God;
- v. 9b in Rom 15:3: Here Paul adds immediately: "For Christ did not please himself; but, as it is written, 'The insults of those who insult you have fallen on me'";
- v. 22, the first in the cursing stanza, in Rom 11:9-10: Here Paul is dealing with the failure of Judaism to recognize Jesus as their messiah. Romans 11 begins with the question: "I ask, then, has God rejected his people?" The answer is: "By no means!" (v. 1). Evidently, the curse is not the final word, nor is one to interpret this cursing too simplistically;
- v. 24 in Rev 16:1: Here one does not find a direct quotation but a very similar phrase and certainly the same idea, as angels pour seven bowls of plagues upon the earth.
- v. 25 is said to reach fulfillment in the death of Judas Iscariot (Acts 1:20).

The frequency of lines from Psalm 69, including lines from the cursing section, demands some explanation of the cursing or vindictive explosion of hate and revenge in the book of Psalms.

The reasons to be presented here do not all carry equal weight. Some, and especially the latter ones, will hopefully shed light on the discussion at hand. No single reason, nor any number of them, however, will ever suffice for the tragic reality of hatred. Yet if God is real, one would think, then, that there must be some relationship between God and such reality. Moreover, if with Wisdom God's providential care "reaches mightily from one end of the earth to the other, / and . . . orders all things well" (Wis 8:1), then between one end and the other must be included the evil and sad presence of violence.

Biblical Style, Exaggeration, and Rhetoric

Every culture, to some degree, has ways exaggerating matters out of all proportion. When the sage who composed Psalm 37 in the typical style of Wisdom literature, known for its moderation and middle-class values, declares, "I have been young, and now am old, / yet I have not seen the righteous forsaken / or their children begging bread" (Ps 37:25), one is inclined to ask, "Really? Where have you been?" Jeremiah and especially Job expand this short query into long books which even argue against God because of innocent suffering. Jesus too followed the patterns of speech of his people by birth when he declared: "Whoever comes to me and does not hate father and mother, wife and children, brothers and sisters, yes, and even life itself, cannot be my disciple" (Luke 14:26). Even today some racial or ethnic groups seem to be more reserved and cautious, while others seem to be more spontaneous and excitable. Semitic people, among whom are included the ancient Israelites or the modern Arabs, fall into the latter category. They are eloquent in their verbal responses.

Some nations speak a language punctuated with many more exclamation marks than others. They also may be characterized by expressions or words whose primary sense denotes violence. American English belongs to this type. A sport like baseball, carefully regulated with precise rules, can sound violent to the uninitiated: "hit" the ball; "strike" out; the "batter"; a "foul." Other American sports like football and boxing pit the players against one another with physical force. Thus, the violent imagery of the Israelite culture and language should not come as a surprise to listeners and readers, but at the same time, it cannot be overlooked hermeneutically. One graphic example of the use of violent imagery in the psalms is found in Ps 137:9: "Happy shall they be who take your little ones / and dash them against the rock!" Historically these lines say: may the enemy city be captured. "Rock" designates the city walls: "little ones," the city's soldiers who are stationed on or within the walls to defend it. Rushing and battering the city walls usually meant death to its defenders. Like the language of American baseball, these lines are not to be taken literally as the smashing of infants against rocks.

Sacred Warfare and Ritual Curses

The title for this section may seem to be an open exaggeration. The Hebrew term is *herem,* literally to consecrate so thoroughly to God as to ban completely from any other use. When a war or a military excursion was so consecrated, the army was forbidden from taking any booty or leaving alive any person. Everything—and every person—was sacrificed to God. Another more realistic term is extermination warfare.

Herem wars were fought in the ancient Near East. This fact is recorded in ancient documentation. In the Bible there are only two examples: one in the days of Joshua when Israel was beginning to occupy the land (Josh 6:21; 8:24-29; 10:28-40; 11:10-21) and the other in the war of King Saul against the Amalekites (1 Samuel 15). This latter case is the most difficult one to deal with. As will be mentioned later, the Bible can record an event without necessarily approving it. Saul, however, was deposed by the prophet Samuel for not fulfilling the *herem* war to the last person. The Amalekites carried the stigma of being Israel's worst enemy. Even Moses fought against them in the Sinai wilderness (Exod 17:8-16). Balaam, on seeing Amalek, voiced this oracle: "Then he looked on Amalek, and uttered his oracle, saying: 'First among the nations was Amalek, / but its end is to perish forever'" (Num 24:20). Amalek, accordingly, became a symbol like the Huns or the Nazis; one can never compromise or even deal with such evil people.

The rabbis offer this interesting and very instructive piece of advice. Should someone meet an Amalekite, that person is bound to kill the Amalekite. (It is outside the story to explain how one recognizes an Amalekite.) Since one is obliged to execute the Amalekite, the faithful Jew is instructed to bind the Amalekite with ropes and chains, lest he escape. In the meanwhile the Jewish man is told to seek out a holy and prudent rabbi. This rabbi will search the Torah for further enlightenment and is certain to find a valid reason for releasing the Amalekite alive. However, in the meanwhile the law remains intact: every Amalekite must die. The important principle here makes clear that Scripture is always to be interpreted, and new interpretations from the ancient Torah are always possible.

The *herem* war occupies sections of Deuteronomy, a book otherwise conspicuous for compassion. One reads:

> When you draw near to a town to fight against it, offer it terms of peace. If it accepts your terms of peace and surrenders to you, then all the people in it shall serve you at forced labor. If it does not submit to you peacefully, but makes war against you, then you shall besiege it; and when the LORD your God gives it into your hand, you shall put all its males to the sword. You may, however, take as your booty the women, the children, livestock, and everything else in the town, all its spoil. You may enjoy the spoil of your enemies, which the LORD your God has given you. Thus you shall treat all the towns that are very far from you, which are not towns of the nations here. But as for the towns of these peoples that the LORD your God is giving you as an inheritance, you must not let anything that breathes remain alive. You shall annihilate them—the Hittites and the Amorites, the Canaanites and the Perizzites, the Hivites and the Jebusites—just as the LORD your God has commanded, so that they may not teach you to do all the abhorrent things that they do for their gods, and you thus sin against the LORD your God (Deut 20:10-18).

Other, similar legislation occurs in Deuteronomy 7, where it contrasts sternly with some of the most touching sentences of God's tender love for Israel:

Deut 7:1-2 and 16	Deut 7:6-7
"When the LORD your God brings you into the land that you are about to enter and occupy, and he clears away many nations before you—the Hittites, the Girgashites, the Amorites, the Canaanites, the Perizzites, the Hivites, and the Jebusites, seven nations mightier and more numerous than you—and when the LORD your God gives them over to you and you defeat them, then you must utterly destroy them. Make no covenant with them and show them no mercy. . . . You shall devour all the peoples that the LORD your God is giving over to you, showing them no pity; you shall not serve their gods, for that would be a snare to you."	For you are a people holy to the LORD your God; the LORD your God has chosen you out of all the peoples on earth to be his people, his treasured possession. It was not because you were more numerous than any other people that the LORD set his heart on you and chose you—for you were the fewest of all peoples.

It is as true in the human world as in the animal world. Where love is most tender—parents for children; mates or spouses for their partner—jealousy and anger, hatred and fear flare up most fiercely.

Another explanation also helps. By the time prophets and Levites were making the final redactions of Deuteronomy, during the reform of King Josiah (2 Kgs 22:8–23:27) and during the Babylonian Exile, Israel no longer possessed the military capability of waging war against any foreign nation. Their helpless posture continued during the post-exilic age up until the time of the Maccabean revolt in 167 B.C.E. As this is discussed in the two books of Maccabees, Israel never attempted the *herem* method of warfare. One can conclude that the *herem* or extermination war became a biblical symbol of a spiritual warfare against immorality and against any compromise of the Torah. Here, a comparison to Paul's words seems appropriate:

> Therefore take up the whole armor of God, so that you may be able to withstand on that evil day, and having done everything, to stand firm. Stand

therefore, and fasten the belt of truth around your waist, and put on the breastplate of righteousness. As shoes for your feet put on whatever will make you ready to proclaim the gospel of peace. With all of these, take the shield of faith, with which you will be able to quench all the flaming arrows of the evil one. Take the helmet of salvation, and the sword of the Spirit, which is the word of God (Eph 6:13-17).

This same explanation applies to the oracles against the enemies in prophetic literature (Isaiah 13–23; Jeremiah 46–51). This literature dates from an age of almost complete non-militarization on Israel's part. One may still prefer non-militarization of Israel's language, but such an ideal is asking too much even of the Gospels and other parts of the New Testament. At this juncture, Jesus' words as recorded by Luke come to light:

Do you think that I have come to bring peace to the earth? No, I tell you, but rather division! From now on five in one household will be divided, three against two and two against three; they will be divided:
father against son
and son against father,
mother against daughter
and daughter against mother,
mother-in-law against her daughter-in-law
and daughter-in-law against mother-in-law (Luke 12:51-53).

In Luke 22:36 and 38, Luke depicts Jesus and his listeners in a candid exchange: "He said to them, 'But now, the one who has a purse must take it, and likewise a bag. And the one who has no sword must sell his cloak and buy one. . . .' They said, 'Lord, look, here are two swords.' He replied, 'It is enough'" (Luke 22:36, 38).

Finally, the curse psalms may have developed from the ritual curses in ancient Israel. These were ceremonies for formal excommunication of sinners or to quarantine people with leprosy and contagious diseases (Leviticus 13–14). People who refused to follow the legal procedures were issued a formal directive: "As for anyone who presumes to disobey the priest appointed to minister there to the LORD your God, or the judge, that person shall die. So you shall purge the evil from Israel. All the people will hear and be afraid, and will not act presumptuously again" (Deut 17:12-13). One is left with the impression that capital punishment never had to be carried out for this crime. In the case where people falsely bore witness against their neighbor, the identical punishment would be inflicted on them. It is in this context that the *lex talionis* is quoted: "life for life, eye for eye, tooth for tooth, hand for hand, foot for foot" (see Deut 19:21). Deuteronomy also contains a series of ritual blessings and curses, to announce a high code of morality for God's elect people.

All of these examples advise listeners and readers to interpret the curse psalms carefully in their historical and literary contexts, with apt attention to their hermeneutical implications.

A Record of Events

This next principle for interpreting the curse psalms is a slippery one, difficult to put into use. This danger of misapplication does not deny its validity. Put simply: the Bible can record an event but not approve of it. It happened and thus finds a place in tradition. Genesis 12 comes to mind. Here the two sides of Abraham (then called Abram) come into focus. Abraham as led by God turns out to be a heroic man; Abraham as led by himself degenerates into a fearful, despicable man. The patriarch and his wife follow God's direction: "Now the LORD said to Abram, 'Go from your country and your kindred and your father's house to the land that I will show you'" (Gen 12:1). Without a moment's hesitation, Abraham and his family set out for the land that God will show them. Later when a famine appears in the land, Abram decides to desert the Promised Land—a failure in faith—and to migrate into Egypt. His instructions to Sarai cannot be defended on any account:

> When he was about to enter Egypt, he said to his wife Sarai, "I know well that you are a woman beautiful in appearance; and when the Egyptians see you, they will say, 'This is his wife'; then they will kill me, but they will let you live. Say you are my sister, so that it may go well with me because of you, and that my life may be spared on your account" (Gen 12:11-13).

A similar story occurs for Abraham and Sarah in chapter 20 and for their son Isaac and his wife in chapter 26, where the Bible condemns the ploy of wife turned "sister" to protect the husband's life.

In Genesis 12, however, the story stands without comment. The storyteller may be letting the listeners come to their own judgment about how wrong it is. Out of respect for the patriarch, the text remains politely silent. Yet the juxtaposition of incidents where Abraham is led by God and where Abraham is led by Abraham clearly though reverently speaks its message.

At times the Bible records anger, jealousy, and other base emotions on the assumption that the reader has enough common sense and wholesome morality to reject such actions. Must the obvious be said? If God views Moses as "very humble, more so than anyone else on the face of the earth" (Num 12:3), then the same God can hardly praise the violent reactions of the curse psalms.

In sum, the principle of interpreting the Bible needs to be done with care of the biblical world and its cultures and religious influences.

From Sin to Sorrow to Purification

As mentioned already in discussing the curse psalms, a sense of reality pervades the Bible. Reality dictates that sin or any abuse of the body or mind, emotions or talents inevitably brings sorrow. The reverse, however, is not equally true. Suffering does not prove that the individual suffering person has sinned. Psalm 7 takes up explicitly the case of innocent suffering:

> O LORD my God, in you I take refuge;
> > save me from all my pursuers, and deliver me. . . .
> O let the evil of the wicked come to an end,
> > but establish the righteous,
> you who test the minds and hearts,
> > O righteous God (Ps 7:1, 9).

The entire book of Job struggles with the agonizing question "Why me?" without settling it. It comes again to the surface in the Gospels. When a blind man appeared along the way, Jesus' disciples asked him, "'Rabbi, who sinned, this man or his parents, that he was born blind?' Jesus answered, 'Neither this man nor his parents sinned; he was born blind so that God's works might be revealed in him'" (John 9:2-3).

One part of Jesus' answer, to show forth God's works, serves as a guide to the next section of the discussion of the curse psalms. Suffering, even as the aftermath of personal sin, need not destroy someone; it can purify the sinner. Suffering activates an inner dynamism, enabling a person to resolve not to do this or that again, to be more cautious in the future. Unfortunately, a person at times may have to hit bottom to come up.

Jeremiah, the prophet who strongly influenced Psalm 69,[1] develops this idea that suffering, induced by sin, can take on a disciplinary, even transforming force. In an oracle, he delivered to his listeners the thought and intention of their God:

> Your wickedness will punish you,
> > and your apostasies will convict you.
> Know and see that it is evil and bitter
> > for you to forsake the LORD your God;
> > the fear of me is not in you, says the Lord GOD of hosts (Jer 2:19).

Later on in the same chapter the prophet again delivers God's word to the people:

---

[1] The many parallels between Psalm 69 and Jeremiah seem to indicate the influence of prophet on the psalm: Ps 69:1-3 and Jeremiah 38; Ps 69:3 and Jer 45:3; Ps 69:7a and Jer 15:15; 20:8; Ps 69:8 and Jer 12:6; Ps 69:19-20 and Jer 18:23; 23:9; Ps 69:22-29 and Jer 18:21-22; the term "cities of Judah," which appears in Ps 69:35 and over twelve times in Jeremiah.

> In vain I have struck down your children;
>> they accepted no correction.
> Your own sword devoured your prophets
>> like a ravening lion (Jer 2:30).

The word *yasar*, "punish," "correct," "chastise," is an important word in the Wisdom literature[2] and a key to the theology of Jeremiah, especially as this unfolds in chapters 30–31. Here one reads:

> I will chastise you in just measure,
>> and I will by no means leave you unpunished.
> For I will restore health to you,
>> and your wounds I will heal, says the LORD (Jer 30:11c, 17a).

> Indeed I heard Ephraim pleading:
> "You disciplined me, and I took the discipline;
>> I was like a calf untrained.
> Bring me back, let me come back,
>> for you are the LORD my God" (Jer 31:18).

Although Jeremiah could not stop Israel from plunging sinfully and recklessly into the fiery cauldron of Jerusalem's destruction and the Babylonian Exile, the people remembered his words and found strength and consolation in them. God was present with them in their suffering. Not even the chaotic whirlwind destroying Jerusalem and sweeping the people off to a foreign land could separate Israel from God's care and God's plans.

The influence of Jeremiah appeared in the preaching of Second Isaiah, one of the great prophets of the Exile. (See Isaiah 40–55.) Among his most poignant pieces, called the Suffering Servant songs, he picks up the key word, *yasar*, of Jeremiah to show how an innocent person, suffering in the midst of a sinful people, becomes a leaven of faith and hope and offers a mysterious yet steady sense of purpose:

> But he was wounded for our transgressions,
>> crushed for our iniquities;
> upon him was the punishment that made us whole,
>> and by his bruises we are healed (Isa 53:5).

While this theology of Jeremiah and Second Isaiah—that suffering can be transforming—does not show up explicitly in Psalm 69, still the influence of Jeremiah was impacting the psalm in other significant ways.[3] It seems possible to assert, at least as a working hypothesis, that the curses of

---

[2] The Hebrew verb *yasar* occurs eleven times in Wisdom literature. The corresponding noun, *mûsar*, "correction," "discipline," "chastisement," occurs thirty-six times.

[3] See n. 1 above.

Psalm 69 are couched in a context that the suffering inflicted by sin on wicked persons can be purifying for them.

Atonement by Union, Not by Substitution

We already took note how Jeremiah and Second Isaiah were so closely bonded with all Israel, that Israel could say:

> He was despised and rejected by others;
> > a man of suffering and acquainted with infirmity;
> and as one from whom others hide their faces
> > he was despised, and we held him of no account.
> Surely he has borne our infirmities
> > and carried our diseases;
> yet we accounted him stricken,
> > struck down by God, and afflicted.
> But he was wounded for our transgressions,
> > crushed for our iniquities;
> upon him was the punishment that made us whole,
> > and by his bruises we are healed (Isa 53:3-5).

The innocent, afflicted by the pain of Israel's sins, do not take that pain away from sinful Israel. The quotation from the second part of Isaiah's prophecy comes from the time of the Babylonian Exile. In chapter 54 the prophet recognizes the continuing sorrow of the people in exile, their memories haunted by barbarous scenes of military invasion of their homeland, the fiery torch set to their glorious temple, the desolate trek into a foreign land. There is hope, only if the people believe. The prophet speaks with the image of a widow without her children or any other consolation:

> For the LORD has called you
> > like a wife forsaken and grieved in spirit,
> like the wife of a man's youth when she is cast off,
> > says your God.
> For a brief moment I abandoned you,
> > but with great compassion I will gather you (Isa 54:6-7).

Returning to the initial quotation from Second Isaiah (53:3-5), one can see that the servant endured the burden of their sins and sorrows, with a sense of hope and the promise of new life.

The same is true for the Christian community today, redeemed by the suffering and death of Jesus. As seen in a previous chapter that dealt with Psalms 2 and 110 and the new birth through the Spirit, Christians bear the marks of Christ's suffering (Gal 2:19), specifically, every time they embrace and live out the redemptive and liberating mission of Jesus. Rather, Jesus suffers in and with our suffering; Jesus dies in and with our dying. Consequently, Christian resurrection is a resurrection to new life in and with the powers of Jesus' resurrection:

> Therefore we have been buried with him by baptism into death, so that, just as Christ was raised from the dead by the glory of the Father, so we too might walk in newness of life. For if we have been united with him in a death like his, we will certainly be united with him in a resurrection like his (Rom 6:4-5).

Because of this intimate bonding with Jesus—also like that of exiled Israel with the Suffering Servant—pain and agony are magnified. The presence of the prophet Isaiah among the exiles was like that of Jesus in his own day. Isaiah heightened his people's conscience about justice and compassion; they remembered their dignity and freedom; they longed for good health and full life. Jesus was continually conscious of his mission; it was a fire burning in his bones; he experienced an anguish to achieve this baptism (Luke 12:49-50). Jeremiah too declared that he could not be silent with such a fire within his heart and bones (Jer 20:9). Yet the words and actions of both Jesus and Jeremiah precipitated struggle and controversy, opposition and rejection. Jealousy and anger flared. The closer the bonding, the more intense the hostility. The "healthier" the good person and the more poisonous the wicked, the more violent the reaction.

The curse psalms voice the most agitated rejection of poisonous injustice and sinful oppression. These psalms enabled Jesus' disciples to understand his most angry moment—of all places, in the house of God. Here in the temple precincts Jesus did what he never did on any other occasion:

> Making a whip of cords, he drove all of them out of the temple, both the sheep and the cattle. He also poured out the coins of the money changers and overturned their tables. He told those who were selling the doves, "Take these things out of here! Stop making my Father's house a marketplace!" (John 2:15-16).

The Gospel of John at this point quotes, as pointed out earlier in this discussion, from one of the cursing psalms, Psalm 69: "Zeal for your house will consume me" (John 2:17; cf. Ps 69:9). The "house" of God turned out to be more than the Temple. Jesus replied to those who challenged his authority "to do these things": "Destroy this temple and in three days I will raise it up." John then reflected: "But he was speaking of the temple of his body. After he was raised from the dead, his disciples remembered that he had said this; and they believed the scripture and the word that Jesus had spoken" (John 2:21-22).

Jesus likens the Temple, contaminated by evil, greedy people, buying and selling their goods, to his own body. The violence now erupts in the human flesh and heart of Jesus. Earlier violence was mostly outside his sacred person, as when Jesus with a whip of cord drove money-changers and other money-minded people from the Temple. Now the righteous anger rages in his very person. For this reason Paul writes: "For our sake he made him to be sin who knew no sin, so that in him we might become the righteousness of God" (2 Cor 5:21). In Galatians, he also states: "Christ redeemed us from the curse of the law by becoming a curse for us—for it is written, 'Cursed is everyone who hangs on a tree'" (Gal 3:13). The curse of sin clashed with the holiness of God in Jesus on the cross. Each by contrast made the other ever more wicked and ever more pure.

The curse psalms bring such a clash of goodness and evil immediately in God's presence. Goodness, with anger and outrage, with "a whip of cords," is driving evil out of God's Temple. If we return for a moment to the example of a healthy human body that has been infected with poison, there is no "nice" way of expelling the foreign, destructive material. Neither was the cross "nice." The agonizing, tortured, heavily bleeding Jesus on the crucifixes of Peru is far closer to the reality of Calvary than the jeweled or sanitized crucifixes of many other parts of the world. The curse psalms belong to the fierce reality of sin—holiness like the crucifixes of Peru. Good people participate in the reuniting of wicked people with God, and such is Jesus, goodness par excellence, the ultimate place in his sacred person for atonement and sanctification of all men and women, not by suffering as a substitute for sinful people but rather by being plunged into their midst. The curse psalms express such a movement when goodness in the midst of wickedness thoroughly expels all evil. Goodness is so intimately interlocked with evil, that in time, in the curse psalms, all one sees on the surface is evil.

Liturgy for Dehumanized, Oppressed People

The cursing verses of the psalm are now missing in the readings of the Church's liturgy. Since Vatican II, they cannot be found any more at Mass or in the Christian Liturgy of the Hours. The decision to delete these lines was wise. Even with explanation the lines remain baffling and disturbing. How much more perplexing will they be to people uninitiated in Bible study? Yet the Christian community cannot deny, and therefore should not completely bypass, the presence of curse psalms in the Bible.

Parts of the psalms seem so emotional and so violent as to have lost contact with the normal human condition and likewise, at times, with oppressed people who have been completely dehumanized and reduced to animals fighting for survival. Such situations include the Nazi concentration camps, the gulag of Solzhenitsyn, and the flaming hell prisons in deserts. Here prisoners or inmates are tortured and victimized by jailers; they also turn against one another. They are abused sexually and frequently, so that they have no decent self-respect left. They are numbed into carelessness. Deprived of proper food and sufficient sleep, overworked and worn down physically, they no longer have the strength to stand erect physically or morally.

These outcasts have been so dehumanized that they cannot pray. A person must be human—and humanly awake—to pray. No one prays in the obscurity of his or her sleep, or in the fright and terror of an imminent crash, or under the appalling and helpless agony of continuous, shameful abuse.

A very learned and respectful person was once involved—innocently— in an automobile crash, fatal to the other driver who recklessly ran a red light at night. Whenever a similar crash was reenacted on TV, this person was overtaken again by the memory and lost all self-control. He shouted and cried and shook all over. Perhaps not as totally as that, each person has certain sensitivities, physically and emotionally, which cannot be touched. These are raw nerves where the pain is so intense that every rational inhibition collapses; at such moments the response comes from naked, blind force.

In conclusion, is it asking too much, that once a year, for only thirty minutes, churches and congregations voice the "prayer" of these humans reduced by torture to savage animals? The curse psalms come from the tortured people of Israel; the Bible gives them their day in court, that is, in the public assembly of the community at prayer. Perhaps as communities plan such annual prayer sessions, they may want to include photos of contemporary torture and personal testimonials. Let the shock impact the conscience of comfortable Christians. Perhaps the liturgy or service might end in silence. Little or no commentary is needed. Prayer in this moment may even be out of place. After all, the condition is too dehumanized for prayer. The sense of prayer comes from the realization that the curse psalms belong to the biblical tradition and are themselves inspired.

Chapter Eleven

Psalms for Reconciliation

O Israel, hope in the LORD!
  For with the LORD there is steadfast love,
    and with him is great power to redeem.
It is he who will redeem Israel
  from all its iniquities (Ps 130:7-8).

A Christian tradition separates apart "seven penitential psalms" (Psalms 6; 32; 38; 51; 102; 130; and 143). St. Augustine was probably acquainted with this category. In monasteries, monks and nuns often recite these seven psalms every Friday in honor of Jesus' death on the cross for sinners.

Without neglecting the other penitential psalms, attention is drawn to Psalm 51, the *miserere* or great cry for mercy. From the earliest ages of the Christian Church it has been the prayer frequently recited during Lent and especially during Holy Week. Complementing Psalm 51 are Psalms 32; 38; and 130.

Psalm 32 shows up prominently in some Byzantine rites, where the priest recites it three times as a way of personal purification before conferring the sacrament of baptism. Some Jewish people recite Psalms 32 and 38 for night prayer on Mondays and Wednesdays, begging God to break the silence and dangers, the howling voices and nightmares of darkness. Psalm 38, according to its title in the Aramaic Targum, accompanied the daily memorial offering in the Temple (Lev 6:7-16).

Psalm 130 provides one with the material for the *De Profundis*. Especially in the tradition and practices of the Order of Preachers, founded by Dominic de Guzman (1215 C.E.), members of the Order recited Psalm 130 while walking from one observance to another. For this reason that part of the cloister which led from the chapter room to the refectory or dining room was given the name of *De Profundis.* Psalm 130 has become a part of many people's daily prayer. The opening words of both Psalms 51 and 130 in the ancient Latin version—*Miserere* and *De Profundis*—have become part of almost every language of the world. It is very possible that they predate Jerome (+ 420 C.E.) and belonged to the earliest, very popular Latin text of Western Christianity called Vetus Latina.

First it is necessary to recognize the way in which the penitential psalms, especially Psalms 32, 38, 51, and 130 blend individual piety with the justice concerns of prophecy and with the public ritual of the Temple. This interaction assures a strong, healthy spirituality, so that personal sincerity keeps a heart and soul within external activity, while the latter prevents individual piety from degeneration into navel gazing and selfish or even morbid subjectivism. Then Psalm 51 can lead listeners and readers through the steps for forgiveness and reconciliation.

Interaction of Priests and Public Speakers

The initial reading of Psalms 32, 38, 51, and 130 leads one along a distinctively individual pathway. Not only do the psalms resonate, like Psalms 42–43, with a strong nostalgic memory of temple ritual, but they end up at the Temple. This point calls to mind Psalms 15 and 24 and how they provide the ultimate ritual at the temple gate for receiving the once guilty person back into full communion with all Israel (see Chapter 4 of this book).

Echoes of Prophecy

It is sometimes obvious but at other times difficult to detect the influence of prophecy upon the psalms. Or perhaps one should say that the degrees of certitude vary. In the case of Psalm 38, sickness has overwhelmed the psalmist. Certain lines connect with a verse in the prophecy of Isaiah:

Psalm 38:3, 5a, 7b	Isaiah 1:6
There is no soundness in my flesh because of your indignation; there is no health in my bones because of my sin. My wounds grow foul and fester . . . there is no soundness in my flesh.	From the sole of the foot even to the head, there is no soundness in it, but bruises and sores and bleeding wounds; they have not been drained, or bound up, or softened with oil.

While the psalmist is bemoaning his or her severe pain and serious illness, Isaiah is proclaiming:

> Ah, sinful nation,
>> people laden with iniquity,
> offspring who do evil,
>> children who deal corruptly,
> who have forsaken the LORD,
>> who have despised the Holy One of Israel,
> who are utterly estranged! (Isa 1:4).

Even more specifically Isaiah twice condemns the people of Jerusalem for neglecting orphans and mistreating widows (Isa 1:16, 23). The prophet also condemns the greedy people, because "everyone loves a bribe / and runs after gifts" (Isa 1:23).

Other parallels between Psalm 38 and prophecy come to attention, this time with Jeremiah. One instance is rather certain:

Psalm 38:1	Jeremiah 10:24
O LORD, do not rebuke me in your anger, or discipline me in your wrath.	Correct me, O LORD, but in just measure; not in your anger, or you will bring me to nothing.

Because this passage of Jeremiah, however, became almost a standard piece of language in the psalms of lament (see Pss 6:1; 27:7-9; 79:8; 85:4), a moment of hesitation arises. Does the influence come from other psalms, that is, from Israel's tradition of prayer, or is it to be traced back to Jeremiah? Still more difficult is the line: "I groan because of the tumult of my heart" (Ps 38:8b). What comes to mind are the short poetic pieces in Amos, Jeremiah, and Joel, found again in Ps 22:2:

> And he said:
>> The LORD roars from Zion,
>>> and utters his voice from Jerusalem;
>> the pastures of the shepherds wither,
>>> and the top of Carmel dries up (Amos 1:2).

> You, therefore, shall prophesy against them all these words, and say to them:
>> The LORD will roar from on high,
>>> and from his holy habitation utter his voice;
>> he will roar mightily against his fold,
>>> and shout, like those who tread grapes,
>>> against all the inhabitants of the earth (Jer 25:30).

The LORD roars from Zion,
>and utters his voice from Jerusalem,
>and the heavens and the earth shake.
But the LORD is a refuge for his people,
>a stronghold for the people of Israel (Joel 3:16).

My God, my God, why have you forsaken me?
>Why are you so far from helping me, from the words of my groaning?
>(Ps 22:1).

A refrain like this one combines prophecy and temple liturgy, so that cries for social justice and personal honor, for Israel and its poor ones, reverberate within many sectors of Israelite life.

It is particularly in Psalm 51 that the anthological style becomes evident. The psalm certainly has its own unique character. All the parts snap together and follow in good sequence. Yet in some other ways Psalm 51 appears to be an anthology, interweaving various prophetical lines and phrases. Some of the cross-references become visible from comparing the text of the psalms and that of prophecy.

Psalm 51:3-4

For I know my transgressions,
>and my sin is ever before me.
Against you, you alone, have I sinned
>and done what is evil in your
>>sight,
So that you are justified in your
>sentence and blameless
>when you pass judgment.

Isaiah 59:12-13

For our transgressions before you
>are many,
>and our sins testify against
>>us . . .
Our transgressions are indeed with us,
>and we know our iniquities:
transgressing, and denying the LORD,
>and turning away from
>>following our God,
talking oppression and revolt,
>conceiving lying words and
>>uttering them from the
>>heart.

Jeremiah 14:20-21

We acknowledge our wickedness,
>O LORD,
>>the iniquity of our ancestors,
>>for we have sinned against you.
Do not spurn us, for your name's sake;
>do not dishonor your glorious
>>throne;
remember and do not break
>your covenant with us.

Psalm 51:5	**Jeremiah 3:25**

Indeed, I was born guilty,
    a sinner when my mother
        conceived me.
	Let us lie down in our shame, and
	let our dishonor cover us; for we
	have sinned against the LORD our
	God, we and our ancestors, from
	our youth even to this day; and we
	have not obeyed the voice of the
	LORD our God.

Psalm 51:6, 10	**Ezekiel 36:25-26**

You desire truth in the inward being;
    therefore teach me wisdom in
        my secret heart.
Create in me a clean heart, O God,
    and put a new and right spirit
        within me.
	I will sprinkle clean water upon you,
	and you shall be clean from all your
	uncleannesses, and from all your
	idols I will cleanse you. A new heart
	I will give you, and a new spirit I will
	put within you; and I will remove
	from your body the heart of stone
	and give you a heart of flesh.

Psalm 51:11	**Isaiah 63:10-11**

Do not cast me away from your
    presence,
and do not take your holy spirit
    from me.
	But they rebelled
	    and grieved his holy spirit;
	therefore he became their enemy;
	    he himself fought against them.
	Then they remembered the days of
	    old,
	        of Moses his servant.
	Where is the one who brought them
	    up out of the sea
	    with the shepherds of his flock?
	Where is the one who put within
	    them
	        his holy spirit. . . .

The parallel between the psalm and the third section of Isaiah (Isaiah 56–66) helps in identifying the *terminus a quo,* the earliest *terminus* or time from which the psalm originated. Isaiah 56–66 reflects the time when Israel first returned from exile (537 B.C.E.). Some poems, like the lovely, poignant prayer in Isa 63:7–64:11, still reel under the tragic sight of the ruined Temple:

> Our holy and beautiful house,
> > where our ancestors praised you,
> has been burned by fire,
> > and all our pleasant places have become ruins (Isa 64:11).

Other poems in Isaiah 56–66 date from after the reconstruction of the Temple (520–515 B.C.E.) and seek to cleanse the narrow, self-serving spirit of devotion, as in Isa 57:1-13, by throwing open the temple doors so that "my house shall be called a house of prayer / for all peoples" (Isa 56:7c).

From Psalm 51 itself, especially its concluding prayer for the rebuilding of the walls of Jerusalem (Ps 51:18), we identify the *terminus ad quem* or time beyond which the composition of the psalm cannot extend—the reconstruction of the walls by Nehemiah in 445 B.C.E. (Neh 2:17). To be still more precise is difficult; a date around 500 B.C.E. seems appropriate.

The larger context of chapters 59 and 63:7–64:11 in Isaiah leads to a time of widespread deceit and social injustice, like that found in Psalm 12:

> For your hands are defiled with blood,
>   and your fingers with iniquity;
> your lips have spoken lies,
>   your tongue mutters wickedness.
> Their feet run to evil,
>   and they rush to shed innocent blood;
> their thoughts are thoughts of iniquity,
>   desolation and destruction are in their highways.
> See, the LORD's hand is not too short to save,
>   nor his ear too dull to hear (Isa 59:3, 7, 1).

While the wickedness thickens in Isaiah 59 and "we stumble at noon as in the twilight, / among the vigorous as though we were dead" (59:10b), the prophet enables the psalmist to find refuge in one of the more beautiful, penitential prayers of the entire Bible (Isa 63:7–64:11). It rests upon YHWH's favors or bonds of love and the memory of YHWH's glorious deeds. The same opening verse repeats the recollection of YHWH's "mercy" and "great kindness," words found in the opening line of Psalm 51's appeal for pardon. The breakdown of trust and concern in the social fabric of Israel does not result in a collapse of faith but in a still stronger, even a still more gentle response in the prophet:

> It was no messenger or angel
>   but his presence that saved them;
> in his love and in his pity he redeemed them;
>   he lifted them up and carried them all the days of old
> But they rebelled
>   and grieved his holy spirit;
> therefore he became their enemy;
>   he himself fought against them (Isa 63:9-10).

The final lines of this long, penitential prayer in the prophecy of Isaiah breaks down every barrier. It rends the heavens and makes the mountains quake (Isa 64:1 in some translations). The prayer concludes:

> There is no one who calls on your name,
>> or attempts to take hold of you;
> for you have hidden your face from us,
>> and have delivered us into the hand of our iniquity (Isa 64:7).

The references in Psalm 51 to other prophets, Jeremiah and Ezekiel, lead to the heart of all prophecy: the interior renewal of the covenant. The reconstruction of the social order will not last without a firm underpinning of interior renewal. While Jeremiah 31 speaks of inscribing the "new covenant with the house of Israel and the house of Judah upon the heart," Ezekiel typically adds a more explicit, liturgical touch:

> I will sprinkle clean water upon you, and you shall be clean from all your uncleannesses, and from all your idols I will cleanse you. A new heart I will give you, and a new spirit I will put within you; and I will remove from your body the heart of stone and give you a heart of flesh. I will put my spirit within you, and make you follow my statutes and be careful to observe my ordinances (Ezek 36:25-27).

Memories of Temple Liturgy

This allusion to Ezekiel in Psalm 51 brings up another important aspect of the penitential spirit, especially in Psalms 32 and 51. As in the case of Psalms 42–43, the liturgy provides the language to speak of absence from it. Separation from the liturgy intensified the longing for it, for in sanctuary liturgy each Israelite felt the strong bonds of family and tribe. To be excluded from the sanctuary was to lose membership in Israel and to be deprived of union with God. The psalmists, accordingly, made use of temple language to describe this loss and isolation, hoping thereby to overcome the loneliness and in some mystic way at least to participate with all Israel in the liturgy.

Psalm 32 was composed in gratitude for being admitted to a service of forgiveness and reconciliation within the community. It follows the stages of a sanctuary or temple ceremony:

vv. 1-2: blessing	Happy are those whose transgression is forgiven, whose sin is covered. Happy are those to whom the LORD imputes no iniquity, and in whose spirit there is no deceit.
vv. 3-5: confession by the penitent	While I kept silence, my body wasted away through my groaning all day long.

For day and night your hand was heavy
upon me;
my strength was dried up as by the heat
of summer.
Then I acknowledged my sin to you,
and I did not hide my iniquity;
I said, "I will confess transgressions to
the LORD,"
and you forgave the guilt of my sin.

v. 6: prayer to God by
the priest

Therefore let all who are faithful
offer prayer to you;
at a time of distress, the rush of mighty
waters
shall not reach them.

v. 7: prayer of the
penitent person, possibly
referring to night vigil
of prayer in the Temple

You are a hiding place for me;
you preserve me from trouble;
you surround me with glad cries
of deliverance.

vv. 8-10: instruction by
the priest

I will instruct you and teach you the way you
should go;
I will counsel you with my eye upon you.
Do not be like a horse or a mule, without
understanding,
whose temper must be curbed with a bit
and bridle,
else it will not stay near you.
Many are the torments of the wicked,
but steadfast love surrounds those who
trust in the LORD.

v. 11: concluding hymn

Be glad in the LORD and rejoice, O righteous,
and shout for joy, all you upright in heart.

Psalm 33 may have been added at a later date, to continue the hymn
of thanksgiving briefly introduced in Ps 32:11.[1] Psalm 33, among other

---

[1] Psalm 33 is a hymn of praise that ascribes the creation of the world to God's word. It
seems to have been influenced by Israel's Wisdom traditions. The call to sing a "new song"
(v. 3) elsewhere occurs only in exilic and post-exilic hymns (Isa 42:10; Pss 40:3; 46:1; 98:1;
144:9; 149:1). Thus Psalm 33 is normally dated in the post-exilic age, although there are also
good reasons for an early date. It seems to have been attracted to its present position by the
final verse of Psalm 32.

things, praises Y<small>HWH</small>'s creative power. Ps 51:12 recognizes the absolute need of God's action as Creator for the sinful but now forgiven person to be renewed completely. Such transformation does not come simply from human effort, no matter how great the good will.

Echoes of temple liturgy do not reach us as distinctively or as abundantly from Psalm 32. Yet they are clearly enough present. Already noted is the dependence of Psalm 51 upon prophecy, particularly prophetic texts about social justice, prayer, and the interior covenant of the heart. The psalmist then must have participated in temple rituals where these prophetical books took shape and were preserved. Sections of Psalm 51 carry the imprint of temple services:

vv. 1-2: Introductory Call for Mercy	Have mercy on me, O God, according to your steadfast love; according to your abundant mercy blot out my transgressions. Wash me thoroughly from my iniquity, and cleanse me from my sin.
vv. 3-5: Confession of Sin	
v. 3: sin consciousness	For I know my transgressions, and my sin is ever before me.
v. 4: confession	Against you, you alone, have I sinned, and done what is evil in your sight, so that you are justified in your sentence and blameless when you pass judgment.
vv. 5-6: maturity	Indeed, I was born guilty, a sinner when my mother conceived me. You desire truth in the inward being; therefore teach me wisdom in my secret heart.
vv. 7-9: Prayer for Forgiveness and Reinstatement in Temple Assembly	Purge me with hyssop, and I shall be clean; wash me, and I shall be whiter than snow. Let me hear joy and gladness; let the bones that you have crushed rejoice.
vv. 10-12: Prayer for Personal Renewal	Create in me a clean heart, O God, and put a new and right spirit within me. Do not cast me away from your presence, and do not take your holy spirit from me.

Restore me to the joy of your salvation,
  and sustain in me a willing spirit.

vv. 13-17: Thanksgiving

Then I will teach transgressors your ways,
  and sinners will return to you.
Deliver me from bloodshed, O God,
  O God of my salvation,
  and my tongue will sing aloud of your
    deliverance.
O Lord, open my lips,
  and my mouth will declare your praise.
For you have no delight in sacrifice;
  if I were to give a burnt offering, you
    would not be pleased.
The sacrifice acceptable to God is a broken
  spirit;
  a broken and contrite heart, O God, you
    will not despise.

vv. 18-19: Additions: Prayer
for the Temple and the City

Do good to Zion in your good pleasure;
  rebuild the walls of Jerusalem,
then you will delight in right sacrifices,
  in burnt offerings and whole burnt
    offerings;
  then bulls will be offered on your altar.

Psalm 130 moves noticeably from a personal cry to God and a personal waiting upon Yhwh to a wish and a prayer for all Israel. Thus an answer comes to the fervent hope of the psalmist:

I wait for the Lord, my soul waits,
  and in his word I hope;
my soul waits for the Lord
  more than those who watch for the morning,
  more than those who watch for the morning (Ps 130:5-6).

Personal Piety

Temple liturgy broke the dismal silence and isolation of the psalmist. At this point one sees, moreover, that prophecy made another important contribution. While the Temple reunited the sinful, penitent person with Israel, prophecy ensured that a healthy individualism was not lost. A sense of personal responsibility comes frequently to the surface of the psalmist's words. Prophecy requires an honest admission of guilt from a sinful person.

In no way is the sinner allowed to shift the blame to all the people or to the ancestors. Both Jeremiah and especially Ezekiel condemn the use of an ancient proverb:

> In those days they shall no longer say:
> "The parents have eaten sour grapes,
> and the children's teeth are set on edge" (Jer 31:29).

> What do you mean by repeating this proverb concerning the land of Israel, "The parents have eaten sour grapes, and the children's teeth are set on edge"? (Ezek 18:2).

Both prophets insist: if a person's teeth are set on edge and his or her lips are puckered, then it was that person who did wrong and ate the sour grapes. This honest admission of personal guilt rings out in Psalm 51 by the continual use of the first-person singular noun: have mercy on me; my offense; my guilt; cleanse me; my offense. Yes *I* acknowledge: *my* sin is before *me* always; etc.

The personal bonding of the psalmist with God reaches a crescendo in the poignant language of Ps 51:6, which addressed God (here translated literally from the Hebrew): "Against you, against you alone have I sinned, / and that deed evil in your eyes I did." This verse calls to mind two verses in Matthew's Gospel where Jesus is depicted as stating: (1) "And the king will answer them, 'Truly I tell you, just as you did it to one of the least of these who are members of my family, you did it to me'" (Matt 25:40); (2) "Then he will answer them, 'Truly I tell you, just as you did not do it to one of the least of these, you did not do it to me'" (Matt 25:45). This urgent desire for full, personal union with God shows up in a touching way within the penitential prayer of Psalm 38:

> O Lord, all my longing is known to you;
> my sighing is not hidden from you (v. 9).
> But it is for you, O LORD, that I wait;
> it is you, O LORD my God, who will answer (v. 15).

The second line of verse 15 about answering or listening as well as the anxious entreaty at the end, "make haste to help me, / O Lord, my salvation" (v. 22) recalls key phrases in Psalm 22, specifically, verses 1-2 and verses 19-21. Psalm 22, as pointed out earlier, moves with a strong interaction between "I, the psalmist," and "you, my God."

Before turning to Psalm 51 for the stages of forgiveness and reconciliation, two points made in Psalms 32; 38; and 130 need consideration: (1) the necessity to wait upon YHWH, and (2) the hopelessness, left to oneself, of getting out of the depths of sin. Sinful people cast themselves into a pit, too deep to climb out by themselves. The opening words of Psalm 30 in the ancient Latin text, as already remarked, reverberate through the languages of the world: *De Profundis*—"Out of the depths I cry to you, O Lord." These "depths," according to the prophet Isaiah, were inhabited by demons like Rahab and the dragon (Isa 51:9). The mighty arm of YHWH must intervene to crush Rahab, pierce the dragon, and dry up the surging waters of the great deep before the redeemed can pass on their way to safety and be fully redeemed. Prophecy continues to declare the impossibility of sinners saving themselves:

> and a pit dug deep in Shittim;
>> but I will punish all of them (Hos 5:2).
> They have deeply corrupted themselves
>> as in the days of Gibeah;
> he will remember their iniquity,
>> he will punish their sins (Hos 9:9).

The same desperate need for God's intervention finds a grateful voice in Psalm 18:

> He reached down from on high, he took me;
>> he drew me out of mighty waters.
> He delivered me from my strong enemy,
>> and from those who hated me;
>> for they were too mighty for me (Ps 18:16-17).

Because God alone saves, the sinner must wait upon God. God, not the sinner, decides when mercy overtakes the wicked person to stir a change of heart and sorrow for sin. God also decides how long it is necessary for the sinner to wait. In such waiting a person becomes better disposed to accept, appreciate, and act upon the gracious invitation of divine grace. Four times in two verses Psalm 130 enunciates this necessary disposition:

> my soul waits for the Lord
>> more than those who watch for the morning,
>> more than those who watch for the morning.
> O Israel, hope in the LORD!
>> For with the LORD there is steadfast love,
>> and with him is great power to redeem (Ps 130:6-7).

The same attitude brings peace to the sinner: "But it is for you, O LORD, that I wait; / it is you, O LORD my God, who will answer" (Ps 38:15).

Stages of Forgiveness and Reconciliation

Psalm 51, along with other penitential psalms, helps one to reconstruct the different moments in moving from sin to forgiveness and reconciliation. Earlier in this chapter Psalm 51 was quoted according to its major stages. These stages followed the liturgy of temple services of prayer and thanksgiving. Now attention is given to the message of each stage.

Prophetic Setting of the Title (Ps 51:1-2)

The title of Psalm 51 is longer than usual. In the Hebrew text, it is subdivided into verses 1-2. It reads:

> For the leader.
> A Psalm of David, when the prophet Nathan came to him, after he had gone in to Bathsheba (Ps 51:1-2).

After David's sin of adultery with Bathsheba and his effective way of arranging for the murder of her husband Uriah, the Lord sent Nathan to David (see 2 Samuel 12:1). Nathan disarms David by telling a story about a wealthy person who took a poor man's only possession, a ewe lamb, a delight of the poor man's children, and had it killed, to prepare a meal for a visitor. David became "greatly kindled against the man. He said to Nathan, 'As the LORD lives, the man who has done this deserves to die'" (2 Sam 12:5). The account continues with strong emphasis, especially in the Hebrew grammar: "Then Nathan said to David: 'You are the man!'" (2 Sam 12:7, Heb.). The title stresses personal responsibility and personal guilt, but another prophetic tradition emerges in the title.

Psalm 51, except for the title, never alludes to the sin of adultery. The psalm introduces sexuality but differently. The title seems to suggest that every sin is symbolically an adultery because of the intense, intimate love of God which sin always violates. The title thus introduces a prophetic tradition which reaches back at least as far as Hosea (around 750–721 B.C.E.) and was continued by other prophets after Hosea within the northern tradition, namely Jeremiah (627–587 B.C.E.), Second Isaiah (Isaiah 40–55; 550–537 B.C.E.), and Third Isaiah (Isaiah 56–66; around 500 B.C.E.). By the time of the Exile, moreover, this epithet of YHWH, Spouse of Israel, had become common property of southern prophets as well, as we see in the preaching of Ezekiel (593–571 B.C.E.). In most of this long tradition, the prevalent context came from an Israel sinful and indifferent or else sad and demoralized.

In reference to his own broken marriage, Hosea states: "The LORD said to me again, 'Go, love a woman who has a lover and is an adulteress, just as the LORD loves the people of Israel, though they turn to other gods and love raisin cakes'" (Hos 3:1). Agonizing over the repeated infidelity of his wife Gomer, Hosea thinks of Israel's frequent wandering away from YHWH and of the Lord's way of alluring her into the desert and speaking to her heart (Hos 2:16, NRSV 2:14). Hosea draws from the memories and experience of his own marriage as well as from the love of the Lord for Israel during the days of Moses, to speak in the language of idyllic love, of honeymoon days. A later editor of Hosea's preaching summarized this lovely, heart-breaking yet reconciling tradition, as YHWH speaks again to Israel: "And I will take you for my wife forever; I will take you for my wife in righteousness and in justice, in steadfast love, and in mercy. I will take you for my wife in faithfulness; and you shall know the LORD" (Hos 2:19-20).

The tradition continues before the Exile with Jer 2:2-3 and during the Exile with Isa 54:1-8. In post-exilic Israel, perhaps very close to the composition of Psalm 51, Third Isaiah writes of Zion as YHWH's bride:

> You shall no more be termed Forsaken,
> > and your land shall no more be termed Desolate;
> but you shall be called My Delight Is in Her,
> > and your land Married;
> for the LORD delights in you,
> > and your land shall be married.
> For as a young man marries a young woman,
> > so shall your builder marry you,
> and as the bridegroom rejoices over the bride,
> > so shall your God rejoice over you (Isa 62:4-5).

Through the love of YHWH, Jerusalem becomes the happy mother of many children:

> Who has heard of such a thing?
> > Who has seen such things?
> Shall a land be born in one day?
> > Shall a nation be delivered in one moment?
> Yet as soon as Zion was in labor
> > she delivered her children.
> Rejoice with Jerusalem, and be glad for her,
> > all you who love her;
> rejoice with her in joy,
> > all you who mourn over her—
> that you may nurse and be satisfied
> > from her consoling breast;
> that you may drink deeply with delight
> > from her glorious bosom (Isa 66:8, 10-11).

The title of Psalm 51 then begins the process of forgiveness and reconciliation by enabling the sinful person to recall the infinite, compassionate love and total fidelity of YHWH toward Israel. This tradition, we have seen several times in this book, rests upon the revelation of God to Moses on Mount Sinai:

> The LORD passed before him, and proclaimed,
>   "The LORD, the LORD,
> a God merciful and gracious,
> slow to anger,
> and abounding in steadfast love and faithfulness,
> keeping steadfast love for the thousandth generation,
> forgiving iniquity and transgression and sin,
> yet by no means clearing the guilty,
> but visiting the iniquity of the parents
> upon the children
> and the children's children,
> to the third and the fourth generation" (Exod 34:6-7).

Sin is to be gauged not simply by the external act but by the tender, intimate love of God which is offended. While sin is initiated by ourselves, forgiveness must begin with God who, like the father in Jesus' parable of the prodigal son, is already waiting at a distance for the wayward son and at the first sight rushes to embrace his son, throwing his arms around him and kissing him (Luke 15:20). Faith, implanted by memories of forgiveness in the history of Israel and by personal experience, is already drawing sinful persons back to God before the latter ever begin to confess their sin. The prophetic tradition of the title reaches beyond parental love to that between spouses, a love far more intimate and compelling, deeper in its hurts, more daring in its requests, more abiding in its memories. God is continuously sustaining these memories and so is taking the divine initiative in recalling the sinful person.

Call for Mercy

After the setting, Psalm 51 properly speaking begins with a poignant, humble, repeated cry for mercy. The literary form for each of the two verses deserves attention. Hebrew grammar allows the poet to put the verb at the beginning and end of each verse, while the words for mercy in verse 3 and for sin in verse 4 come next to each other and occupy the center spot. Put in diagram form, it reads in Hebrew:

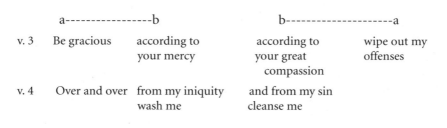

	a---------------b		b---------------------a	
v. 3	Be gracious	according to your mercy	according to your great compassion	wipe out my offenses
v. 4	Over and over	from my iniquity wash me	and from my sin cleanse me	

The grammar sets up a tension between God's intimate love and the willful sinfulness of the creature. In the first line sin and separation occupy the outer edge, in the second line purification is there. In the first line God's intimate love is at the center, in the second line sinfulness corrupts the heart. At the heart is the clash between God's great, loving compassion and the psalmist's sinfulness.

Still other striking ways of uniting with God and being torn apart become apparent in studying the diagram. While in verse 3 the words for mercy and compassion emphatically denote close bonds of blood, the verbs "have mercy" and "to wipe out my offenses" speak of distance and even stridently of rebellion. The Hebrew word for mercy is the familiar one, *hesed,* one of those words unlocking the deeper meaning of many biblical experiences and present in that basic text of Exod 34:6, which includes this description of YHWH, "abounding in steadfast love and faithfulness." As mentioned several times over in this book, *hesed* or mercy always presumes a close bond, usually among blood members of the same extended family or tribe, sometimes to people who bind themselves by treaty or contract. The other central word in verse 3, "merciful," translates the Hebrew *rahamîm.* When this word appears in the plural, as here, it means "compassion" or "warm or loving mercy," but in the singular (the basic form of the word) it refers to the "womb" where a child develops and comes to birth. God therefore forgives in the loving, tender, slow, nourishing way of a pregnant woman.

Forgiveness, moreover, remains a continuous promise, because we never stop being a "blood relative" of God. God always recognizes in us a part of the divine self; divine blood, if we stay with the image of the Hebrew language, courses spiritually through us as it does through God. In accord with this symbol and its deeper, realistic meaning, the prophet Isaiah wrote to console Israel, on the edge of despair and giving up on God:

> Thus says the LORD:
> The wealth of Egypt and the merchandise of Ethiopia,
>   and the Sabeans, tall of stature,
> shall come over to you and be yours,
>   they shall follow you;
>   they shall come over in chains and bow down to you.
> They will make supplication to you, saying,
>   "God is with you alone, and there is no other;
>   there is no god besides him."
> Truly, you are a God who hides himself,
>   O God of Israel, the Savior.
> All of them are put to shame and confounded,
>   the makers of idols go in confusion together (Isa 45:14-16).

The reality turns out to be bolder and more startling than the symbol.

The paradox returns when one looks at the verbs at the beginning and end of the Hebrew structure in verse 3. The request, "be gracious," translates the Hebrew *hanah*—the origin of the rather common name Hannah or Anna, the name of the mother of the prophet Samuel (1 Sam 1:2, 19-28) and of the mother of Mary and grandmother of Jesus. While *hesed* is restricted to members of the extended family and would not be shown to outsiders, no matter how kind a person was to them, *hanah* carries a wide, generic reach. This calls to mind the birth names or nicknames with which only closest friends or at times only members of a family will use in addressing someone. Such are the words *hesed* and *rahamîm*. The word now under consideration, *hanah*, can include the distant stranger and be used by everyone.

The tension between intimate bonding and distant contact becomes all the more severe when one turns to a key term found in verse 3: "transgression." The Hebrew word here, *pesha'*, denotes rebellion and rupture, a burning of bridges, a cutting away, a violent separation. Because of rebellion, peoples once bonded by treaty turn to savage war, even destroying cities and deporting the remnant who survive the long siege and angry assault of the walled city.

The opening verse of Psalm 51 therefore declares, from the human viewpoint, the deliberate rupture from God; from the divine side, one is consoled that God cannot give up and abandon the lost sheep, the lost coin, or the lost child (cf. Luke 15). The penitential Psalm 51 sets out to resolve this tension. The resolution continues with deliberate pace in the next verse, which concludes the introduction of Psalm 51. Again the tension of straying away from a loving God continues. The two words for sin are classic ones in the Hebrew language. The first, *'awon*, bespeaks something malformed, crooked, or bent: a situation which does not conform with what society considers normal (see Job 15:5; 20:27; Jer 11:10; 14:7; 16:17). The other word for sin, *hatta'*, in its elementary meaning, refers to an arrow that misses its target or to a traveler who wanders off and gets lost (see Judg 20:16; Job 5:24; Prov 8:36). If one attaches these words for sin with the metaphor behind the "great compassion" (*rahamîm*) in the preceding verse, what results is the agony of a pregnant mother whose embryo is badly lodged in the womb, refuses to proceed to birth or proceeds in the wrong way—like a child rupturing the womb. Sin is thus crooked and wrongly directed.

Such a condition demands immediate, energetic action, exactly what is found in the verbs at the beginning and at the end of verse 4 in the Hebrew. So insistent is the opening phrase that it succumbs to tautology, yet without being verbose. In Hebrew, there are two words at the beginning: (1) "many times over" or "over and over again," and (2) "wash me." Yet the latter verb, wash or *kabas,* includes many different stages of washing clothes in cold, running water. Usually in this and most world cultures it is a woman's duty. She repeatedly pushes the soiled clothes into the water and out again, each time wringing out the water with some of the dirt. She will also beat the wet clothes with a wooden paddle or else hit them against rocks, again to submerge them in the cold water. Finally, after a final plunge into the water and a thorough wringing, the woman stretches the clothes out upon rocks to dry and bleach in the strong sunlight. No more vigorous word comes to mind. Here is a willingness to submit to the most thorough purification, as echoed in Psalm 12: "silver refined in a furnace on the ground, / purified seven times" (v. 6). A similar idea is also found in Isaiah:

> I will turn my hand against you;
> > I will smelt away your dross as with lye
> > and remove all your alloy (Isa 1:25).

If bonding with God through grace is as intimate as an unborn child with its mother, then the return to grace after sin will have to be equally thorough and reach into every fiber of a person's being.

The final phrase in the introductory couplet of Psalm 51 seeks to restore the sinful person to full membership within the community. Then the blood bond of the extended family is completely in place once again. The verb "to cleanse," *taher,* is the standard word for ceremonial cleanliness and full membership, without shame or fear, within the community of Israel, in its dwellings and in the Temple or house of God. This word adds a distinct nuance: it not only implies cleanliness but it declares that the "clean" person is no longer suspected of spreading disease. There is no fear of contagion anymore. Forgiveness, therefore, like sin is a social concern and affects the entire community. There is no such thing, simply and exclusively, as a "private" sin of an "individual." The prophetic background insists upon the social dimension as much as it stresses personal obligation and intimate bonding with God and with one's neighbor.

Confession of Sin (Pss 51:5-8; 32)

The opening verses, then, of Psalm 51 set the tone or spirit. They serve like a song for introducing a liturgical service, whether this ceremony be the Eucharist, a penitential rite for the forgiveness of sin and for reconciliation with the Church and with one another, or a ritual for anointing the sick and the aged. Verses 3 and 4 express the profound biblical theology of sin and forgiveness in a nontheological way, without the serious precision of defining the conditions essential for a sin to be serious and without stipulating in legal or canonical terms the conditions required by the priesthood for declaring a person purified and acceptable within temple services. This psalm begins by looking away from the Torah and such passages as Num 5:5-10 or even by leaving aside for the moment the final ritual of reconciliation at the temple gate in such psalms as Psalms 15 and 24. The opening verses of Psalm 51 set up a bridge between the theology of sin and forgiveness and the reception of that forgiveness in the sinful person. This bridge spans the distance between theory and life, first in the title (vv. 1-2) by insisting upon the intimate bond of love between God and the people Israel, and second in the introductory prayer (vv. 3-4) by admitting the frightful and disturbing rupture inflicted upon such love by sin and therefore the long, painful process of reconciliation and renewal.

The psalm now proceeds with an honest confession: "Indeed, I was born guilty, / a sinner when my mother conceived me" (v. 5). What an oppressive weight is lifted off a close relationship, whether in family or in friendship, when a person who has offended another is able to say what he or she did, and simultaneously show how much he or she has suffered in his or her heart because of the offensive deed. Verse 5 responds to the necessity of honest and open confession; verse 6, to the need of the guilty party to communicate the depth of his or her own personal suffering because of the sin.

The second of the penitential psalms (Psalm 32) allows for a longer reflection on the necessity of confessing one's sins. The following lines voice the reaction of every confessing person:

> While I kept silence, my body wasted away
> through my groaning all day long.
> For day and night your hand was heavy upon me;
> my strength was dried up as by the heat of summer.
> Then I acknowledged my sin to you,
> and I did not hide my iniquity;
> I said, "I will confess my transgressions to the LORD,"
> and you forgave the guilt of my sin (Ps 32:3-5).

The key idea in Psalm 32 is to admit one's fault. Various phrases within the psalm develop this theme:

- "kept silence . . . body wasted away" (v. 3);
- "acknowledged my sin" (v. 5);
- "did not hide my iniquity" (v. 5);
- "I will confess my transgressions" (v. 5);
- "you forgave the guilt of my sin" (v. 5).

The preceding Psalm 31 recognizes this nonscientific yet realistic way of saying, "I suffer all over but especially in the deepest part of myself." Psalm 31 states:

> Be gracious to me, O LORD, for I am in distress;
>> my eye wastes away from grief,
>> my soul and body also.
> For my life is spent with sorrow,
>> and my years with sighing;
> my strength fails because of my misery,
>> and my bones waste away (Ps 31:9-10).

The climactic line declares how "my bones waste away," better translated, "my bones are crushed and ground to powder" like bones in the jaws of a dog. See Mic 3:1-3.

The second and fourth phrases in the previous quotations from Ps 32:3-5, "I acknowledged my sin . . . . I will confess my transgressions . . ." lead into a very ambiguous, yet illuminating terrain of Hebrew words. The word here translated "acknowledge" comes from the root *yadah,* which has various meanings:

In Gen 29:35, Leah, in giving birth to her fourth son, declares: "This time I will praise the *Lord.*" Therefore, she names the boy "Praise" or "Judah," from the root *y(j)dh.* In Gen 49:8, Jacob's testament to his twelve sons plays on this meaning of Judah: "Judah, your brothers shall praise you." In Prov 28:13, there occurs a meaning very close to Psalm 32, where *yadah* must be translated "confess": "No one who conceals transgressions will prosper, / but one who confesses and forsakes them will obtain mercy." In Ps 118:1, a major song of thanksgiving begins with a variation of *yadah:* "O give thanks to the LORD, for he is good; / his steadfast love endures forever!"

Acknowledgment, as painful as it may be, in laying bare one's guilt, releases a person of shame and regret, and a sense of relief and happiness flow out. Such an immediate and spontaneous response to a happy situation is what the Bible suggests as "praise." It relies upon total openness and honesty (in a sinful situation, it presumes confession of one's guilt), it reveals God's wonderful presence (it easily becomes "praise"), and its natural response becomes the best way of saying "thank you" (and so it is the major biblical word for gratitude). In returning to Ps 32:5, one notes that there is a double use of this same word *yadah:* "acknowledge" and "confess." Thus, the psalm moves almost at once into praise, joy, and gratitude:

> Therefore let all who are faithful
>> offer prayer to you;
> at a time of distress, the rush of mighty waters
>> shall not reach them.

You are a hiding place for me;
>   you preserve me from trouble;
>   you surround me with glad cries of deliverance.
Be glad in the LORD and rejoice, O righteous,
>   and shout for joy, all you upright in heart (Ps 32:6-7, 11).

Finally, in this same Psalm 32 there is the phrase: "you forgave the guilt of my sin" (v. 5b) This phrase brings to mind another essential of reconciliation, God's way of initiating and completing the return to grace. No person, in the area of his or her sinfulness, independently decides when and how he or she will seek forgiveness and be reconciled with God and with his or her community. One needs to respond to God's initiative. Reconciliation is a conscious choice on the part of the one in need of reconciliation, and it is a divinely bestowed free gift of grace that God bestows on the one seeking reconciliation.

Unlike the composer of other psalms, the author of Psalm 51 does not openly declare that he is "wretched" and "close to death" (see Ps 88:15), or that he is "struck with terror" and "weary" with "mourning" (Ps 6:3, 6). Nor does the psalmist state simply, like Ps 38:18, "I am sorry for my sin." Psalm 51 instead features a more personal acknowledgment of one's transgression. In this psalm, the psalmist addresses God directly:

> Have mercy on me, O God,
>   according to your steadfast love;
> according to your abundant mercy
>   blot out my transgressions.
> Wash me thoroughly from my iniquity,
>   and cleanse me from my sin (Ps 51:1-2).

This personal acknowledgment of sin, admitted to God, continues in verses 3-4:

> For I know my transgressions,
>   and my sin is ever before me.
> Against you, you alone, have I sinned,
>   and done what is evil in your sight.

And what will God's response be? Here one needs to recall the Bible's central, unifying, and supporting position of all biblical theology. God revealed the mystery of divinity to Moses at Mount Sinai by declaring:

> The LORD passed before him, and proclaimed,
>   "The LORD, the LORD,
>   a God merciful and gracious,
>   slow to anger,
>   and abounding in steadfast love and faithfulness . . ." (Exod 34:6).

It is God's revelation of such love to the psalmist that prompts and sustains all the stages of reconciliation. Because the psalmist participates in such tender love, the poet experiences the pain caused by sin. Among these parties offended is God. Never is any human act so privatized that God is left out. If God is present, as is always the case, God cannot be present in a neutral, distant, or even purely objective way.[2] God is happy or full of grief, but never a passive observer. Because of this faith, the psalmist must confess as done to God whatever was done to the neighbor. God, in fact, is the absent neighbor.

---

[2] The Hebrew word *paqad* has various meanings: "to visit," "to appoint," "to punish," etc. Its root meaning, however, seems to be "to attend to with care" or "to concern oneself with."

Chapter Twelve

Wisdom Psalms

The earth, O LORD, is full of your steadfast love;
teach me your statutes.
Teach me good judgment and knowledge.
For I believe in your commandments (Ps 119:64, 66).

Wisdom was associated very early with royalty in Israel (cf. 1 Kgs 4:29-34, a section that concludes, "People came from all the nations to hear the wisdom of Solomon; they came from all the kings of the earth who had heard of his wisdom"). As in other countries, finishing schools for noble youth must have existed at the royal capital and in the post-exilic age the synagogues must have served as places both of worship and of instruction. The clearest reference to such schools occurs in Sir 51:23: "Draw near to me, you who are uneducated, / and lodge in the house of instruction." The attitude of school and instruction can be characterized as traditional, reflective, moderate, and refined. "Traditional" does not necessarily mean an attachment to covenant theology, or to the great religious symbols of Israel like the exodus out of Egypt, settlement of the land, or establishment of the Davidic dynasty. In fact, these essential ingredients of Israel's religion seldom if ever enter the classic piece of Wisdom literature, the book of Proverbs. Only the very late books of Sirach (ca. 190 B.C.E.) and the Wisdom of Solomon (ca. 50 B.C.E.) blend these aspects of Israel's sacred history with instruction. Wisdom literature is traditional in the sense of incorporating age-old common sense, family loyalty, conscientious work, dependability, keen insight, well-tested prudence, and long experience. Therefore, the attitude tended to be reflective and rational. The positions have been thought out, even over generations of time, and further refinement has come from each new re-experience of the problem or situation. People formed in this background tend to be moderate, calm, and self-controlled.

The radical threats of the prophets do not echo in Wisdom literature, nor do we find the stern laws of the Torah about clean and unclean. Wisdom received its authority in the community from human experience; genera- || tion after generation has testified that "it works." When all is said and done, this type of authority is probably more demanding and unbending than any other, be this other priestly or prophetic.

Wisdom literature seeks the harmonious, stable order of life. It stands against chaos and violence. While the hymns, especially those that derive their motivation from God's creative action over the universe, portray YHWH as supreme victor over the angry sea and the roaring storms of the winter season (Pss 29; 89:9-13), wisdom finds itself in the presence of the creator "like a master worker," "daily his delight," and "rejoicing before him always" (Prov 8:30). Despite this attitude of being reflective and "rational," nonetheless wisdom always implies ultimate mystery, secretly in God's control. In Prov 8:22-31 wisdom rests with God before creation; the same is found to be the case in Sirach 24. The same aspect of mystery will show up in sapiential aspects of Psalm 139: "Even before a word is on my tongue, / O LORD, you know it completely" (v. 4).

In content, the Wisdom psalms tend to contrast the just and the wicked; one of their ways of inculcating wisdom is to stress the inevitability that the wicked are punished and the just rewarded. The dedicatory psalm for the entire Psalter stresses this iron law of retribution (Psalm 1). These psalms will offer solid advice about one's conduct, yet frequently lead the discussion to the "fear of the Lord."

The Wisdom psalms, like the other sapiential literature of the Bible, are rich in their rhetorical elements. For example, the rhetorical elements are shared with the other Wisdom literature of the Bible. In the Wisdom psalms one finds such features as:

(1) The "better" sayings:
Better is a little that the righteous person has
  than the abundance of many wicked.
For the arms of the wicked shall be broken,
  but the LORD upholds the righteous (Ps 37:16-17).

(2) Numerical sayings:
Once God has spoken;
  twice have I heard this:
that power belongs to God,
  and steadfast love belongs to you, O Lord.
For you repay to all
  according to their work (Ps 62:11-12).

(3) The *ʾashre* or "happy" sayings:
Happy are those
> who do not follow the advice of the wicked,
or take the path that sinners tread,
> > or sit in the seat of scoffers (Ps 1:1).

(4) The acrostic or alphabetic psalms (Psalms 34; 37; 111; 112; 119; 145).

When one compares the Wisdom psalms with the Wisdom literature generally in the Bible, one finds the psalms to be more conscious of God's presence in daily life. One would presume that the schools and synagogues developed an attitude of prayer and produced their own standard prayers. While the hymns of praise and the prayers of supplication respond more with adoration and stunned silence, with excitement and outrage, the Wisdom psalms reply with reflection and calm strength, with moderation and appreciation for the learning experience.

The fact that a Wisdom psalm not only inaugurates the entire series of psalms but also that it was placed here at the beginning of the Psalter in the final stages of the formation of the canonical text shows that the sages exercised more than their share of influence over the book of Psalms.

Psalm 1: Introducing a Book of Prayers

If the Psalter were compiled during the post-exilic age (539 B.C.E. onward) as the principal song book of the Jerusalem Temple, this introductory psalm would be a reminder that neither the Psalter nor the Temple belonged exclusively to Israelite priests and other religious leaders. Psalm 1 is rightly considered a sapiential psalm with close ties to such books as Proverbs which speak seldom of liturgical matters, not even of Israel's great historical moments, the basis of theology and worship. Sapiential literature remains close to the everyday world of human existence and seeks to live here in a godly way. Psalm 1, therefore, does not ring with the glorious tones of a sanctuary hymn like Psalms 8 or 29, or echo salvation history like Psalms 104; 105; and 114; yet it shows a close association with Israel's sacred institutions. It reminds us that Israel's liturgy ritualizes God's redeeming presence in secular life and is to be judged acceptable or not by its impact on justice and sincerity. Thereby liturgy and the psalms offer true worship to God.

Psalm 1 was added late to the Psalter. Some New Testament manuscripts and early ecclesiastical writers seem oblivious of Psalm 1 and refer to Psalm 2 as the first psalm (cf. Codex Bezae; Origen on Acts 13:33). When one of the final editors of the Psalter added Psalm 1, this person linked it carefully with Psalm 2. The first psalm begins and the second ends with "Happy" or "Happy are all . . . ," a literary device called "inclusion." Because Psalm 2 originally belonged to the coronation of a new king, Psalm 1 is thereby associated with the Davidic royalty at Jerusalem. There are associations with still other parts of the Bible. Some connection exists between Psalm 1 and Jer 17:5-8, and there is a remote possibility of some relation of Ps 1:3 with the poetry of an Egyptian scribe, Amen-en-Opet. Psalm 1 also harmonizes with deuteronomic literature in Joshua and the book of Deuteronomy, literature that resonates the theology of the northern kingdom, which was closer to Moses and less centralized or less controlled than the religious situation at Jerusalem. In many subtle ways then, Psalm 1 represents a medley of many biblical traditions, more secular than sacred, yet always related to the way of God's direction, goodness, and care. The author may not have been a great poet, thinker, or moralist. The psalmist may have been a person of experience, reflection, and moderation, but most of all a person of strong conviction, totally dedicated to YHWH in the path of daily life.

The redactor integrated Psalm 1 with the five books that comprise the Psalter. The opening phrase of Psalm 1, "happy are those," or better translated in a less liturgical way, closer to the Hebrew *²ashre,* "How happy that one," is found toward the end of the first two books: Ps 41:1 within Psalms 1–41; Ps 65:4 within Psalms 42–72. It also occurs in the final psalm of the third and fourth books (Psalms 73–89 and Psalms 90–106—cf. 89:15 and 106:3), and it appears very often in the fifth book, Psalms 107–150, eight times in Psalm 119 alone. The psalm is divided into verses 1-3, the way of the just; verses 4-5, the way of the wicked; verse 6, the concluding judgment on the two ways. In contrast with the pre-exilic age (before 587 B.C.E.) and its struggle between Israel and the Gentile non-elect people, this psalm, perhaps by prophetic or sapiential influence, identified the crucial struggle as that within Israel between the just and the wicked.

"Happy" translates the Hebrew word *²ashre* (not the more liturgical, ritualistic word *baruk*—cf. Psalm 104), closely connected with right living in one's daily life. The word occurs often in the Hebrew Bible, many times in the Psalms and in other Wisdom literature, especially in the oldest section of Prov (14:21; 16:20; 20:7). The "happy" person fears God (Ps 112:1; Prov 28:14), behaves righteously (Ps 119:1-2), cares for the poor (Ps 41:1; Prov 14:21), and follows YHWH's instructions (Prov 29:18). Because of association with Wisdom literature, the word might even be translated: "How envious" or "to be envied" is that person.

Another key term in Psalm 1 is "the way." The word "way" (in Hebrew, *derek*) came into popular use with the later prophets, Jeremiah and especially Ezekiel (107 times); Second Isaiah considers it to be the way of YHWH (Isa 55:9) along which the exiles return to their Promised Land (Isa 40:3) and so retrace in spirit the first Exodus out of Egypt (43:16, 19). It becomes even clearer that this way belongs to YHWH and can be found only by obedient faith and humble submission to divine guidance. People are never the master of this right way, only YHWH. Psalm 1 ends by stating: "for the LORD watches over the way of the righteous, / but the way of the wicked will perish" (v. 6). One finds here an unusual, even intriguing combination of practical common sense (very visible in the Wisdom books) and the mysterious guidance of YHWH (prominent with the prophets). Again one finds the ecumenical or inclusive attitude of Psalm 1.

The Law of the YHWH extends beyond the Mosaic Torah or the first five books of the Bible, even though this Law is always based on the Mosaic covenant, is mediated through the Holy Scriptures, and ought to be the subject of continuous meditation, day and night, or as Deut 6:7 stated: "Recite them to your children and talk about them when you are at home and when you are away, when you lie down and when you rise." The Hebrew word "meditate" *(hgh)* means to mumble, sigh, whisper, or reflect aloud (see Psalms 9; 16); it presumes a visible manifestation (Isa 3:14; 8:19; Ps 90:9; Josh 1:8), and therefore it commits a person totally, body and mind, as YHWH's way sinks deeply within. Therefore, one's "delight" in the Law of YHWH reveals an interior peace and satisfaction that center upon the person of YHWH (Pss 19:8-9; 119:2, 10). This interior satisfaction in YHWH orients one to the proper meaning of "the fear of the LORD" (Ps 19:9; Prov 1:7), a healthy fear, lest one stray from the heart's greatest delight. Such wandering, unfortunately, is easily possible when one is successful (Ps 37:7-9).

A steady momentum moves the psalm forward:

> They are like trees
>   planted by streams of water,
> which yield their fruit in its season,
>   and their leaves do not wither.
> In all that they do, they prosper (Ps 1:3).

This impetus toward a final, permanent state of justice—a divine gift where one has been transplanted by YHWH "by streams of water" may be at least a vague, intuitive glimpse of the eschatological judgment in fleeting perception of the messianic community. This sense of God's final judgment is hidden within the comparison of the wicked to "chaff" (v. 4), which occurs with fierce finality in Zeph 2:3; Isa 17:13.

In Hebrew, Psalm 1 begins with *aleph,* the first letter of the Hebrew alphabet, *'ashre*; its final word, *to'bed,* starts with the last letter of the alphabet, *taw.* The letters *aleph* and *taw* symbolize all the letters and words in between. Psalm 1 thereby embraces the entire Psalter, even all the Holy Scripture. Psalm 1, moreover, places listeners and readers of its message in meditation day and night, and reaches beyond time.

Psalm 49: The Common Lot of Humanity

The first group of psalms from the guild of Korah ends on a melancholy note with Psalm 49, although there is a flash of hope in the extraordinary line, verse 15: "But God will ransom my soul from the power of Sheol, / for he will receive me." This psalm asserts that wealth and in fact every human resource pass away and cannot give true wisdom and absolute security. The thought remains within Israel's traditional view that rejected personal immortality (see Psalms 6; 16; and 39). Yet because this psalm is composed in the style of proverbs—for that matter, like Psalm 1—it could risk: (1) contradictory statements: compare verses 8-9 that no one "should live on forever and ever and never see the grave," with verse 15: "But God will ransom my soul from the power of Sheol." Or compare verse 14

> Like sheep they are appointed for Sheol;
> > Death shall be their shepherd;
> straight to the grave they descend,
> > and their form shall waste away;
> Sheol shall be their home.

with Ps 23:1: "The LORD is my shepherd, / I shall not want"; (2) contrasting statements: compare verse 15, above, with verse 7, "no ransom avails for one's life"; (3) disconcerting statements, especially in the refrain, verses 12 and 20, "they are like the animals that perish" (cf. Eccl 3:19; Job 18:3). With such an enigmatic style the psalmist offers an insight, reaching toward personal immortality: "But God will ransom my soul from the power of Sheol" (v. 15).

This Wisdom psalm is generally divided as follows: the long introduction (vv. 1-4); the discussion of transitory wealth (vv. 5-9, 16-20); and the inevitability of death (vv. 10-13, 14-15). Verses 12 and 20 serve as a baffling refrain:

> Mortals cannot abide in their pomp;
> > they are like the animals that perish (Ps 49:12).
> Mortals cannot abide in their pomp;
> > they are like the animals that perish (Ps 49:20).

The long, solemn introduction of this psalm, with even the summons for musical accompaniment ("I will solve my riddle to the music of the harp," v. 4b), seems to lead nowhere. The final line endorsed the orthodox theology of Israel: that death and Sheol lie beyond the presence and power of YHWH: each human being is like the beasts that perish (v. 20b; see Psalm 16). One of the key phrases in the psalm, "to ransom" one's life from death, reminds us of Jesus' statement: "For the Son of Man came not to be served but to serve, and to give his life a ransom for many" (Mark 10:45). Verses from 1 Peter also come to mind: "You know that you were ransomed from the futile ways inherited from your ancestors, not with perishable things like silver or gold, but with the precious blood of Christ, like that of a lamb without defect or blemish" (1 Pet 1:18-19). The solution to wealth and the false hopes that it engenders is not more silver and gold, but the bond of love.

Psalm 119: A Meditation on God's Law

This longest psalm of the Psalter meditates upon the "law," externally in a highly structured way, but thematically in a completely unstructured way. The eight lines of each stanza (doubled in most English translations) begin with the same letter of the Hebrew alphabet, so that all twenty-two letters have a complete stanza in the order of the alphabet (see Psalms 9–10). Each of the 176 lines contains one of eight synonyms for law—with two exceptions. In verse 90 a ninth synonym for law occurs, and no synonym at all is found in verse 122. The long psalm blends almost every type or style, again with the exception that the great moments of Israel's history are totally absent. The dominant forms are sapiential (beginning with v. 1) and lament (vv. 22, 23, 25 as examples), but also praise (vv. 7, 164, 171, etc.), confidence (vv. 50, 56, etc.), and prayer (vv. 10, 17, etc.). Yet the psalm's audience meets none of the excitement and community participation of the hymn, none of the intense agony of the laments.

Verses 1-8

> Happy are those whose way is blameless,
>   who walk in the law of the LORD.
> Happy are those who keep his decrees,
>   who seek him with their whole heart,
> who also do no wrong,
>   but walk in his ways.
> You have commanded your precepts
>   to be kept diligently.
> O that my ways may be steadfast
>   in keeping your statutes!
> Then I shall not be put to shame,
>   having my eyes fixed on all your commandments.
> I will praise you with an upright heart,
>   when I learn your righteous ordinances.
> I will observe your statutes;
>   do not utterly forsake me (Ps 119:1-8).

As in the case of Psalm 96, Psalm 119 reveals long meditation upon the treasury of biblical tradition. The favorite book seems to be Deuteronomy, then Proverbs, Job, Jeremiah, Ezekiel, and finally, in a lesser way, Isaiah 40–55. Psalm 119 inserts a word for "law" in every line but one, has no allusions to the most important legal corpus in Israel, the Priestly tradition or "P" of the Pentateuch. Furthermore, it does not refer to the covenant and draws very little from the historical books of the deuteronomic tradition (Joshua-Judges-Samuel-Kings). The following verses are examples of how Psalm 119 alludes to other biblical traditions:

Ps 119:2	Deut 4:29
Happy are those who keep his decrees,	From there you will seek the LORD your God, and you will find him if
who seek him with their whole heart.	you search after him with all your heart and soul.

Ps 119:70	Isa 6:10
Their hearts are fat and gross,	Make the mind of this people dull,
but I delight in your law.	and stop their ears,
	and shut their eyes,
	so that they may not look with their eyes,
	and listen with their ears,
	and comprehend with their minds,
	and turn and be healed.

Ps 119:76	Isa 51:3
Let your steadfast love become my comfort	For the LORD will comfort Zion;
	he will comfort all her waste places,
according to your promise to your servant.	and will make her wilderness like Eden,
	her desert like the garden of the LORD;
	joy and gladness will be found in her,
	thanksgiving and the voice of song.

Ps 119:85	Jer 18:20

The arrogant have dug pitfalls for me;
    they flout your law.
	Is evil a recompense for good?
	    Yet they have dug a pit for my life.
	Remember how I stood before you
	    to speak good for them,
	    to turn away your wrath from them.

Ps 119:89	Isa 40:8

The LORD exists forever;
    your word is firmly fixed in heaven.
	The grass withers, the flower fades;
	    but the word of our God will stand forever.

Psalm 119 infuses a new character into these allusions. While most of these texts are community oriented—even those of a sapiential nature—Psalm 119 is intent upon personal, individual piety. According to a word that occurs within its lines (*siah,* "to meditate," in vv. 15, 23, 27, 48, 78, 148), one ought to go over in thought, muse on, linger upon, even to mumble the sound repeatedly. In this way biblical texts sink deeply into one's subconscious with new life and coloration.

Verses 89-96

> The LORD exists forever;
>   your word is firmly fixed in heaven.
> Your faithfulness endures to all generations;
>   you have established the earth, and it stands fast.
> By your appointment they stand today,
>   for all things are your servants.
> If your law had not been my delight,
>   I would have perished in my misery.
> I will never forget your precepts,
>   for by them you have given me life.
> I am yours; save me,
>   for I have sought your precepts.
> The wicked lie in wait to destroy me,
>   but I consider your decrees.
> I have seen a limit to all perfection,
>   but your commandment is exceedingly broad (Ps 119:89-96).

Because of the frequent interaction with the book of Deuteronomy, the psalm may have originated in the contemplative background of a preacher of the word of God. According to Deut 31:9-13, Levites were to preserve the Law, read it before the people, and explain its impact upon their daily lives, that the peoples and "their children, who have not known it, may hear and learn to fear the LORD your God, as long as you live in the land that you are crossing over the Jordan to possess" (v. 13). However, because Psalm 119 ignores the stipulations of the covenant Law and never quotes from it, it is also possible that the poem was composed among the disciples of the sages, in a school similar to the one conducted by Jesus ben Sirach (Sir 51:23). In this case one is dealing with a more private, less temple or sanctuary orientation to religious practice.

If Psalm 119 never quotes from the Priestly tradition, perhaps the most important part of the Mosaic Torah or Law, one needs to inquire what the psalmist really meant by "law." It is a way of life, learned and integrated by the Law of Moses but not identifiable with it; it is a keen sensitivity to oral traditions as these transmit the ideals, the sorrows, and the struggles of Israel's ordinary folk; it is personal dedication to what one perceives to be the best, not just conformity to a legal code; it is not searching the past but living in the present moment where God is to be found and where ancient traditions take on a new vitality; it is satisfaction even within monotonous daily life, not with a frenetic drive for excitement and wondrous deeds; most of all, it is seeking God with one's whole heart (v. 2; cf. Deut 6:5, "You shall love the LORD your God with all your heart, and with all your soul, and with all your might.")

Verses 33-40

> Teach me, O LORD, the way of your statutes,
> > and I will observe it to the end.
> Give me understanding, that I may keep your law
> > and observe it with my whole heart.
> Lead me in the path of your commandments,
> > for I delight in it.
> Turn my heart to your decrees,
> > and not to selfish gain.
> Turn my eyes from looking at vanities;
> > give me life in your ways.
> Confirm to your servant your promise,
> > which is for those who fear you.
> Turn away the disgrace that I dread,
> > for your ordinances are good.
> See, I have longed for your precepts;
> > in your righteousness give me life (Ps 119:33-40).

Several themes emerge from Psalm 119:

- the spirit of receiving the Law from the Lord, not from books or scrolls, as in verse 19: "I live as an alien in the land; / do not hide your commandments from me" (see also vv. 11-12);
- the study of the Law, therefore, leads personally to God. Of particular interest is the subtle way by which the psalmist is drawn immediately to YHWH, as in verse 2: "Happy are those who keep his decrees, / who seek him with their whole heart" (see also v. 10);
- perseverance and self-control characterize obedience to YHWH. The psalmist confesses in verses 33-34:

> Teach me, O LORD, the way of your statutes,
> and I will observe it to the end.
> Give me understanding, that I may keep your law
> and observe it with my whole heart.

Under the control of the alphabetical style, emotions never get out of hand.

- the Law is a source of genuine, lasting joy: verses 14, 16:

> I delight in the way of your decrees
> as much as in all riches.
> I will delight in your statutes;
> I will not forget your word.

- prayer is addressed to God in order to keep the Law:

> Let your steadfast love come to me, O LORD,
> your salvation according to your promise.
> Remember your word to your servant,
> in which you have made me hope (vv. 41, 49).

This prayer is to continue through the night (vv. 55, 62, 147) and "Seven times a day I praise you / for your righteous ordinances" (v. 164);

- the Law is an important part of conversion and religious fervor, as one sees in verses 67 and 176:

> Before I was humbled I went astray,
> but now I keep your word.
> I have gone astray like a lost sheep; seek out your servant,
> for I do not forget your commandments.

According to the psalm, every "letter" is a gift from God and contains an inexhaustible meaning. God's Law is made known to people in the deepest levels of their conscience. When one realizes that God is speaking in the silence of one's heart, one needs to listen attentively. The repetition of letter by letter, line by line, yet seemingly getting nowhere, can quiet one's heart in the richness of the present moment, filled with God's presence.

Chapter Thirteen

Thanksgiving Psalms

Praise is due to you,
O God, in Zion;
and to you shall vows be preformed,
O you who answer prayer!
To you all flesh shall come.
You crown the year with your bounty;
your wagon tracks overflow with richness.
The pastures of the wilderness overflow,
the hills gird themselves with joy,
the meadows clothe themselves
with flocks,
the valleys deck themselves
with grain,
they shout and sing together
for joy (Ps 65:1-2, 11-13).

In the Psalter, prayers of thanksgiving are the least numerous of all the prayers. They are found in Mesopotamia and Egypt and in ancient Israel (cf. Exodus 15; Judges 5). They are usually in the domain of individual piety, so far as grammar is concerned ("I") (cf. Psalms 18 and 30). The structure of these psalms combines hymns and supplication. God is being thanked for delivering one from sorrow and danger. The introduction may resemble the first part of a hymn; it is addressed either to God, the object of gratitude, or to the community that witnesses the ceremony of thanksgiving or even joins in it. The body of the psalm is developed in narrative style: dangers, attacks, persecution, confession of faults, expressions of weakness or innocence. The psalmist recounts God's saving intervention.

Finally, the psalm looks toward the future with confidence. Often enough a formula of liturgical blessing can occur here.

Psalms of thanksgiving accompanied the liturgical *todah* or thanksgiving sacrifice. At this time part of the sacrificial animal was burned in adoration, symbolizing one's total dedication to God, and the remaining part of the food contributed to the sacred meal, to be consumed by the offerer and entire family (Lev 7:12; 22:29-30). These psalms are frequently enough associated with vows made during a time of misfortune (Pss 66:13; 116:17-19).

Psalm 65: Blessed Be the Creator

The unity and momentum of Psalm 65 are detected in three key places. First, in verse 3: "When deeds of iniquity overwhelm us, / you forgive our transgressions." Second, in verse 6: "By your strength you established the mountains; / you are girded with might." And third, in verse 10:

> You water its furrows abundantly,
> > settling its ridges,
> softening it with showers,
> > and blessing its growth.

The psalm moves from prayer to answer to action. A further development becomes apparent: in verses 3-4, God hears our prayer and forgives sins, drawing the people closely to the divine presence in the sanctuary; in verses 6-8, God answers by quieting the roaring chaos of the world. The psalm modulates from personal forgiveness to universal peace, from the Jerusalem Temple to its surrounding courtyard, the world. In verses 10-13, God visits the world with life-giving water, which one is tempted to think originates within the sanctuary (cf. Ezekiel 47 or Ps 46:4). This sequence is a reminder of the high holy days in the month of Tishri (September–October), particularly from Yom Kippur on 10 Tishri to Tabernacles or Booths on 15–22 Tishri, from at-one-ment and forgiveness to thanksgiving for the year's harvest and prayer for rain to break the long dry season (cf. Psalm 67). During the octave of Tabernacles the pouring of water was a prominent feature of the ritual at the beginning of each new day. Psalm 65 possibly occupied a prominent place in these pilgrimage festivals in the month of Tishri. This fact may explain why the title to the psalm links it with David in Hebrew, but with Jeremiah and Ezekiel and the return from exile in the Greek, with David who first marched into Jerusalem after conquering the city and with the exiles who return to the Holy City to re-create their life. All three persons, David, Jeremiah and Ezekiel, are associated closely with sin and its forgiveness, Jeremiah also with new life (chs. 30–31) and Ezekiel with the reconstruction of the Temple (chs. 40–48).

The structure of the psalm is clear: in verses 1-4 God hears prayers, forgives sin, and by the beauty of God's holy Temple, one is moved to joy; in verses 5-8 God as Creator overcomes chaos and settles the universe in secure and joyful peace; in verses 9-13 God as Giver of Rain makes the earth fertile, decked with grain and bounding for joy. The reference to sin in verse 3 suggests that this psalm is less a hymn of praise (the early hymns would not deal with sin) and much more a prayer of thanksgiving:

> O you who answer prayer!
> To you all flesh shall come.
> When deeds of iniquity overwhelm us,
>> you forgive our transgressions.
> Happy are those whom you choose and bring near
>> to live in your courts.
> We shall be satisfied with the goodness of your house,
>> your holy temple (Ps 65:2-4).

In accord with the ancient Greek and Syriac versions, the opening line is usually read, as in the NRSV, "Praise is due to you, / O God, in Zion"; yet the Hebrew reads, "For you silence is praise, O God, in Zion," the attitude of ecstatic wonder over what God is about to do, coupling with the later line, "You still the roaring of the seas" (v. 7). In verse 2 "all flesh" may indicate the weakness of sinful Israel. Verse 3, "when deeds of iniquity overwhelm us," suggests the burden of weight that sin creates. Verse 4 is also rich in covenant and ritual allusions: "happy" (see Ps 1:1); "you choose" (cf. Deut 7:7-8); "live in your courts," possible for all Israelites (cf. Psalms 15 and 24 which speak of entering the courts of the Temple after a ritual of purification/forgiveness); "the goodness of your house," probably a reference to the sacred meals (cf. Ps 22:26, "the poor shall eat and be satisfied" within the assembly of worship).

Verses 5-8 celebrate not only God's responsiveness to humankind but also God's strength:

> By awesome deeds you answer us with deliverance,
>> O God of our salvation;
> you are the hope of all the ends of the earth
>> and of the farthest seas.
> By your strength you established the mountains;
>> you are girded with might.
> You silence the roaring of the seas,
>> the roaring of their waves,
>> the tumult of the peoples.

> Those who live at earth's farthest bounds are awed by your signs;
>   you make the gateways of the morning and the evening shout for joy.

These lines have the hallmark of Israel's great hymns, like Psalms 29 or 89:5-18 (see also Psalm 8), with the hymnic participle—establishing the mountains, quieting the roar of the sea—God's magnificent, even fearful and awesome display of power over all chaotic forces, the shout of joy from morning till evening.

Verses 9-13 proclaim God's benevolent care for the natural world:

> You visit the earth and water it,
>   you greatly enrich it;
> the river of God is full of water;
>   you provide the people with grain,
>   for so you have prepared it.
> You water its furrows abundantly,
>   settling its ridges,
> softening it with showers,
>   and blessing its growth.
> You crown the year with your bounty;
>   your wagon tracks overflow with richness.
> The pastures of the wilderness overflow,
>   the hills gird themselves with joy,
> the meadows clothe themselves with flocks;
>   the valleys deck themselves with grain,
>   they shout and sing together for joy.

Here the perfect tense of the Hebrew verb is employed, the narrative style of praise: if God visits the earth with rain and enriches it with new life, it is done so perfectly that the results continue from harvest to new planting, from the early rains in October–November to the late rains in March–April. Again there is a joyful shout to conclude the psalm.

By drawing upon pagan mythology in verses 5-8, and linking the Jerusalem Temple with the universe, by dwelling upon the blessings of the earth's harvest, Psalm 65 enabled Israel to glimpse its world mission even from the beginning. Only at rare moments, as in the final poems of Second Isaiah (Isaiah 40–55), did a faithful Israelite begin to see the consequences of its mission and to break through the more narrow bonds of election that separated Israel from all other nations. Such flashes of insight are crucial for future development. Biblical religion is glimpsed as the center of world religions; the covenant God is the source of forgiveness and new life for everyone, whether "There is no longer Jew or Greek, there is no longer slave or free, there is no longer male and female; for all of you are one in Christ Jesus" (Gal 3:28).

Christian tradition has linked Psalm 65 with the liturgy for the deceased. The dead are to receive full purification from sin, to be called into the blessedness of the heavenly sanctuary, and to find their entire world recreated and transformed.

Psalm 66: Blessed Be the Redeemer

Come and see what God has done:
> he is awesome in his deeds among mortals.
He turned the sea into dry land;
> they passed through the river on foot.
There we rejoiced in him,
> who rules by his might forever,
whose eyes keep watch on the nations—
> let the rebellious not exalt themselves.
Bless our God, O peoples,
> let the sound of his praise be heard,
who has kept us among the living,
> and has not let our feet slip.
For you, O God, have tested us;
> you have tried us as silver is tried.
You brought us into the net;
> you laid burdens on our backs;
you let people ride over our heads;
> we went through fire and through water;
yet you have brought us out to a spacious place (Ps 66:5-12).

What is most effectively achieved in Psalm 66 is the actualization or reliving of God's redemptive acts, particularly the exodus out of Egypt and the crossing of the River Jordan, within the *contemporary* situation of the Israelite nation and the individual worshiper. Unlike much of modern biblical study, the psalm does not attempt to recapture the historical setting of the past but rather enables the ancient act of God to become an important ingredient of the later age. One is reminded of the well-known "today" passages in Deuteronomy, i.e., "The LORD our God made a covenant with us at Horeb. Not with our ancestors did the LORD make this covenant, but with us, who are all of us here alive today" (Deut 5:2-3); or one thinks of the answer given to the child who asks, "What is the meaning" of this liturgical action:

> When your children ask you in time to come, "What is the meaning of the decrees and the statutes and the ordinances that the LORD our God has commanded you?" then you shall say to your children, "We were Pharaoh's slaves in Egypt, but the LORD brought us out of Egypt with a mighty hand. The LORD displayed before our eyes great and awesome signs and wonders against Egypt, against Pharaoh and all his household" (Deut 6:20-22).

The psalmist is not constrained to remain within ancient liturgical formulas and actions, but rather was creative enough to adapt the community ritual of verses 1-12 to personal, individual needs (vv. 13-20, where the plural changes to the singular "I"). Important liturgical actions presume a right attitude within each individual worshiper before God. While remaining within the main lines of the ancient liturgy, one finds strong personal convictions and individual consecration expressed through the sacrifices and holocausts.

The psalm is too general to determine what may have been the serious trial for the nation (vv. 10-12) and for the individual psalmist (vv. 18-19). The contact with Isaiah and Jeremiah (vv. 10-11 and Isa 1:25; Jer 6:29; 9:6) and with Second Isaiah's theme of the new exodus (v. 6 and Isa 43:16-21) inclines us to a date during the Exile or immediately afterwards, but the reasons are not absolutely compelling.

The structure of Psalm 66 is complex yet clear. Verses 1-4 are an introductory hymn of praise:

> Make a joyful noise to God, all the earth;
>> sing the glory of his name;
>> give to him glorious praise.
> Say to God, "How awesome are your deeds!
>> Because of your great power, your enemies cringe before you.
> All the earth worships you;
>> they sing praises to you,
>> sing praises to your name."

Verse 1: To call upon *all the earth,* which appears again in verse 4, is more hyperbole than realism, and is suited to enthusiastic praise; yet the later reference to the Exodus involves other nations besides Israel and so may tilt the scale again toward some general type of universal call. Israel's religion was so rooted in world history that sooner or later its covenant election was bound to be thrown open to all nations. It is interesting to note that this enlargement of the covenant did not come principally from Israel's religious resources but more from Israel's international involvement.

The hymn of praise is followed by a grateful remembrance and a reliving of God's deliverance at the exodus and the River Jordan. These two great acts are associated in Psalms 114 and 136 (see also Isa 43:16-21). With stylistic elegance, there is a second call to praise in verse 5. This call to praise is very similar to Ps 46:8. The psalm turns quickly from the past to the present moment and the present place of worship: "There we rejoiced in him, / who rules by his might forever" (vv. 6b-7). The emphasis is surely on *"we"* who worship and rejoice, and the notion of *forever* is similar to Isa 43:18-19:

Do not remember the former things,
>> or consider the things of old.
I am about to do a new thing;
>> now it springs forth, do you not perceive it?
I will make a way in the wilderness
>> and rivers in the desert.

God's dominion over the chaotic forces of the sea and river, derived from Canaanite mythology, is folded into God's mighty act of saving Israel (cf. Isa 51:9-10).

Verses 8-12 express a community thanksgiving:

Bless our God, O peoples,
>> let the sound of his praise be heard,
who has kept us among the living,
>> and has not let our feet slip.
For you, O God, have tested us;
>> you have tried us as silver is tried.
You brought us into the net;
>> you laid burdens on our backs;
you let people ride over our heads;
>> we went through fire and through water;
yet you have brought us out to a spacious place.

This communal expression of thanksgiving is followed by an expression of individual thanksgiving:

I will come into your house with burnt offerings;
>> I will pay you my vows
those that my lips uttered
>> and my mouth promised when I was in trouble.
I will offer to you burnt offerings of fatlings,
>> with the smoke of the sacrifice of rams;
I will make an offering of bulls and goats.
Come and hear, all you who fear God,
>> and I will tell what he has done for me.
I cried aloud to him,
>> and he was extolled with my tongue.
If I had cherished iniquity in my heart,
>> the Lord would not have listened.
But truly God has listened;
>> he has given heed to the words of my prayer (Ps 66:13-19).

The abundant thanksgiving offerings can make one think of a prominent person like a king or high priest. The confession of faith in these verses recalls Ps 22:22-31. Liturgical words and cultic actions have centered Israel's entire redemptive history in the person of each worshiper. Verses 16-19 are held together by the word listen: the psalmist asks "all you who fear God" to "come and hear," but at the source of the praise and gratitude is the fact that "God has listened; he has given heed to the words of my prayer" (v. 19). Instruction is not a primary purpose of liturgy, but it happens in the midst of enthusiastic praise and gratitude. The phrase "Blessed be God" expresses both recognition and affirmation of God's wondrous actions (cf. Exod 18:10-12). Such actions are characteristic of God's care of God's people throughout the ages. Gratitude is capped with God's covenant promise:

> The LORD passed before him, and proclaimed,
>> "The LORD, the LORD,
>> a God merciful and gracious,
>> slow to anger,
>> and abounding in steadfast love and faithfulness,
>> keeping steadfast love for the thousandth generation,
>> forgiving iniquity and transgression and sin,
>> yet by no means clearing the guilty,
>> but visiting the iniquity of the parents
>> upon the children
>> and the children's children,
>> to the third and the fourth generation" (Exod 34:6-7).

This psalm was linked very early with the resurrection of Jesus, as we learn from the title in the Latin Vulgate, *Canticum Psalmi Resurrectionis.* This relationship is not surprising in view of the link between the paschal mystery of the Exodus (v. 6) and Jesus' death and resurrection, and because of verse 12 in the psalm: ". . . you have brought us out to a spacious place." The references to "all the earth" (vv. 1 and 4) induced early patristic writers to associate the psalm with the feast of the Epiphany when foreigners came to worship the newborn king (Matt 2:1-12). Mystics like Paul of the Cross considered Psalm 66 to be a favorite on account of the transition from overwhelming sorrow and intense interior searching to a profound union with God and a new, secret peace.

Psalm 67: Thanksgiving for the Harvest

> May God be gracious to us and bless us
>> and make his face to shine upon us,
> that your way may be known upon earth,
>> your saving power among all nations.
> Let the peoples praise you, O God;
>> let all the peoples praise you.

Let the nations be glad and sing for joy,
>for you judge the peoples with equity
>and guide the nations upon earth.
Let the peoples praise you, O God;
>let all the peoples praise you.
The earth has yielded its increase;
>God, our God, has blessed us.
May God continue to bless us;
>let all the ends of the earth revere him (Ps 67:1-7).

As in Psalm 65, the psalmist in this psalm turns gratefully to God after a bountiful harvest. The good fruits of the earth unite people of every race and background; a strong universal note is perceived here. In fact, future blessings, even messianic ones, are portrayed as an abundance of earthly produce. In Hos 14:6,

[God's] shoots shall spread out;
>his beauty shall be like the olive tree,
>and his fragrance like that of Lebanon.

In Amos 9:13 one hears:

The time is surely coming, says the LORD,
>when the one who plows shall overtake the one who reaps,
>and the treader of grapes the one who sows the seed;
the mountains shall drip sweet wine,
>and all the hills shall flow with it.

The classic text of Isa 45:8 comes to mind:

Shower, O heavens, from above,
>and let the skies rain down righteousness;
let the earth open, that salvation may spring up,
>and let it cause righteousness to sprout up also;
I the LORD have created it.

Gradually the messianic sweep of Israel's mission became associated with the harvest festival of the year, Tabernacles or Booths, 15–22 Tishri in today's September–October (cf. Psalm 65; also Zech 14:17). Again, the world mission of Israel was perceived more through God's action across the world in rain and fertility—or in international politics—than in purely religious sources. It is equally clear that the hidden presence of God in nature and politics would remain too obscure without an explicit revelation to Israel about her role of being God's elect people with a mission.

The structure of this prayer of thanksgiving for bountiful crops is easily detectable in English translation: verses 1-3, a general statement of God's way across the earth; verses 4-5, a recognition by the nations of God's fidelity; verses 6-7, the specific goodness of God in the harvest. The refrain (vv. 3 and 5) needs to be added after verse 7.

The universal reach of Psalm 67 is also evident in the large number of words that parallel Ugaritic, a Northwest Semitic language. It is possible that a poem, strongly non-Israelite in influence, was later introduced in verse 2 by the priestly blessing of Num 6:24-26, felt still later the impact of Second Isaiah's outreach of the nations, and reached its final form during a peaceful period of the post-exilic age.

The opening verse, taken from the priestly blessing of Num 6:24-26, would have been recited by the priest in attendance. God's blessing is most manifest in life, especially in the family (Psalm 128) but also in food (Ps 132:15), dew (Ps 133:3), rain (Hos 6:3), etc. For God to shine God's face on someone means special delight in that person and gracious generosity (Pss 4:5-6; 27:7; etc.). One is further reminded that each earthly blessing should redound upon others and become a means of proclaiming salvation to all peoples. One's material generosity ought to become a means of good news that celebrates God as the gift-giver and God's people as sharers in and sharers of God's goodness.

Psalm 118: A Liturgy of Thanksgiving

This psalm turns out to be very complex, not on purpose, of course, nor because of the psalmist's ineptitude, but on account of adaptation to liturgical ceremonies at the Jerusalem Temple and also on account of re-interpretation by the rabbis and New Testament writers. Explained as simply as possible, Psalm 118 belongs to the entrance liturgy, possibly at the Temple gate called "Gate of Righteousness" (see v. 19). Ancient and modern practice indicates that gates or decorative arches within a sacred area can be given special names. At Mount Sinai, along the four thousand steps leading to the top, a pilgrim passes through "the Door of Confession," where the monk St. Stephen heard confessions and granted absolution. Psalm 118, along with Psalms 15 and 24, provides an entrance liturgy on the occasion of solemn thanksgiving to God.

Psalm 118 may have been sung when pilgrims gratefully came to Jerusalem for the feast of Tabernacles, the final harvest festival: verse 15 refers to "the tents," the booths in which pilgrims lived during the eight-day festival; verse 24, to the refrain, "let us rejoice" ("grant salvation"); verse 27 to lights, prominent at the feast of Tabernacles; and to the "lulab," or bundle of "branches" from myrtle, willow, palm, and citron (Lev 23:40). Recited also on the feast of Passover, Psalm 118 accompanied the rite of filling the fourth cup of wine (Mark 14:26).

Psalm 118 can be divided into five units: verses 1-4; verses 5-20; verses 21-25; verses 26-27; and verses 28-29. The first unit is a communal thanksgiving, consisting of two traditional formulas: "O give thanks to the LORD," and "His steadfast love endures forever."

Verses 1-4

> O give thanks to the LORD, for he is good;
>> his steadfast love endures forever!
> Let Israel say,
>> "His steadfast love endures forever."
> Let the house of Aaron say,
>> "His steadfast love endures forever."
> Let those who fear the LORD say,
>> "His steadfast love endures forever."

In Psalm 136 "love" explains the entire history of the cosmos and of Israel; Psalm 118 unites this national and even cosmic history of the Lord's goodness to the help given to individuals. The refrain echoes the basic quality of the covenant and its God (Exod 34:6-7).

Verses 5-21

> Out of my distress I called on the LORD;
>> the LORD answered me and set me in a broad place.
> With the LORD on my side I do not fear.
>> What can mortals do to me?
> The LORD is on my side to help me;
>> I shall look in triumph on those who hate me.
> It is better to take refuge in the LORD
>> than to put confidence in mortals.
> It is better to take refuge in the LORD
>> than to put confidence in princes.
> All nations surrounded me;
>> in the name of the LORD I cut them off!
> They surrounded me, surrounded me on every side;
>> in the name of the LORD I cut them off!
> They surrounded me like bees;
>> they blazed like a fire of thorns;
>> in the name of the LORD I cut them off!
> I was pushed hard, so that I was falling,
>> but the LORD helped me.
> The LORD is my strength and my might;
>> he has become my salvation.
> There are glad songs of victory in the tents of the righteous:

"The right hand of the LORD does valiantly;
　　the right hand of the LORD is exalted;
　　the right hand of the LORD does valiantly."
I shall not die, but I shall live,
　　and recount the deeds of the LORD.
The LORD has punished me severely,
　　but he did not give me over to death.
Open to me the gates of righteousness,
　　that I may enter through them
　　and give thanks to the LORD.
This is the gate of the LORD;
　　the righteous shall enter through it.

Verses 5-21 are an individual thanksgiving sung either by the king or as an interaction between various categories of people with priest and congregation. In verse 5 "distress" is similar to Ps 116:3; Lam 1:3. The phrase "set me in a broad place" reflects the desire of nomads to roam the open spaces of the wilderness, a wish deeply imbedded within the blood and bones of Israel.

The reference to "all nations" in verse 10 may designate the king as speaker, but it could equally apply to individual travelers or merchants harassed by foreigners on their way to Jerusalem. In verse 10, "in the name of the LORD" is a phrase associated with covenant. According to the covenant, it was God's "vocation" or "promise" to bring Israel through difficulties to peace (see Ps 113:1-3).

Verses 14-16 echo lines found in Moses' song of praise and victory in Exodus 15:

The LORD is my strength and my might,
　　and he has become my salvation;
this is my God, and I will praise him,
　　my father's God, and I will exalt him.
Your right hand, O LORD, glorious in power—
　　your right hand, O LORD, shattered the enemy.
You stretched out your right hand,
　　the earth swallowed them (Exod 15:2, 6, 12).

The entire history of Israel converges within this moment of thanksgiving and praise. In verse 18 the word "punished" found in the phrase "the LORD has punished me severely" reflects sapiential piety (Prov 3:11-12) which was given a firm rooting in prophetic preaching and then in popular piety by Deuteronomy (Deut 4:36; 8:5) and by Jeremiah (Jer 2:19; 31:18; specifically, thirty-one times in Jeremiah). See also Pss 7; 50:16-21.

Verses 21-25

> I thank you that you have answered me
>> and have become my salvation.
> The stone that the builders rejected
>> has become the chief cornerstone.
> This is the Lord's doing;
>> it is marvelous in our eyes.
> This is the day that the Lord has made;
>> let us rejoice and be glad in it.
> Save us, we beseech you, O Lord!
>> O Lord, we beseech you, give us success!

Verses 21-25 express the community's praise and prayer. In verse 22, the statement about the stone being rejected sounds like an ancient proverb: that which is precious can be despised by some persons but given a place of fundamental importance by other persons of faith. In verse 25, the phrase "save us" was first a cry for help (Pss 12:1; 28:9) or for mercy (2 Sam 14:4); later it became a solemn acclamation that God has indeed saved and granted victory. On the feast of Tabernacles it was sung each day as the congregation encircled the altar and on the octave day seven times. That laity could come this close to the altar would point to pre-exilic times; later, only priests were permitted in what became the courts of the priests.

Verses 26-27

> Blessed is the one who comes in the name of the Lord.
>> We bless you from the house of the Lord.
> The Lord is God,
>> and he has given us light.
> Bind the festal procession with branches,
>> up to the horns of the altar.

Verses 26-27 are a blessing that recall the "priestly benediction" in Num 6:24-26.

Verses 28-29

> You are my God, and I will give thanks to you;
>> you are my God, I will extol you.
> O give thanks to the Lord, for he is good,
>> for his steadfast love endures forever.

Verses 28-29 serve as a conclusion to the psalm. These verses would be sung by an individual (v. 28) and by the entire congregation as well (v. 29).

With respect to New Testament theology, Psalm 118 occupies an important place. The idea of verse 6, "with the Lord on my side," enters the final chapter of Hebrews, urging Christ's disciples to fulfill faithfully the laws of hospitality and basic morality, despite the cost. Verse 24, "This is the day that the LORD has made; / let us rejoice and be glad in it," helps to describe a vision of heaven, the marriage feast of the lamb (Rev 19:7). Quoted most frequently are verses 22-23:

> The stone that the builders rejected
> > has become the chief cornerstone.
> This is the LORD's doing;
> > it is marvelous in our eyes.

Verses 25-26 are also frequently quoted: "Save us. . . . / Blessed is the one who comes in the name of the LORD." These two verses are used in Matthew's Gospel in the parable of the vine dressers (Matt 21:42-43). Here the word could indicate continuity (Matt 21:42-43). In this case "stone" indicated the continuity of God's kingdom from earlier Scriptures to the new age (as in Isa 28:16-17) and its strength to withstand all opposition (as in Dan 2:44). Mark 12:10-12 relates the passage of Ps 118:22-23 more closely with the death of Jesus, caused by ungrateful, jealous people. Luke 20:16-18 cites the same passage more with the necessity of making a clear decision for or against Jesus. The context of the quotation in Acts 4:11 is explicitly: "This Jesus is 'the stone that was rejected by you, the builders; / it has become the cornerstone.'" Acts adapts the passage from Psalm 118 by speaking of a stone that was "rejected," like the Suffering Servant in Isa 53:3. Each of these citations must be studied in their own context. Thus, one can conclude that not only Psalm 118 occupied an important place in teaching about the death and resurrection of Jesus, but also that the Old Testament psalm was re-read within a new context that presumed faith in Jesus as Messiah, and was used to delve more deeply into this mystery.

Verses 25-27 are introduced into Jesus' triumphal entry into Jerusalem, again with a slightly different nuance in Mark 11:9; Matt 21:9; Luke 19:38; John 12:13. Verse 26 is also cited when Jesus weeps over Jerusalem (Matt 23:37-39 and Luke 13:34-35).

And finally, both the Eastern and Western Churches of today have appointed Psalm 118 to be sung on Easter as a reminder that "This is the day that the LORD has made; / let us rejoice and be glad in it" (v. 24).

Questions for Reflection

Chapter 1:

1. Do the psalms lead me to God? How is God portrayed in the psalms? In what ways do the psalms connect with my life experiences? How are my life experiences and those of the psalmist different?

2. Are the diverse ways of organizing and numbering the psalms bothersome? How does my response to this organization reflect my own approach to life? Am I "overly organized" or "flexible"?

3. The psalms are often read and interpreted within the liturgical life of the Christian community. How can I read and interpret them in an informed way for myself?

Chapter 2:

1. Where have I heard God's voice (in the psalms, for instance) today?

2. Can I imagine myself as part of the liturgical procession of Psalm 95? Where do I stand? What do I see?

3. When I read or hear the psalms, what particular word or words strike me? Why do some words or ideas stand out while others do not?

Chapter 3:

1. Israel adopted Canaanite poetry and practices and saw them as valid ways of expressing one's experience of YHWH. In what ways do I experience God's presence and power outside traditional Christian forms of prayer and worship? How do I experience God working in and through other cultures, faiths, and religious expressions?

2. When do I experience God in such a way that I want to shout out words of praise or give expression to wonder?

3. In what ways does the natural world proclaim the presence of God? Have I ever reflected on Psalm 8 under a starry sky, Ps 19:1-6 at a sunrise, or Psalm 29 during a thunderstorm?

Chapter 4:

1. In what way(s) do I participate in salvation history and the divine work of redemption and liberation? How do the psalms help me to remember what happened to Israel, to Jesus, to the early Church?

2. What do I experience after repeating a phrase (or psalm) again and again, such as in Psalm 136? What images come to mind?

3. Psalm 46 can be a powerful prayer in times of trouble and insecurity. Where do I see myself in this psalm? What does Psalm 46 tell me about God? About myself?

Chapter 5:

1. What would the metaphorical expression "YHWH is king" mean for people today?

2. According to Psalms 96–99, what does God's "justice" mean? How do I share in the divine and human responsibility to practice justice?

3. In what way(s) could the psalms be "new songs" today?

Chapter 6:

1. How am I called and chosen by God? What qualities of leadership am I asked to display? How can Psalms 2 and 110 draw these qualities out from me?

2. What kind of promises does God make? What happened to the promises made to David as recorded in Psalm 89? Can any of them apply to me?

3. In what way am I begotten of God? How is God experienced in and through me today?

Chapter 7:

1. How does God show kindness and fidelity in my life?

2. Can I relate to Ps 44:23-26? Does God ever seem asleep in my life? How do I deal with the feelings of God's seeming absence?

3. What strikes me in Psalm 12? How do I allow God's promises to comfort me when I am anxious or in distress?

Chapter 8:

1. Have I ever felt as desperate or as abandoned as the author of Psalm 22? Could I be as serene in the midst of such troubles?

2. How can memories of my encounters with God help me to persevere in difficulties? Which memories or images in Psalms 42–43 appeal to me?

Chapter 9:

1. Has sickness or pain ever seemed like a burden to me? When does any part of Psalm 38 describe or speak to my own situation?

2. How can I entrust my pain or sickness to God? How would I pray Psalm 6? Which words or phrases strike me?

3. What does it mean for me to be searched and known by God? Am I comfortable with God's intimate knowledge of me and my life? What part of Psalm 139 speaks directly to me?

Chapter 10:

1. Have I ever felt angry enough to curse others and wish them harm? In reading Ps 58:6-11, do I feel embarrassment or agreement? Why?

2. How do I feel when I read Ps 137:9? Why can such words be a problem in prayer? Why might they sometimes be necessary in prayer?

3. Why might someone pray Ps 139:19-24? Can the venting of strong negative feelings begin a process of healing and reconciliation?

Chapter 11:

1. When have I ever felt healing and peace after admitting a fault or failing? Does Psalm 32 ring true for me?

2. Does any part of Psalm 130 speak to me? When do I trust in God and wait for divine compassion?

3. Is the image of washing or cleaning in Psalm 51 appropriate when speaking of sin and forgiveness?

Chapter 12:

1. How does Psalm 1 speak to me? Does the image of the tree and the clear division between good and evil make sense to me, or is the division not as clear-cut as the psalm suggests?

2. In my opinion, does Psalm 49 express wisdom or cynicism? Why? In what way can these words be described as wise?

3. What is my attitude toward Torah? Toward God's word? Are there benefits to a healthy and integrated sense of intellectual and spiritual discipline? If so, what are these benefits?

Chapter 13:

1. In what way does Psalm 65 speak to me? How do I show gratitude to the God of compassion?

2. What are the great deeds that God has done in my life? What part of Psalm 66 strikes me? In what ways do I appreciate the blessings God has bestowed on me?

3. Does liturgy/ritual/worship help me to be grateful to God? In what way? Do I appreciate the wonderful deeds of God described in Psalm 118? How do I give expression to my appreciation?

Index of Psalms